Before Auschwitz

Before Auschwitz

What Christian Theology Must Learn from the Rise of Nazism

PAUL R. HINLICKY

CASCADE *Books* • Eugene, Oregon

BEFORE AUSCHWITZ
What Christian Theology Must Learn from the Rise of Nazism

Copyright © 2013 Paul R. Hinlicky. All rights reserved. Except for brief quotations in critical publications or reviews, no part of this book may be reproduced in any manner without prior written permission from the publisher. Write: Permissions. Wipf and Stock Publishers, 199 W. 8th Ave., Suite 3, Eugene, OR 97401.

Cascade Books
An Imprint of Wipf and Stock Publishers
199 W. 8th Ave., Suite 3
Eugene, OR 97401

www.wipfandstock.com

ISBN 13: 978-1-62032-103-4

Cataloguing-in-Publication data:

Hinlicky, Paul R.

    Before Auschwitz : what Christian theology must learn from the rise of Nazism / Paul R. Hinlicky.

    xii + 234 p. ; 23 cm. Includes bibliographical references and index.

    ISBN 13: 978-1-62032-103-4

    1. National Socialism and Religion. 2. Theology, Doctrinal—Germany—History—20th century. 3. Protestant churches—Germany—History—20th century. I. Title.

BR 856 .H57 2013

Manufactured in the U.S.A.

In Memoriam:

Samuel Štefan Osuský
Confessor of the Faith, 1888–1975

Contents

Preface | ix
Acknowledgments | xi

Introduction
    Can Theology Learn from Its Past? | 1

Chapter One
    Hitler's Theologians | 14

Chapter Two
    The Peril of Conservative Apologetics | 44

Chapter Three
    Seeing How We Saw | 68

Chapter Four
    The Not So Strange Theology of Adolf Hitler | 99

Chapter Five
    Contested Topics in Theology | 141

Conclusion
    Inheritance, Decay, and Renewal | 188

Appendix
Samuel Štefan Osuský, "The Philosophy of Bolshevism, Fascism, and Hitlerism" (1937) | 193

Bibliography | 221
Index of Subjects and Names | 229

Preface

My father was a veteran of World War II. As his son I grew up fascinated with the great military campaign in which he had played a part to defeat Nazi Germany. It was all very grand and glorious to a boy awakening to the wider world in the early 1960s. I remember, however, how I came to learn of the Holocaust in connection with Adolf Eichmann's capture, trial, and execution. When I asked my father about it, I recall, he would only shake his head and sigh at "man's inhumanity to man." *Homo lupis hominis.* My father did not like to talk about the war. He always said that there are two kinds of veterans: those who have seen war and only want to forget it and those who only talk about war because they never really experienced it. Only later in life did he share some of his experiences from the war, always, however, in the context of how it had changed his life by leading him to his calling to the pastoral ministry. To do good, he thought, after seeing so much killing and destruction. Nothing seemed more self-evident to me growing into adulthood, as a result, and finding my own way to the ministry after him, than that our precious Christianity was opposed to Nazism and all its wicked works and ways. Maybe growing up in a Slovak Lutheran immigrant ghetto reinforced this. Yet as I grew and learned, the question even then nagged at me: how could this have come from the land of Luther?

Such convictions and such questions have never left me. What is now laid before the reader reflects a lifetime of meditation—I do mean, religiously, *meditation*—as well as inquiry. The truth is that a decent person hardly dares to write about such matters, holy ground to the aggrieved but source of continuing shame to the children of the perpetrators to the third and fourth generation. I do not know whether anything helpful or hopeful can be written about the failures, by and large, of Christian people to recognize the devil disguised as an angel of light (2 Cor 11:14), but for the sake of our seeing today more clearly and judging tomorrow more precisely by staying more awake and alert when the hour of testing falls (Mark 14:37–38) as

Preface

surely it does, I put away reservations. Naturally, I think that what I offer to the reader in this book advances the argument about what Christian theology must learn from the rise of Nazism. That is for the reader to judge. But I worry that the warning embodied in it, like that made by Samuel Štefan Osuský in 1937, will fall on deaf ears.

Paul R. Hinlicky
Epiphany, 2013

Acknowledgments

I HAVE BEEN BLESSED FOR over thirteen years now to teach in the "up and coming" liberal arts curriculum of Roanoke College. In these years I have taught various iterations of the college's course, cross-listed in both Religion and History, on the Holocaust, both singly and in a team with my younger colleague in the History Department, Rob Willingham. He has read and commented on portions of this book, giving his approval to the project, though not necessarily to the theological conclusions to which I come nor the moral judgments that I make on the way. I am grateful for his moral passion, keen intelligence, and delightful friendship. My cup runs over with outstanding colleagues. I am particularly grateful to Bob Benne (who was moved to share fascinating anecdotes from his student years in postwar Germany about some of the theologians discussed in this book). He read the entire draft with interest and approval, dissenting only and sharply at a first draft of my concluding words. Our debates continue. Likewise Gerald McDermott was particularly generous also in reading the entire draft and saving me from inconsistencies and infelicities. Those that remain are the author's fault alone. Brent Adkins, too, even after the exhaustion we shared after recently concluding a co-authored book, took the time to nose around in my draft and express general approbation, albeit tempered by a decided lack of enthusiasm for the Nolte/Safranski/Aschheim reading of the Nazified Nietzsche. As above, the debate continues. I am also indebted to several colleagues from beyond the borders of Roanoke College. Fritz Oehlschlaeger, my friend and a remarkable lay theologian, makes his living teaching English at Virginia Tech. He has been generous beyond telling in providing both substantive feedback and the kinds of organizational and compositional suggestions at which an accomplished teacher in his field excels. Any befuddlements in what follows due to style and organization are solely to be laid at the author's feet. Michael DeJonge of the University of Southern Florida, whom I first

Acknowledgments

met at a Bonhoeffer conference two years ago in Flensburg, delivered an intellectually powerful analysis of the initial draft that both corroborated and subtly corrected one of my chief operating ideas; that is acknowledged below in the footnotes. I very much look forward to this young scholar's promising research on the "Lutheran" Bonhoeffer. Once again the apple of her father's eye, Sarah Hinlicky Wilson, gave the author the kind of sophisticated theological feedback both needed and desired, namely, from one not overly familiar with the explosion of literature in the field studied in this book, but greatly concerned with its implications for church and theology, particularly concerning method in today's rampant theological confusion. Jeffrey Martin, who runs the Interlibrary Loan Desk at Roanoke College, has graciously assisted time and again this behind-the-technological-curve professor who never remembers to return borrowed books on time. He sought and found for me whatever obscure titles I requested. Kudos to him! Spouse Ellen of more years than we care to count any more was as always patient, kind, interested, and pleased to play a supporting role. Thank you, Ellen. I would also like to thank Dean Richard Smith of Roanoke College, who granted me sabbatical leave for 2012-13 to work on this book and several other projects to which I now turn, grateful for the opportunity given me to express my thoughts on this still most vexing matter of modern times.

Excerpts from a book review by the author of Colin Kidd, The Forging of Races, appearing in Chapter Five, were first published in *Sixteenth Century Journal* (Summer 2008) XXXIX/2 513–14; likewise excerpts from the author's Introduction to Osusky's "Pastoral Letter on the Jewish Question" appearing in Chapter Three were first published in *Lutheran Quarterly* (Autumn, 2009) 332–34. The Appendix giving Osusky' 1937 lecture, "The Philosophy of Boshevism, Fascism and Hitlerism," first appeared in Two Parts, *Lutheran Forum* (Winter, 2009) 50–58 and (Spring, 2010) 50–58. All are republished here with permission.

Introduction

Can Theology Learn from Its Past?

WHEN WE ASK FOR the sources of the Final Solution[1] in the realm of human ideas we set sail on treacherous waters, where self-serving rationalizations lurk behind the most placid surfaces of scholarship. We cannot be naïve about this, even in one's own case. Especially in theology, the challenge is rather to demonstrate the discipline's critical power, including especially its power of self-criticism. Good criticism moves the argument forward to the benefit of all. But sadly, people use the Holocaust to smear others in contemporary fights that have more to do with posturing than pursuit of truth. The source of the Holocaust is, say, Christian Fundamentalism, or rather, Nietzsche, the self-proclaimed Antichrist. There is, say, a straight line running "Luther-Bismarck-Hitler,"[2] or rather "Darwin-Nietzsche-Hitler."[3] Unsurprisingly these facile characterizations correspond to contemporary culture wars, especially in North America. In our culture, Nazis have become the image of evil incarnate; the tendency

---

1. Any contemporary writer in this field is immediately confronted with the problem of naming the event. The convention in English for a long time has been to use the term, *Holocaust*, and I defer to this customary usage. An alternative is the word derived from Hebrew, *Shoah*. Substantively in this book I am trying to understand the mind of Nazis and their Christian sympathizers (in order better to oppose it!) and thus whatever of the terms I use I am referring to the *Endlösung*, not primarily to the experience of it by Jews and others.

2. So William Shirer influentially argued in *The Rise and Fall of the Third Reich*. See Chapter 2 below for Uwe Simon-Netto's critique of Shirer.

3. Richard Weikart's otherwise impressive documentation of intellectual history, *From Darwin to Hitler,* comes perilously near to arguing this. The insinuation is clearly there. See the discussion in Chapter 4 below.

is to demonize them as agents of virtually supernatural evil—for popular example, in Spielberg's *Indiana Jones* movies. We casually call our liberal gun-confiscating or conservative anti-abortion political opponents "Nazis." Apart from the dishonor this abusive language does to the memory of those actually murdered under the Nazi horror, and the fallacy of illicitly generalizing a particular evil of historic proportions, such demonizing is self-serving in yet another deleterious fashion. It does not achieve historical understanding of the Nazi evil as a human possibility nor does it realize the moral possibility of genuine disagreement and precise critique. Rather it perpetuates the very bad theology which permitted Nazis in the first place to construct perceived enemies as incorrigibly malevolent and nigh unto omniscient in cunning. As Michael Burleigh reflects at the end of his weighty *The Third Reich: A New History* (new, in that it takes the Nazi "worldview" seriously in the way this book also intends to do): Contemporary ideological appropriation and abuse of the Holocaust in our culture wars "trivializes" this unprecedented atrocity by "reducing" it "to the cultural climate and personalities of our time, hav[ing] little to do with the enormity of the event itself, about which there should be no confusion."[4]

The title of this book contains, then, this supposition: in the English speaking world, especially in North America and in the field of theology, recent inquiry into the meaning of the Nazi murder of over five million Jews and other racial-political "undesirables" suffers frequently from a subtle methodological difficulty, namely, the "retrospective fallacy," sometimes also called "presentism." Unlike the historical actors in church and society during the 1920s and 1930s in Germany, our inquiry today benefits from certain knowledge of the outcome of events. Indeed, it is just this knowledge of the Holocaust's singular and unprecedented wickedness on the soil of a philosophically modern, progressively Christian culture that evokes the moral imperative, *Never again!* In turn this moral interest arising from the outcome of Nazism quite properly motivates historical inquiry. We trouble ourselves with this awful business because we are convinced that we can learn from it in ways that contribute to preventing its recurrence. We are not, then, passive observers in this historical inquiry but highly motivated and interested agents. Just this interest, however, complicates inquiry. Above and beyond the dry, dusty work of establishing a baseline of factual knowledge, in the narratives we construct when we "connect the dots" between established facts to tell a story of the passage from Hitler's political beginnings in Bavaria after World War I all the way to Auschwitz, we are

---

4. Burleigh, *The Third Reich*, 811.

actively answering our own burning questions about fellow human agents: What were they thinking? How could they have thought these things? How could they have acted on these thoughts?

To answer these questions well, however, we have to bracket the very moral judgment and especially the corresponding repugnance that provoked our inquiry in the first place. This entails a certain kind of suffering, a patience, a listening to others whom we would just as soon shoot as they so mercilessly shot and then gassed the innocent and defenseless. By an act of suffering imagination, then, we have to enter into the world in which these actors lived. In doing this, we assume our common humanity with these agents of the past whom we study—with Nazi murderers. Inevitably then our inquiry into them becomes simultaneously an inquiry into ourselves: Could I have thought their thoughts? Could I have acted on them? If we recoil at this point on account of our well-justified repugnance and adopt an air of self-evident superiority to these human possibilities for evil, we cut short the very learning that would profit us the most, namely, when we the questioner becomes the questioned (cf. 2 Sam 12:7). It is said that the first victim of war is truth. This holds also for polemical historiography.

This is admittedly risky business—to empathize humanly with agents of brutal cruelty, thereby to enter a vortex as we contemplate living in their world, caught up in their passions and acting on their ideas. "To understand all is to forgive all or, perhaps, to *despise* all," Nietzsche once commented. Historical relativism that normalizes the Nazi "Final Solution" then passes into a cynicism that concludes that we are all Nazis in a way—this is a temptation that necessarily accompanies serious inquiry into serious human moral calamity in rigorous historical consciousness. But it is only a temptation, not a necessity. "If everyone is guilty, then no one is guilty"—so Hannah Arendt wrote in her study of Eichmann on trial in Jerusalem, rightly admonishing us to think after the agents of evil, not in order to excuse them, but rather to judge precisely and deeply.[5] That is surely the true point in avoiding the retrospective fallacy: we resist the temptation to "demonize" fellow human beings, criminals though they are, in order to hold them along with ourselves morally accountable as human beings, though naturally just this accountability entails a viable distinction between perpetrator and victim. It was, by contrast, precisely Nazis who literally and all-too-readily "demonized" Jews and others until they could think of their massive murder as like the work of a cancer surgeon removing a tumor. Just such emotionally understandable but intellectually irresponsible distancing

---

5. Arendt, *Eichmann in Jerusalem*, 277–79.

by way of demonization is what we must avoid if we are to learn anything for ourselves in telling the story of the moral abyss of Nazi Germany.

Fundamental to our common humanity is that we are historical "patients," that is to say, "agents" only as we ride the wave of history that first forms us and then propels us along. Fundamental to this "patiency," as I have discussed in other works,[6] is ignorance of the future. We cannot synthesize the infinity of data in any moment to prognosticate reliably what will be tomorrow. We have to act, then, not only within the parameters of that particular wave of history that first forms and bears us along, but we have to act here without knowing just how that wave will come to shore and so how our own dreams, hopes, fantasies, and plans will or will not be realized. Not even our post-Auschwitz imperative, *Never again!*, causes these waves of history to stand still or its storms to cease. In making historical judgments—as we historians too are in the thrall of that wave of history we ride—we do not by righteous indignation rise above to some superior vantage point from which to judge *sub specie aeternitatis* but rather only make a little history in our own little way—for good or for ill or more usually for some confused and confusing combination of good and ill. We make history in this way too when subtly we allow our passion for justice to override judgment and moral purpose to pass into after the fact moralizing that ironically perpetuates a vicious cycle of *ressentiment*—think of the vindictiveness of the Versailles Treaty and the German resentment of it on which Hitler so masterfully played, not least because he himself so bitterly felt it. Discipline fails, then, when we do not by the act of historical imagination allow to voices of the past their own ignorance of the outcome of their actions and thus their own risks and ventures. Equally, we cheat ourselves by such anachronism. We learn nothing from the past when already we know what "they" should have done. At worst we turn the past into an old-fashioned Bible from which we can proof-text any and all of our preconceived notions, albeit trumpeted now as a bold stand for justice, with which to denounce contemporary opponents and so to confirm us in our own sense of moral superiority—which is in fact a dangerous moral complacency.

I use then throughout this book the notion of "retrospective fallacy" along the foregoing lines, though the notion itself would be fallacious if I did not make explicit here some key qualifications. All history is written retrospectively. There is no fallacy contained in the perspective of the present as such, but rather the temptation that attends all perspective, namely, to absolutize itself by employing in judgment criteria or concepts or insights

---

6. See especially Hinlicky, *Luther and the Beloved Community*, 93, 144, 303, 323, and 374.

unavailable to other, in this case, past actors. Furthermore, "fallacy" is a notion borrowed from syllogistic logic where it denotes errors in inference, but history does not always follow logic and history writing is more of an inductive art than a deductive science. Hence my use of "fallacy" here is analogical. I am not so much arguing against inferential errors in reasoning by this terminology as against a moral stance that moralizes rather than judges justly and precisely by criteria immanent to the situation, according to possibilities available in a horizon of the past. History consists in complicated, interpretative judgments about the relation of facts to one another by the mediation of human agents whose vision is historically constrained by immanent horizons of possibility. The "fallacy" in mind here is the error of anachronism in the narrating of these interactions in history by importing our present horizon and superimposing it upon a past one. The retrospective fallacy then is a hermeneutical error, an imperialism of the present in which the historian's labor of love to know the past in its own particularity, its "otherness," succumbs to a narcissism that discovers only its mirror image in the past and thus learns from the past only what is already known. Anachronism is erroneous in the sense that by imposing the present horizon of possibilities on the past it necessarily misses the target, that is, the actual decisions human actors made according to their own horizons. These decisions are the very thing that could teach us something. Missing this also forfeits an ethical commitment, also pertinent to scholarship, to regard ourselves with those past actors as members of a common humanity.[7] The solution to the retrospective fallacy, then, is better intellectual history than that which rides roughshod over the perplexities faced by past agents on account of the imposition of a simplifying scheme derived from present-day certitudes.

I argue in this book that we *liberals* —for that, going back to Locke and Jefferson, is what virtually all of us North Americans are, though in different ways—that *we* liberals do not already know better because we habitually blind ourselves to our deep and categorical dependence on triumphing

---

7. I am grateful to Michael DeJonge (personal correspondence, 1/4/13) for a stimulating critique of the notion of "retrospective fallacy." I am indebted to some of his suggestions that are embedded in this paragraph, though naturally I alone am responsible for this formulation. I am also happily dependent on my colleague, the philosopher Monica Vilhauer's lucid and compelling exposition in *Gadamer's Ethics of Play* for any number of notions employed in what follows, specifically "the claim to truth" (5–6), tradition as appropriation (16, 56), achieving disagreement (90) and more broadly, the problem of ethical conditions. Likewise I alone am responsible for the use of made of these ideas. I have also found very helpful Jens Zimmermann, *Recovering Theological Hermeneutics*.

capitalism,[8] just as fascists (and communists) once so clearly saw about us; that fascism just so is an endemically modern possibility; that we too then can be seduced in times of crisis; that times of catastrophic crisis are impending because of unsustainable contradictions in modernity obscured by just this moral complacency; that we are closer then to fascism than indignant moralizing about the past comprehends; that, although the devil never shows its face twice in exactly the same way, the particular hubris of grasping after "final solutions" along biopolitical[9] lines—that is, the "racially scientific" version of fascism that was Nazism—is and remains near at hand today, within our horizon of possibilities unrecognized in just the ways that it was unrecognized by Germans "before Auschwitz."

To be sure this thesis immediately perplexes by its use of the term, "liberal," to characterize author and reader (on the assumption that we will be predominantly North Americans and also, today, post-Holocaust Western Europeans). Chapter 3 below is devoted to making my meaning clear. There the attempt is to juxtapose the filter through which Americans in particular read events during the rise of Nazism to the way in which those events were perceived indigenously. The point is to show the mismatch between American constructions of the modern "left/right" binary derived from Locke and Jefferson, not to mention the communist "left/right" binary derived from one reading of the French Revolution, with Nazi self-understandings as progressive, revolutionary, modern, scientific and in all these ways not only continuous with but in fulfillment of "the Enlightenment" (as Adorno and Horkheimer ruefully realized in the immediate postwar years). Nazis also regarded themselves along the same lines as theologically revisionist. Here a further conventional, but no less slippery use of the word, "liberal," is found in the term, "liberal Protestantism," which emerges as a key consideration in the research reported below in Chapter 1. Recent scholarship, as we shall see, finds considerable continuity between the theological liberalism, as it is called, of the nineteenth century and the emergence of German Christianity

---

8. For the non-teleological, that is to say, non-Hegelian/Marxist notion of capitalism that I employ in this book, and for the Deleuzian account of its insidious nature and savage consequences, see Bell, *Liberation Theology after the End of History*, and my review essay, to which Bell responded, in the online October, 2010, *Journal of Lutheran Ethics* (http://www.elca.org/What-We-Believe/Social-Issues/Journal-of-Lutheran-Ethics.aspx) Vol. 10, Issue 10. This book is not the place to make a full-blown argument about how the juggernaut of savage capitalism is overwhelming just those American traditions, especially symbolized in Lincoln and King, that could and should constrain it.

9. On Agamben's concept of the "biopolitical" see the analysis in Adkins and Hinlicky, *Rethinking Philosophy and Theology with Deleuze*, 114–20, 178, 203, and 234. More immediately see the important study of Friedlander, *The Origins of the Nazi Genocide*.

in support of Nazism during the time of its ascendancy. I do not argue against the fact of this connection but about the sense of it in tandem with an overriding purpose in this book, which is to explode as clichés substituting for thought such left/right binaries by unearthing the anomalies they embody. If I am successful in this we will apprehend how our intramural quarrels both politically and theologically collaborate in self-serving, unilluminating if not obfuscating reductions that do not penetrate to perception of the unsustainable juggernaut that is driving our world relentlessly on towards catastrophe, as dramatically instanced in Nazism (but also in Stalinism and at Hiroshima)—a point I will argue in the Conclusion with the help of the Italian philosopher, Giorgio Agamben.

In historical fact, until very late in the game after the rise of Nazism —that is, with the decision to invade the Soviet Union in June of 1941 in an act of total war and the subsequent construction of the factory-efficient death camps when mass shootings by the *Einsatzgruppen* (the special SS killing squads) behind the Russian front proved too distressing, even for the killers[10]—no one, not even Hitler and his henchmen, knew that Auschwitz and its kindred killing machines would be the *Endlösung* of the "Jewish Question" that Hitler intended since he had captured the leadership of the National Socialist German Workers Party twenty some years earlier. Ghettoization of the Jews and other racial inferiors, pending deportation, was the dominant model among Nazis, until the Wannsee Conference in early 1942 settled upon that "final" solution of the gas chambers, although, as mentioned, the SS killing squads following the Russian front had already begun shooting Jews in mass alongside Soviet commissars and others in the intelligentsia of conquered lands. But it was at Wannsee that Jews were finally singled out as "the top priority of Nazi destruction."[11] Extermination by gassing in the "T-4" program had been a late domestic experiment (January 1940), not on Jews, but on Germans mentally ill, the biopolitical *Lebens unwertes Lebens* (life unworthy of living). Only in the spring of 1942 did Auschwitz become fully functional as a factory of death whose primary victims were to be the Jews of all of Europe.

To be sure, as we will study in detail in Chapter 4, Lucy S. Dawidowicz passionately argued in her classic account, *The War against the Jews, 1933–45*, the "intentionalist"[12] interpretation of the Holocaust: "history begins in

10. See Fritz, *Ostkrieg*, and Rhodes, *Masters of Death*.

11. Bergen, *The Holocaust*, 164. We will encounter Bergen's work further in Chapter 1. For fuller accounts see Crowe, *The Holocaust*, 234–39, esp. 238 and Dwork and van Pelt, *The Holocaust*, 280–284.

12. "[Hans] Mommsen even coined the term 'intentionalist,' used pejoratively to distinguish those historians who believe that intentions have consequences for history

the minds of men and women."[13] Had Germans read *Mein Kampf* and taken it seriously they could have known that Hitler intended to remove Jews and others from his Third Reich and would or should already then have stopped him in his tracks when first steps were taken early on in the suspension of civil liberties, the boycott of Jewish businesses, and the promulgation of racial laws. They could or should have known how improbably he combined Wall Street capitalism and Moscow Bolshevism together in a secretive, world conspiracy to justify this attack on Jewry. They could or should have known that he scorned parliamentarianism as inimical to national unity and purposeful action and did not shy from revolutionary terror and agitprop to accomplish his ultimate purpose of conquest for *Lebensraum* (living space) in an allegedly scientific-Darwinian competition of races for survival. For all these reasons, Germans could and should have known, so Dawidowicz argues, that Hitler was not a liberal, that Hitler was an antisemite, and that Hitler regarded Bolshevism as the mortal rival occupying the land he coveted for German expansion.

The supposition is that we "liberals" would have read *Mein Kampf* and taken it with philosophical seriousness. Although, as we shall see in Chapter 3, there was one prescient contemporary near by, Samuel Štefan Osuský, who in 1937 did read *Mein Kampf* with philosophical seriousness, and as a result did see the disaster that was coming and warned against it, even this did not equate to foreknowledge of Auschwitz. To the contrary, for many in Germany, perhaps most, the rise of Nazism equated instead with national liberation from the equally threatening savageries of Anglo-American capitalism and Moscow communism of which "the Jews" were made a potent contemporary secular symbol.[14] For significant others, pre-eminently Pope Pius XII, it represented the lesser of evils in a world in which, after a Hitler comes to power, only evil choices remained.[15] German Jews, Catholics

---

from the 'functionalists' who see the truth and properly assign the history-making roles to structures and functions." Dawidowicz, *The War against the Jews*, xxix. The new introduction in this edition makes the "intentionalist" case. She tries to avoid the equivocation in the term between the vague sense of a resolve to deal with a problem and the specific sense of a definite plan of action.

13. Ibid., xxxi.

14. For ample evidence of Hitler seen as national savior, also sometimes in the eyes of contemporary American expats, see Nagorski, *Hitlerland*, a book discussed in detail in Chapter 3.

15. Cornwell, *Hitler's Pope*. See also Spicer, *Hitler's Priests*. Since at the time of Hitler's rise, Germany was predominately Protestant, in this book I focus on what the Protestant iteration of Christian theology can learn from the rise of Nazism, though the titles just listed indicate that a parallel inquiry more sophisticated than Rosemary Ruether's jeremiad, *Faith and Fratricide*, is urgently needed, one that does not, however,

of the Center Party betrayed by the Concordat, the moderate Left of the Social Democrat Party, and Communists actively and passively opposed Hitler's National Socialist Revolution, not because they foresaw the Holocaust but because naturally enough the rise of Nazism imperiled their own immediate interests as well as their own alternative plans and purposes for a better future. Even of the few, prescient theologians in Germany like Barth, Bonhoeffer, and Bultmann, who from the beginning summoned to spiritual resistance against Nazism, none did or could have imagined the outcome that actually occurred in the gas chambers. Of these, Bonhoeffer alone passed into active, political resistance within Nazi Germany and that only when his brother-in-law, the military intelligence officer Hans von Dohnanyi, convinced him with physical evidence of the atrocities occurring behind the Russian front.

Of course, from today's perspective in North America with our mantras of tolerance and human rights—which are in part the product of liberal capitalism's triumph over Nazism and since 1989 over Bolshevism—we might retort with Dawidowicz that they should have known already from *Mein Kampf* that Hitler's illiberalism would lead to nothing good. Whether they read *Mein Kampf* or not, there was no secret about Hitler's illiberalism and those in Germany who did indeed suspect nothing good to come of it were more or less helpless effectively to act on that suspicion once Hitler consolidated power. But our after-the-fact moral pronouncement from outside the situation begs two essential questions that actors within it could not beg: first, why historically liberalism on the American model imported to Germany after WW I came into such discredit in the course of the Weimar Republic, and second, why liberals of the Weimar Republic would in any case have taken the apparent ravings of an autodidact seriously—one who by lack of liberal education in critical thinking skills and philosophical hermeneutics had never been required to defend ideas in the trial of peer examination. Liberals, reeling from their own failures in governance, could not believe that the worst elements within Nazism would actually prevail. They latched onto signs of moderation with which Hitler was only too willing to deceive them in his first years in power. They assumed as liberals that sanity would prevail. They saw neither the limits of reason in themselves nor the method in the madness of Hitler.

If we do not beg such questions about the questionableness of liberalism in Weimar Germany, but actually look and see, we discover that in this climate of crisis Christian theologians were seduced, or confused, or on the

---

seek to discredit Cornwell's discoveries by attacking his person, as sadly too many conservative apologists have done.

other side sufficiently alarmed to protest spiritually (though not politically) during the rise of Nazism. The happily seduced and militant minority of the so-called German Christians supported the coordination (*Gleichschaltung*) of church and theology to the Nazi worldview and political order, lending it their spiritual support. The confused majority was reduced to silence that gradually passed into active loyalty and patriotic solidarity once the war began. The alarmed formed the Confessing Church. These protested from the pulpit the Nazification of the faith; some, perhaps even most, opposed Nazism spiritually but supported Nazism politically in a bifurcation that bewilders us today and requires special examination. Some of these were intimidated to silence, or imprisoned, or later drafted and sent to die on the Russian front. Others, perhaps most, rallied patriotically to the war effort later on. Even Confessing Church leader Martin Niemöller, who had skippered a U-Boat in WW I, wrote to Hitler from the concentration camp volunteering to resume command when the war broke out. What can Christian theology today learn from this morass of seduction, confusion, and discernment, not to mention from the manifest limits of spiritual resistance? Those are questions posed and pursued in this book.

Several assumptions being made in what follows, as indicated in this book's subtitle, should also be noted, even if this is not the place to warrant them. First, I assume in what follows that Christian theology is a viable undertaking today, even "after Auschwitz." To a degree, I will actually argue for this assumption in Chapter Five's discussion of theological issues under the heading there of what Karl Barth in 1933 called "theological existence today." But for the most part, I simply assume that it is not idle to ask what Christian theology can learn from the rise of Nazism and the varied responses to it by Christian theologians of that time. Following Rubenstein,[16] not a few self-proclaimed "radical" theologians announced variously the death of God, or that anti-Semitism is the left-hand of Christology,[17] or that only action for social justice could follow after this event since fundamentally it disqualifies Christianity as theology.[18] Manifestly, I do not share such judgments be-

16. Rubenstein, *After Auschwitz*.

17. E.g., Ruether, *Faith and Fratricide*.

18. As in former General Secretary of the World Council of Churches Konrad Raiser's summons in 1995 for the "urgent reordering of the ecumenical agenda away from old doctrinal disputes and unresolvable arguments of the past toward more urgent contemporary issues such as justice, peace and concern for the environment." Cited in George, "Evangelicals and the Present Ecumenical Moment," in ed. Garcia and Wood, *Critical Issues in Ecclesiology*, 60–61. Against Raiser's erection of a false antithesis, George joined his voice to those which have expressed "disquiet and deep concern over what appeared to be the loss of theological substance and Christocentric commitment." I belong to this latter camp, see Hinlicky, "Verbum Externum," in *God Speaks to Us*.

Introduction

cause, second, in writing this book I assume that Christian theology can and must still learn from experience and produce knowledge that makes a difference. Whether that learning is accomplished is for the reader to decide. But methodologically I note with Josiah Royce, as I have argued in detail elsewhere, that theology is "critical dogmatics." As *critical thinking* it does not suffer folly gladly, yet for just this reason hermeneutically it eschews partisan apologetics and partisan polemics alike in pursuit of the truth, and hence *right teaching* (dogma), of the gospel.[19] Neither those who attack nor those who defend succeed in understanding and therefore neither is able to draw any true and helpful lessons for reconstruction "after Christendom" of the church of the gospel in mission to the nations. Theology, as critical dogmatics, conducts inquiry and critique on the level of cultural life, also in the modality of self-examination of its past, in historical theology. As Christian theology, critical dogmatics combats religious experiences and metaphysical motives that arise within the putative domain of the church other than by death to sin in the cross of Christ and resurrection to his faith, hope and love. From chapter to chapter I will make further methodological remarks along these lines as the course of the inquiry requires.

I propose to learn then by pursuing the following set of questions. In the first chapter we will ask what historical scholarship has unearthed in the last two decades or so about "theologians under Hitler," as Robert P. Ericksen put the question in his seminal book by that title.[20] The question taken up in the second chapter is how conservative theologians, who find themselves sore pressed and much afflicted by this new scholarship, have defended their traditional commitments. As a result, we will have to ask whether there is a theological alternative to an historical method intending disillusionment on the one side and mere apologetics on the other. The third chapter seeks to reframe the questions as they have been framed by our complacent and misleading "left/right" binary by listening intently to select contemporaneous witnesses of the rise of Nazism, in this way guarding against the retrospective fallacy. The fourth chapter continues in this vein by asking what can we learn about theology from Hitler himself, who hoped in victorious retirement to return to the religious question and settle it. In the fifth chapter, the ground has been prepared to sketch some fresh answers, clarifying a number of contested theological topics that have emerged from the rise of Nazism and the ambiguous Christian theological responses to it. These topics are the end of Christendom; the problematic relation and distinction of anti-Judaism and anti-Semitism; evangelical mission to the

---

19. Hinlicky, *Beloved Community*, 7–18.
20. Ericksen, *Theologians under Hitler*, a book much discussed in Chapter 1.

nations and the construction of race; Christology and the Jewishness of Jesus; the Two Kingdoms doctrine and political sovereignty; and theological existence or subjectivity. By way of conclusion, as mentioned, I will offer some reflections on the endemic crises of democratic capitalism in our contemporary Euro-America from the perspective of the chastened Christian theology gained from this book's study.

One final note by way of introduction: there is something unseemly in the appearance of yet another English-language book by an American theologian that by focusing attention on someone else's sins de facto deflects attention away from the Trail of Tears and the African Slave Trade. But on reflection, these atrocities are also Euro-American events. A linkage between them and the Holocaust is not blocked by the Atlantic Ocean, but rather navigated by it. As the discussion of Samuel Štefan Osuský in Chapter 3 and the publication of his prescient 1937 lecture in the Appendix indicate, moreover, the present author is biographically and culturally linked to the events in Europe in the middle of the last century. I have accordingly adopted in my writing the neologism, "Euro-America," in order not only to contradict the exaggerations of American Exceptionalists about an American *Sonderweg* (special way), but also to insist that we Americans for the most part still come from Europe, that is, that Europe is still in us, especially so far as we retain the tacit political model of Christendom (on the "right") or parasitically rely on its legacy (on the "left"). I use it, as well, to insist that after Hitler Europeans too see how fatefully we are linked together and how wrong a German *Sonderweg* was then and a European one would be today.

But Native Americans and descendents of the enslaved Africans do not share this history until recently except for the most part as its victims. It is a trap earnestly to be avoided to play genocides off one another. Jewish scholarship has laid the groundwork for today's genocide studies by the work it has done on the Holocaust; this trail-blazing is to its everlasting credit, a real blessing to all nations wrenched out of a singular evil. The "uniqueness" of the Nazi murder of Jews and others is not diminished by attending with equal moral passion and scholarly rigor to other genocides.[21] By way of this note, then, I wish to make a promise eventually to turn attention to the Trail of Tears and the African Slave Trade as the shadow side of American theology. For the present, my own supposition, with Richard L. Rubenstein,[22] is that it is the religious dimension, specifically the Jewish-Christian relation, which makes the Nazi murder of the Jews and others "unique," thus demanding not only historically rigorous inquiry but also

---

21. Rosenbaum, ed., *Is the Holocaust Unique?*
22. Rubenstein, *After Auschwitz*, 45.

theological interpretation that goes to the heart of our respective identities and commitments. Even though I will not answer the theological question of the Holocaust's historical uniqueness in the same way that Rubenstein did, it is fitting to point out that my asking today in this book about theology *before* Auschwitz is only possible and fruitful today because Rubenstein in 1967 asked about theology *after* it.[23]

---

23. "How can Jews believe in an omnipotent, beneficent God after Auschwitz?" Cited from Morgan, *A Holocaust Reader*, 94–95.

Chapter One

Hitler's Theologians

THE MISLEADING POSTWAR NARRATIVE AND THE NEED OF A CORRECTION

ON JANUARY 13, 2002 the *New York Times* published a report, affirmative in tone, on a file of trial evidence that had been prepared by General William J. Donovan's staff after the end of WW II entitled, "The Persecution of the Christian Churches." Supposedly, it documented the Nazi plan to destroy Christianity.[1] The Nuremberg Trials did not pursue this line of inquiry and this file along with others was lodged at Cornell University from the time of Donovan's death in 1959. Rediscovered in 1999, the *Rutgers Journal of Law and Religion*[2] thereafter posted the 108 pages prepared by Donovan's O.S.S. investigators to aid Nuremberg prosecutors. Dated July 6, 1945, the report articulated its operating assumption on its fourth page: "National Socialism by its very nature was hostile to Christianity and the Christian churches. The purpose of the National Socialist movement was to convert the German people into a homogenous racial group united in all its energies for the prosecution of aggressive warfare." Although lost to history until recently, the document's notion of an essential Nazi hostility to Christianity comports with a larger narrative

---

1. *New York Times*, January 13, 2002.
2. "The Persecution of the Christian Churches," 4.

that emerged after the end of the war and has since predominated, namely, that after their Jewish brethren the Christians were next in line for Nazi liquidation, since Nazism was a quasi-religious "totalitarian" movement that pursued its grandiose vision of domination by eliminating rivals in kind step by methodical step. This view of an essential enmity between totalitarian and militaristic Nazism and liberal, peace-loving, tolerant Christianity is still widely shared in North America. Yet empirically things were not so simple.

Since Robert P. Ericksen published his path-breaking *Theologians under Hitler* in 1985, a series of North American historians have followed Ericksen's lead in probing more deeply. Beginning with Ericksen's seminal study, in this chapter we will summarize and analyze these contributions. In keeping with the methodological point made in the Introduction, we will restrict our discussion to these North American authors in order to see, not only what they can teach us about theologians under Hitler, but what we, who write this book and read it, can in the process also learn about ourselves. There is not a seamless unanimity of opinion among these authors about the relation of Nazism and Christianity, but they are united by the basic insight Ericksen gained in his study of Paul Althaus, Gerhard Kittel, and Immanuel Hirsch: "not isolated or eccentric individuals," "not extremists," but intelligent, accomplished Christian theologians and scholars, yet each of these "chose a political stance which ultimately led them to support Adolf Hitler and National Socialism."[3] Flawed though it is in important ways, as we shall see, Ericksen's study undermined the complacent assurances of the predominant, post-war narrative.

In her 1996 book *Twisted Cross*, Doris L. Bergen analyzed the German Christian movement that sought the "co-ordination" of church and theology to Nazism.[4] James M. Stayer in his *Martin Luther: German Saviour* from 2000 exposed the use of the Luther icon by theologians to parse in part their relation to the rise of Nazism.[5] In *Holy Reich* from 2003, Richard Steigmann-Gall pushed Ericksen's breakthrough even further by exorcizing any and all remnants of normative theological judgment about what may properly be called Christian, instead empirically inventorying all who self-identified as Christian. In this way he discovered a great deal of Christian

---

3. *Theologians under Hitler*, 198–99. In this chapter page citations will hereafter be provided in the text by parentheses.

4. Bergen, *Twisted Cross*. In this chapter page citations will hereafter be provided in the text by parentheses.

5. Stayer, *Martin Luther: German Saviour*. In this chapter page citations will hereafter be provided in the text by parentheses.

Nazism.⁶ Finally, in her 2008 study of the German Christian iteration of nineteenth century liberal theology's quest for the historical Jesus, *The Aryan Jesus*, Susannah Heschel exposed the complicity, not of biblicists and fundamentalists, but of liberal Protestant biblical criticism in the service of nazifying the study of Christian origins.⁷

Although published by a North American in this same period, and a book to which I will recur especially in Chapter 5, I do not include in the foregoing list for examination in this chapter Jack Forstman's 1992 *Christian Faith in Dark Times*. The reason is that it is distinguished from these others by its method and intention as "historical theology . . . daring to say what authentic Christian faith means and does not mean, implies and does not imply, here and now."⁸ I mention it here, however, because it serves to set off the non-theological method and intention of our other authors, who, following Ericksen, not only eschew any kind of apologetics for Christian faith, but by objective historical research more or less openly intend the disillusionment of the complacent and inflated narrative articulated in General Donovan's 1945 report. Well-merited disillusionment notwithstanding, as we shall see, a summons to objective historical research is easier claimed than performed. While these historians expressly disavow the retrospective fallacy—in Ericksen's words, "It is hard to provide answers which are objective and which do not rely on hindsight for their verification" (141; cf. 30 in response to Siegele-Wenchkewitz) but accurately display the "complexity of the problem[s]" (70)—my contention will be that these historians have opened up a problematic for Christian theology regarding Christian complicity in Nazism, but not by any means resolved it. Moreover, I will contend that it only can be resolved, as Forstman indicates, by the work of normative theology that is to be sure well informed by history, what I call "critical dogmatics."⁹

ERICKSEN'S THEOLOGIANS UNDER HITLER

Twenty-five some years after Ericksen's book appeared, then, we may firmly and thankfully grant the thesis that he was then seeking to establish about

---

6. Steigmann-Gall, *The Holy Reich*. In this chapter page citations will hereafter be provided in the text by parentheses.

7. Heschel, *The Aryan Jesus*. In this chapter page citations will hereafter be provided in the text by parentheses.

8. Forstman, *Christian Faith in Dark Times*, 245. In this chapter page citations will hereafter be provided in the text by parentheses.

9. See Bielfeldt, Mattox, and Hinlicky, *The Substance of Faith*, 131–90.

Hitler's Theologians

the complicity of mainstream Christian theologians in Nazism. The very premise of this chapter, indeed this book, is the truth of what Ericksen then claimed. What is more interesting to us today, however, is critical reflection on the way Ericksen framed the questions of his inquiry and the theological issues he thereby identified and discussed. The most cognitively troubling of these operating frameworks, in hindsight, is the not uncommon claim in this connection to a moral absolute within history: "Adolf Hitler provides one of the few, clearcut moral quantities in history" (31)—a kind of incarnate Antichrist, as it were, by which to measure evil. What is obscured by this is not the (to us liberals) manifest evil already in Hitler's seizing power and crushing dissent in 1933. But by absolutizing Hitler's (at the time as yet not fully known) evil what is obscured is that mainstream Germans, like Althaus, Hirsch, and Kittel, and not only Germans in the 1930s, found themselves caught between two devils, Hitler and Stalin, and often chose the lesser of these evils according to their own lights and interests.[10] These Christian theologians—indeed the three that Ericksen lifted up for examination—shared a common, vaguely "socialist" opposition to liberal capitalism and thus positively assented to the National Socialist Party platform from 1922 that declared first and foremost for "public need over private greed."[11] This possibility for socialism without Bolshevism helped tip the balance for them towards Hitler's revolution over Stalin's. The Party Platform's vague endorsement of "positive Christianity" likewise seemed to

---

10. It is interesting to note, though there is no indication of it in Ericksen's text, that he wrote simultaneously with the notorious *Historikerstreit* of the 1980s, precipitated by Jürgen Habermas's largely ad hominem attack on Ernst Nolte for, as he charged, historically relativizing, thus normalizing, thus apologizing for Hitlerism as a supposedly rational response to the precedent and threat of Bolshevism. See Knowlton and Cates, eds., *Forever in the Shadow of Hitler?* Nolte certainly overstated his case in speculating about the "true" Nazi intentions. A more defensible thesis is that Hitler, pursuing his own intention of removing Jews from lands claimed for Aryan expansion, hyped the popular fear of Bolshevism (which was also his own) to consolidate domestic support. Eberhard Jäckel puts it well when he wrote in criticism of Nolte and Joachim Fest, who had intervened with perhaps the best defense of Nolte's historical contextualizing of Nazism, that "Hitler often said why he wished to remove and kill Jews. His explanation is a complicated and structurally logical construct that can be reproduced in great detail . . . In contrast, he knew very well how to mobilize for his own uses the fears of the bourgeoisie" (78) regarding Stalinism.

11. Writing as he was in the Reagan era, and before 1989, Ericksen's tendency to diminish the factor of the known reality of Soviet atrocities against the unknown future of Hitler's crimes is understandable as an American academic reaction to Reagan's Manichean rhetoric about the "evil empire." Since then, however, such anti-anticommunism is not historically credible. A series of significant recent titles have made this unmistakably clear. Mazower, *Dark Continent*; Gellately, *Lenin, Stalin, and Hitler*; Snyder, *Bloodlands*.

invite their constructive collaboration in the revolutionary reconstruction of a new Germany. The various ways in the process in which they endorsed, downplayed, or sought to revise Nazi anti-Semitism and other of its unsavory features will be discussed in what follows.

It is appalling, to be sure, to conjure up the same threat of Red Terror that Hitler himself so effectively deployed to the bitter end, but repugnance at this association aside, the fear of Bolshevism with its known atrocities, for example, of the intentional starvation of millions of Ukrainian peasants, the purges and the show trials and the formation of the Gulag, puts our feet back down on the real soil of Germany in the 1930s. Ericksen may be faulted, as we shall see, for regularly diminishing this felt dilemma and reducing it to a reflex of his subjects' supposed "conservativism"—as if even Weimar's Social Democrats, going back to 1919 and their break from the Leninists, had not felt exactly the same dilemma. Recalling from the Introduction the problems that attend any attempt within history to occupy a vantage point superior to history, or an absolute within history, it will suffice in the following to present summaries of Ericksen's evidence and analyses in the cases of Althaus, Hirsch, and Kittel, highlighting the issues raised, and teasing out the ordering principles, such as we have just previewed.

Gerhard Kittel

Gerhard Kittel, internationally renowned as general editor of *The Theological Dictionary of the New Testament*, was a specialist in early Judaism and the origins of Christianity. Kittel was, in Ericksen's judgment, the "sincere" Nazi (75), who took up Nazism as a political Weltanschauung most congruent with his Christian theological convictions, at the same time hoping to influence Nazism to develop in Christian directions. On the basis of his scholarly expertise in early Judaism, Kittel had become convinced that political emancipation and secularization were not only robbing contemporary Jews of their traditional piety but also, in the associated processes of assimilation, diluting Jewish ethnic identity and solidarity (32). His consistent claim was that his work was directed towards providing a Christian and informed, scholarly answer to the so-called "Jewish question." In discussing Kittel's conviction along these lines, Ericksen questions the very propriety of the posing of "the Jewish question" (60). As we shall see in Chapter 3 in our study of the Jewish thinker, Maurice Samuel, however, this question abides.[12] Indeed, it remains at the heart of Judaism itself from the time of

---

12. David Nirenberg's newly published *Anti-Judaism* has come into this author's hands as this manuscript goes to press, too late to take its contents into consideration.

the early rabbis because it is properly speaking a theological question about the vocation of the Jewish people as bearer of Torah values and as such light and blessing to all nations. In our time period, it was asked by all sorts of Europeans and by Jews themselves; indeed, the emergence of Zionism is unthinkable except as a Jewish answer to the "Jewish question." Moreover, today, after Auschwitz, the Jewish question remains; it has neither been answered nor set aside, but internationalized so that it now focuses upon the contested existence of the State of Israel.

In any case, Kittel's answer to the "Jewish question" was in his own "sincere" eyes a severe mercy. He advocated sending Jews back to the ghetto (56), where both piety and peoplehood could be reclaimed. He imagined that his, so to say, apartheid solution could even lead to "a respectful and friendly coexistence of Germans and Jews" (32). He advocated this solution as an alternative to the prospect, which he himself discussed theoretically (55) in order to reject, of the final solution of liquidation. Accordingly, after the war Kittel admitted no guilt or even second thoughts, since, as Ericksen puts it, his distinction between "the vulgar anti-Semitism of Nazi propaganda" and his own position, "Christian in motivation and scientific in method," was "fundamental," not merely to Kittel's post-war self-defense, but to his actual stance within the Third Reich. Of course, presupposed in all this is the viability of the very category of *Volk*. Skeptical though we are today about the reification of ethnicity in this way, Kittel was not merely inventing this concept out of thin air nor borrowing it wholesale from Nazism. As Ericksen's presentation amply shows, Kittel discovered the sense of Jewish peoplehood in the Hebrew scriptures and rabbinic literature and he thought thereby to correct the genetic-racialist interpretation of ethnicity among Nazis with a theological-providential interpretation of the nations or peoples of the earth made by God, as made known by Israel's election.

Kittel, then, like many theological contemporaries, identified with Nazism as "a *völkisch* renewal movement on a Christian, moral foundation" (35). He joined the party, and lent to it his expertise, to combat the vulgar wing. In this combat, of course, he failed and became objectively the servant of that vulgarity. Further, he admitted after the war that he had been bitterly deceived: "the genuine national thoughts which reside in every *Volk* became falsified into a system of imperialistic and megalomaniacal politics of brutality, and the social and socialistic ideal misused as camouflage for lies and corruption. Today I know that my endeavor was based upon the most bitter deception of my life" (43).

A cursory survey, however, indicates weighty reasons why the "Jewish question" in the West and to the West is not overcome.

Note in the citation just made how Kittel complains about the Nazis' abuse of the "social and socialist ideal"; this is generally and rightly considered the standard ideal of progressivism. Yet in Ericksen's judgment we hear repeatedly that it is "apparent that Kittel was very conservative, if not to say, reactionary in his political, social and intellectual attitudes. He rejected the Enlightenment, and with it those ideals of equality and justice admired in the Western world" (44). One has to wonder about the salience of this claim in the 1930s, when the sun still never set on the British Empire and Jim Crow's version of "apartheid" ruled as an established fact of the American way of life, FDR and the New Deal notwithstanding. It is difficult, in any case, to square Ericksen's unqualified judgment with Kittel's credentials as an historical-critical biblical scholar, let alone with his manifest intellectual radicalism in addressing the "Jewish question." Yet again, however, Ericksen tells us that Kittel "entered into the neo-conservative reaction of his generation" after WW I (45), deploying anachronistically a neologism of the Reagan era in which Ericksen was writing. This is said to have taken place, despite Gerhard's upbringing under his father, Rudolph Kittel, at home "in nineteenth century liberal academia" with its "rationalism and tolerance." On the other hand, Ericksen writes that "the younger Kittel shared his father's political conservatism as well as his roots in the pre-war era" (45).

If one finds the play here of the 'liberal—conservative' binary in Ericksen's analysis baffling, it is because Ericksen's deployment of it is confusing. We have here a trope,[13] what Uwe Siemon-Netto will call "cliché thinking" (see Chapter 2 below), just as Adolf Hitler too often appears in his book as the symbol of incarnate evil within history (that is to say, we are provided no analysis of Hitler's theology or of the Nazi Weltanschauung by which to make contextually apt comparisons). Correspondingly, the trope of "the Enlightenment" (likewise given without explication) functions for Ericksen as the icon of progressivism. These tropes, as we shall see again and again, serve to reduce theological questions to existential leaps for Left/Right political options determined upon quite other lines than Forstman's summons to know theologically what is authentically Christian.

Ericksen's conscience as an historian is evident nonetheless when he explicitly states that it would be "too easy to make Kittel the scapegoat or sacrificial lamb" (73). He acknowledges that Kittel was a "genuine Christian

---

13. Sternhell, *Neither Right nor Left: Fascist Ideology in France*. Though devoted to France, where the Left/Right binary originated after the Revolution, this study develops incisive critiques of it. See in addition, Furet, *The Passing of an Illusion,* for examination of the interest served in perpetuating this outmoded binary. The correspondence of Furet with Nolte in the wake of the historians' controversy is illuminating as well; see Furet and Nolte, *Fascism and Communism*.

... a sensitive human being ... academically respected, and took a stance on the Jewish question that was distinct from National Socialist policy. All this cannot and should not be ignored" (73). Ericksen subsequently faults Kittel on two levels. He faults him personally for "opportunism," for "ego involvement and peer pressure," for the "desire to please, to fit in and be acceptable" (74–75), as such forms of complicity are readily imaginable in the consolidated Hitlerland of the later 1930s and beyond. More seriously, however, Ericksen faults the theologian Kittel politically and ethically in that for him the "truth of German experience became the final arbiter of truth in an otherwise relativistic world. In this environment legitimate research could veer into dangerous and tragic paths with no signposts to give warning. Kittel rejected one such signpost, the Enlightenment, with its ideals of equality, basic human rights and tolerance. Christianity had also failed him. It was his misfortune to seize upon the anti-Jewish thread within the Christian tradition to the virtual exclusion of compassion, love and grace" (75). This latter distinction bears the promise of venturing a normative theological judgment and thus making progress in theological knowledge. Unfortunately, the statement as it stands tells us more about Ericksen than about Kittel, as it is imposed from the far distance of contemporary American progressivism and in defiance, or in ignorance, of far more immediate judgments on the ambiguity of the Enlightenment legacy, for pertinent instance, in (the "leftists"!) Adorno and Horkheimer's post-war work.[14] Kittel's work as an historical critic, his vague though avowed socialism, and his claim to have addressed the "Jewish question" with radical intellectual rigor from a dual perspective of Christian faith and scientific method squarely place him within the actual legacy of the Enlightenment as its passes through nineteenth-century German liberal theology. The alternative versions of the Enlightenment for them were Anglo-American individualism, parliamentarianism, and capitalism on the one side and Bolshevism on the other.

Paul Althaus

In this regard Ericksen's treatment of Paul Althaus is marginally more successful. Althaus, like Kittel, is well known in English-speaking circles on account of the translation of his books on Luther's theology and on Luther's ethics. And in fact, Althaus anointed himself, along with Erlangen colleague Werner Elert, as the "authentic voice of Lutheranism" in issuing the *Ansbacher Ratschlag* (the Ansbach Memorandum) in June of 1934, a supposedly pure Lutheran alternative to the Barthian theology of the Barmen

14. Adorno and Horkheimer, *Dialectic of Enlightenment*.

Declaration. The German Christians celebrated Althaus's document "with glee, reprinting it in one of their newspapers under the heading, 'Leading Theologians Refute Barmen'" (87). This little gem of Elert and Althaus gave thanks to God "that he has given to our *Volk* in its time of need the Führer as a 'pious and faithful sovereign,' and that he wants to prepare for us in the National Socialist system of government 'good rule,' a government with 'discipline and honor.' Accordingly, we know that we are responsible before God to assist the work of the Führer in our calling and station in life" (87). What lies behind this enthusiastic endorsement of the National Socialist claim to a revolutionary turning point in German history (with its allusions to the Lutheran confessional writings of the sixteenth century) was, according to Ericksen, Althaus's "desire to make Christianity relevant and attractive to the German people by tying it to völkisch images and issues" (115). Contextual theology, then, together with a correlation to a national liberation movement as a new source of insight into the divine creative work, conditions Althaus's "authentic" Lutheranism. That would be an important and instructive insight into a normatively false theological judgment. Yet again, however, Ericksen names these characteristic progressive theological emphases on context under the assumption that the world sets the agenda for the church as instances of "patriotic, romantic conservatism" (115).[15]

Yet even Althaus's endorsement and theological development of the category of *Volk* as an "order of creation," which Ericksen amply documents (84, 92; 106–8) is hardly stand-pat "conservativism." It is a "progressive" adaptation to supposed cutting-edge advances in evolutionary and anthropological science.[16] But Ericksen does not note how this connects with typically progressive critiques of capitalism and individualism and how modern Nazism borrows from its modern rival, Marxism, the motif of "rebirth" through revolution, through *Volkswerdung* (the process of being formed into a people). Indeed, as we shall see in Chapter 5, Paul Tillich found the deepest failure among his socialist friends and allies in their making just such a facile judgment about Nazism on the basis of dogmatic Marxism.

Ericksen identifies and discusses a number of salient theological topics surrounding Althaus's attempt at völkisch theology. "Salvation history,"

---

15. Compare Ericksen's judgment to Robert Bertram's half-hearted defense of his teacher, Elert, as one who "hoped for a church that could identify with the ethnic-political liberation of his people. He has been likened to a liberation theologian, a title which is anachronistic if apt." Bertram, *A Time for Confessing*, 70.

16. For the immediate context in the rise of social Darwinism, see Weikart, *From Darwin to Hitler*. For broader background to the problem of the rise of scientific racism on the soil of Christian culture, see Kidd, *The Forging of Races*, a book to be discussed below in Chapter 5.

for Althaus, entailed a contemporary affirmation of the biblical God as the living God, the Lord of history, hence theologically the task of discerning "God teaching through history" (85). When remembering the law-gospel distinction of traditional Lutheranism, Althaus could, according to Ericksen's presentation, use this notion critically against the German Christians who interpreted "German history as *Heilsgeschichte*," noting against this christologically that "no *Volk* offers salvation. Only the Christian church does that" (92). Hence for all self-distancing from the Barmen Declaration, Althaus and Elert in the Ansbacher Ratschlag sought a middle way between the Barth circle and the German Christians. Indeed against the latter Althaus rightly saw that the indiscriminate view of revelation as history was a product of nineteenth-century liberal theology as inherited and freshly appropriated by the Deutsche Christen (98)—a judgment with which his rival, Karl Barth, agreed. Hence, by contrast with Barth who spoke a categorical Nein! to the very attempt at engagement here, Althaus tried to develop criteria by which to judge history theologically: Primal Revelation, the Orders of Creation, and the Two Kingdoms. By means of this complex conceptual apparatus, he hoped to discriminate between what is temporal and political on the one side and what is eternal and spiritual on the other, under the traditional Lutheran notion that confusion, rather than the right relation, of time and eternity produces tyranny politically and idolatry theologically. Discovering precisely how these categories failed as theological criteria, then, would be a significant contribution to theological knowledge.

With the help of his Left-Right binary, however, Ericksen handles these notions of Althaus with a crude reduction: "the fundamental, though unexpressed, premise of *Ur-Offenbarung* as developed by Althaus is that God created and approves the political status quo" (100). He cites the Ansbacher Ratschlag as proof: God's law "binds each in the position to which he has been called by God and commits us to the natural orders under which we are subjugated, such as family, *Volk*, race (i.e., blood relation) . . . In that the will of God also meets us continually in our here and now, it binds us also to a specific historical moment . . . " (100). Amalgamating the distinct concepts of Primal Revelation, the Orders of Creation, and the Law of God, Ericksen concludes sarcastically: "According to this theory, God's will equals the situation at any moment, except, of course, for aberrations such as the Weimar years . . ." (100). If that clumsy reduction were not bad enough —Althaus, after all, is being faulted for supporting the revolutionary *Wende* (turning point) of National Socialism!—on the very next page, Ericksen allows that "Althaus argues that this is not a conservative theory, for the natural order is dynamic and ever-changing." That is in fact the true import of the Althaus-Elert claim that God's will meets us in the "here and now" and binds us to just this unique moment of the never ceasing change in which we live, move and have our being. Consequently, just here, as Althaus explains and Ericksen notes, "God may call a person into opposition" (101). But Ericksen's simplistic "conservative-liberal" trope makes a hash of this. In this case it obscures the highly salient fact that in 1934 in Germany it was the Nazis who were dynamic, the change agents, the revolutionaries, whose *Wende* cried out for theological interpretation and judgment of just the kind Althaus attempted with his categories of Primal Revelation, the Orders, and the Kingdoms—notwithstanding his erroneous judgment, as we see in hindsight but on which Ericksen sheds no theological light.

Ericksen virtually despairs of this work of theology. "Unfortunately, this is a very subjective basis for opposing the existing order. Barth no doubt believed he opposed the völkisch idea because directed by God to do so, and Althaus supported it on the same basis. The second ground for opposition to the status quo is no less subjective" (101). Ericksen is certainly in order to raise the question of the "theological subject," what Karl Barth called in these times "theological existence"—a topic to which we will return in Chapter Five. But if once we admit that not all change is for the good, that in some cases the "progressive" thing to do is to resist change, then "opposition to the status quo" cannot function as any kind of illuminating criterion.

All the same, a few pages later Ericksen acknowledged that Althaus in fact turned the "traditional Lutheran views on the state on their head" when he argued for a right to völkisch revolution and so against Luther's belief in a limited state, endorsing instead the total claim of the völkisch State (106). Now Althaus appears as a "progressive" innovator within the "conservative" Lutheran tradition. But not so fast! For Ericksen this complication is only appearance. "Perhaps Althaus' reinterpretation of the *Zweireichlehre* [sic, *Zweireichelehre*, "the Two Kingdom's doctrine"] was not so significant as it first appears. The traditional, non-political stance of the church always supported the status quo, which is a political stance in reality, and it always opposed leftists as a threat to morality and order" (107). This last thought of Ericksen builds upon a statement of Althaus from 1937 that Ericksen had introduced earlier: "The church knows that her God-given responsibility today as yesterday points her into the fight against Bolshevism, against the horrible poison of destruction of all worthy order, all humanity. She belongs on the side of all who conduct this fight with earnestness" (96). Thus in sum "Althaus opposed progressive and revolutionary ideologies of the left which hoped to remake society in a new and better form, and he affirmed the authoritarian and paternalistic emphases of National Socialism" (119). I suppose that in 1986 it was still possible to frame things this way. After 1989 we have to see that in reality Althaus supported progressive and revolutionary ideologies of the "right" that hoped just as much to remake society in a new and better form. And after 1989 we can ask: Just how do Stalin and Hitler differ in their authoritarian and paternalistic emphases?

The tradition of nineteenth-century *Vermittlungstheologie* (mediation theology) in which Althaus stood inclined him to discover in the category of *das Volk* a hitherto overlooked "order of creation." As we have occasion in the following chapters to observe, this fateful move by the self-proclaimed "authentic voice" of Lutheranism by no means reflects the theological legacy of traditional Lutheranism, better represented and developed in the collaborative effort of Dietrich Bonhoeffer and Herman Sasse in the abortive Bethel Confession from the summer of 1933 that took a principled stand against the German Christian "enthusiasm" and named the Jews by name as objects of unjust political persecution.[17] Moreover, when we turn in the next chapter to Uwe Siemon-Netto's treatment of Luther's commendation of "spiritual" resistance over against violent revolution, that is, to nonviolent civil disobedience in the political realm, we will also see how Althaus's theological innovations obscured this possibility in traditional Lutheranism as well.

Immanuel Hirsch

One concession Ericksen makes to the complexity of Althaus's case is to note that the "theme of relevance towards the world is neutral" (117). It can lead either to Immanuel Hirsch's "jump" to the right or to Paul Tillich's "jump" to the left (184), as the treatment of Ericksen's final theologian under Hitler shows. Immanuel Hirsch was not in any ordinary sense a "conservative" theologian, though Ericksen nonetheless links him with Kittel and Althaus in his now familiar trope of "traditional, conservative German Christian values" (189). Intellectually radical like his friend, Paul Tillich, Hirsch found Christianity's traditional dogmas incredible for modern persons (185). Unlike Tillich but with the liberal theology of the nineteenth century, he sought to ground a modern faith perspective on historical knowledge of Jesus of Nazareth—the supposedly "Aryan Jesus" recently discovered by "German theological scholarship" (164, as we may be seen in detail in Susannah Heschel's treatment of Walter Grundmann, discussed below). An expert on the existentialist thought of Søren Kierkegaard, but a follower of the German idealist, Johann Gottlieb Fichte, Hirsch affirmed the Enlightenment as "a pure destructive force" that required of modern theology a fundamental "reformulation as the path ordained of God" in order to "build a new

17. See Hinlicky, "Verbum Externum."

Christian concept of history consistent with the new circumstances and the new understanding" (185), hence a radical revisionism but in recognizable continuity with the liberal theological trajectory of the nineteenth century.

But, according to Ericksen, what this really means is that Hirsch "disliked pluralism and change, the centrifugal forces of modern life. His ideal, therefore, was a society in which a self-aware and unified *Volk* worked together under the authority of a just state. His philosophy of history and theory of knowledge were existential. That is, he believed truth was not empirically verifiable; rather, it had to be individually grasped and then acted upon with courage. It required a leap of faith." One wonders where the error lies in wanting a self-aware and unified people working together under a just government. But the real riddle here—how Hirsch's radical critique approaching "postmodern" perspectives squares with Nazism, say, in parallel with the concurrent political decisionism of Carl Schmitt—[18]goes unremarked, though manifestly Hirsch belongs in the same camp as decisionists like Martin Heidegger and Friedrich Gogarten. This incongruity is all the more surprising, since Ericksen himself emphatically affirms with these existentialist thinkers that "we must act, but we can only do so with fear and trembling" (191), since we cannot know outcomes in advance. How odd, then, that Ericksen finally faults Hirsch, well, for acting, which he construes in Hirsch's case as wanting closure, making a decision as if it actually settled anything. Ericksen describes how Hirsch introduced from Kierkegaard the insight that "reason and freedom lead ultimately to 'the all-encompassing debate about everything . . . ' leading always to crisis and revolution, and this is why it has no unifying, creative power. Instead of being creative, rationalism is ultimately nihilistic, as Nietzsche correctly saw . . . , reveal[ing] only the will to power as the final reality" (151). Not surprisingly, like the other existentialists just mentioned, Hirsch concluded from the unhappy prospect of suicidal nihilism that the only help is a defiant act of will in affirmation of concrete existence, absurd though it be. Hirsch found this will to life in Hitler and his decision for the brute facticity of the blood community of the German *Volk* that Hitler promised to lead to victory. Such was precisely his "new Christian concept of history consistent with the new circumstances and the new understanding" (151).

It is not difficult to see that Hirsch presents Ericksen with his greatest challenge, since he is neither a pietist and biblicist like Kittel nor a neo-Lutheran like Althaus, but a theologian who without equivocation has drunk to the bitter dregs the cup of Enlightenment rationalism ending in nihilism,

---

18. Schmitt, *Political Theology*. For further analysis see "The Occasional Decisionism of Carl Schmitt" in Löwith, *Martin Heidegger and European Nihilism*, 137–69.

yet has drawn from it the politically incorrect conclusion, or rather "leap," in support of Hitler. To be sure, Ericksen from the beginning of his book had discussed a double crisis of modernity: not only the Enlightenment's critique of the antecedent Christian religious tradition, but the critique of Enlightenment rationalism by its children, the "masters of suspicion" Marx, Nietzsche, and Freud. "The lost inheritance of Nietzsche and his disciples was not only traditional Christian culture and values, which Nietzsche rejected altogether, but also any hope of finding a real world beyond the symbolic and relativistic world perceived by our senses" (3). Ericksen rightly located his three theologians in this double-crisis of modernity, and indeed, locates his own work as a contemporary historian venturing moral-political judgments in it as well. This is evident in his concluding statement, "Reason proved inadequate. The crisis of reason, therefore, appears to be real" (199). Existential decision—that is, a non-rational "jump" (184), "Kierkegaard's leap of faith"(177)—is necessary when we face challenges similar to those faced by Hirsch, Kittel, and Althaus. "The present need is for historical insight which is more than relative, which can provide reliable guidelines to the intelligent student of history. But that need remains unmet" (199).

That is a remarkable concession coming at the end of this study. Writing of Tillich and Hirsch, Ericksen concluded, "Approbation or criticism of positions depends finally on personal, subjective judgment" (187)—the very fault Ericksen had found in Barth's and/or Althaus's merely "theological" stances. It is because we own and own up to our own politics of liberal tolerance, then, that we judge Hirsch, Althaus, and Kittel finally wrong: "Perhaps one could insist upon a humanitarian stance in which love or egalitarianism would preclude the most blatant violations of human rights. A strong sense of human rights would certainly have diverted Nazism from committing its worst crimes" (190), though of course with a strong sense of human rights, it would not have been Nazism. What this concession means, then, is that what we have learned through the pages of this study is simply that we have been right all along. "We can best avoid the Nazi error by heavily stressing the values of the liberal, democratic tradition, humanitarianism and justice, and by probing history with a view towards it significance for contemporary decision making" (191). Thus we are empowered to denounce as a Nazi, or a dupe of Nazism, those whom we find to be insufficiently like ourselves politically, so long as we recall with humility that "this conclusion [too] is ultimately exactly like that of Hirsch, an existential decision based upon a leap of faith" (191). We must act with "the possibility of error . . . only in fear and trembling" (191)—so long as we land on the correct side, politically.

This deep agreement with Hirsch complements Ericksen's other major conclusion: "The role of Christianity in history is also called into question by this study" (199, cf. 187 on Hirsch) so far as it supposedly provides a moral guide to political commitment. Hirsch too judged Christian dogma useless, dogmatics as outmoded and incompatible with criticism, Christianity as theology passé. Under this supposition, Christian doctrine appears in this study as but a veneer decorating political decisions formed along other lines (e.g., 100, 120, 183, 186–87) because intellect alone, whether philosophical or theological, cannot decide (124). Ironically, then, even the Enlightenment, not as the truth of rationalism but as a vague symbol of humane values, serves as a tacit criterion (54, 75–76, 191) for correct political engagement, just as "conservative" antimodernism (61, 116, 119) moralism (86, 101, 115, 120, 189), and anti-communism (96, 198) mark tendencies that lead to Hitlerism.

Perhaps historiography cannot do otherwise. But theology can and must do better than this. Notwithstanding the problematic decisionism of his own stance and its reductive tendencies, Ericksen's uncovering of Christian complicity in the rise of Nazism demands the effort, and for this problematic theology is in Ericksen's debt.

DORIS BERGEN'S *TWISTED CROSS*

As if in correction of Ericksen's despair of theology, Doris L. Bergen's *Twisted Cross* proceeds under the hypothesis that study of the theology (such as it was) of the pro-Nazi German Christian Faith Movement would prove instructive. "To me, the German Christian movement embodies a moral and spiritual dilemma I associate with my own religious questions: What is the value of religion, and in particular of Christianity, if it provides no defense against brutality and can even become a willing participant in genocide?" (xi). Thus Bergen follows Ericksen's work opening up the empirical problem of Christian theological complicity in Nazism, though she does not surrender in advance the conviction that Christianity and National Socialism are "two systems of belief that most people would regard as fundamentally irreconcilable" (xi; as we shall see this conviction is the target of Richard Steigmann-Gall's sharp dissent). Holding this conviction, Bergen finds the German Christian effort at the synthesis of "irreconcilable" traditions an interesting topic for investigation and she indeed delivers interesting results. "[T]he movement's attack on church doctrine represented an offensive against the very institutions on which German Christians depended for legitimacy and identity. Devoted to religious revival, they spurned belief. Led by pastors, they denounced the clergy. Rooted in the church, they rejected all manifestations of ecclesiastical order" (173). One telling example she provides from among many: "A German Christian pastor in Bavaria attracted ninety-three youngsters to his confirmation instruction by dropping the required examination . . . It drew exactly the kind of adherents who undermined the [German Christian] movement: people with only a weak link to some aspect of Christian culture, the intellectually lazy, wastrels, thugs" (188). In such ways, "German Christians jettisoned everything theological and moral about Christianity and reduced it to a handful of cultural symbols and practices from their childhoods" (229).

Lebensbezug (relevance to life) is indeed no test of Christian authenticity; in the "successful" confirmation class along the foregoing lines the tail of culture wags the dog of the gospel. But as Klaus Scholder put it, relevance to life was as such the sole theological criterion in German Christianity: The "direct social impulse was characteristic of a whole series of German Christian leaders in the early period. For them the concept of a community of the *Volk* was above all a social concept, the realization of social justice. Certainly it was not accidental that the pastors from the working-class districts were the ones who joined the German Christians . . . 'The German Christians are the SA [storm troopers] of Jesus Christ in the struggle to eliminate physical, social and spiritual distress.'"[19] It is useful here to take a short detour and consult Scholder's analysis of the German Christian Faith Movement, since this exemplary work of postwar German scholarship from the previous generation forms the baseline for further discussions, such as Bergen's, and indeed leads in a direct line to her work.

The first thing to be noted is that the German Christian Faith Movement arose within the Nazi ranks in opposition to the expressly anti-Christian and neo-pagan Weltanschauung articulated in Alfred Rosenberg's *The Myth of the Twentieth Century*: "a new faith: the myth of the blood; the belief that with the blood one is also defending the divinity of human nature." German Christians understood the publication of this book as gauntlet thrown down before them, as "a summons to fight in the NSDAP for a 'German Church' orientation and against a völkisch neo-pagan orientation" (190). In doing so, they sought to defend and define the clause in the Nazi Party Platform in support of "positive Christianity." As such the German Christians are an illustrative case of the perils of systematic apologetics. Second, the doctrine of "totality" in Nazism was understood as a just such a "positive" challenge to overcome traditional Lutheran dualism (193) and achieve "the unity of thinking and doing, of faith and action, of church and politics. German Christianity no longer existed apart from the *Volk* and its history; the

---

19. Scholder, *The Churches and the Third Reich*, *Vol. One*, 212–13. In this chapter page citations will hereafter be provided in the text by parentheses.

Before Auschwitz

German church was no longer just a 'sect,' and the 'tendency to turn away from the world, nature and life' disappeared" (195). Taking over from the rival Religious Socialists the "process of politicizing the churches," German Christians aimed at the "conquest of the church via elections" (196). In this "political theology," as Scholder tags this struggle for power, the hope was cherished "of escaping all theological arguments" (207). Because the "order of the church 'has to conform to the natural conditions established by God in creation and still . . . identifiable today . . . which we find in race and *Volkstum*," discussions "on 'dogmatic questions' were to be avoided at all costs" (208). This avoidance is understandable when we recall that Christian "dogma" has to do with the sinful blindness of fallen creation and its overcoming by the redemptive Incarnation of God in a Jewish man who was crucified by the imperial power, prima facie not themes congenial to "coordination" with Nazism. Nonetheless, "little though they may have reflected or wanted to reflect theologically, the German Christians of the early days were not so far distant from certain theological approaches which at the time were theologically approved of in German Protestantism" (209). What a judgment, as Scholder concludes in the contemporaneous words of Herman Sasse, "upon German theology, upon theological science and theological education, is represented by the fact that the major political theories have gained such authority over even the theologians[!]" (214). It represented an utter loss of theological subjectivity.

With this background in mind, the great advance of Bergen's *Twisted Cross* for our purposes in this study was to have documented the essential role of the German Christian avoidance of dogmatic questions with its roots in nineteenth-century liberal theology—just as the contemporaneous renewer of dogmatic theology and opponent of nineteenth-century liberalism, Karl Barth, expressed the matter when in 1933 he broke his silence and spoke out against the German Christians. "The veriest tyro [British English for "the least beginner"] in theology knows that with their thinking we are dealing with a small collection of odds and ends from the great theological dust-bins (this happy phrase is not mine; I've borrowed it) of the despised eighteenth and nineteenth centuries."[20] Bergen nevertheless rightly demurs from too categorical a judgment here. "Despite affinities and connections, it would be an oversimplification to equate liberal theology and German Christianity," lifting up the counter example of Martin Rade, editor of the *Christliche Welt*, who spoke out against the inhumanity of Nazism (144). We could in this light place Robert Ericksen in the same camp as Rade, since however reduced and simplified, the occasional allusion to the themes of

---

20. Barth, *Theological Existence To-day*, 53.

mercy and compassion in the Christian tradition in fact makes a theologically normative claim that qualifies the utter agnosticism of the existential leap. We shall in any case return to this question of sources in the nineteenth century when we consider Steigmann-Gall's and Heschel's contributions below. For the present, we can focus on the indisputable point that German Christianity sought to evade theology—though, if I may parody Ericksen's statement that a "non-political" stance is in reality a political one, this evasion of theology is itself a theological decision!

What Bergen's mass of evidence shows is that the German Christians were "champions of antidoctrinal Christianity. At the heart of their vision of the church lay not affirmation of certain tenets of faith but the insistence that adherence to particular religious beliefs played no role in determining membership in the spiritual community" (44). Of course, this simply means that other "doctrinal" criteria—racial and political rather than Christological and sacramental—now determined that membership, as known and sanctified by the Creator's *Uroffenbarung*, still visible today in the *Völker*. The tacit contradiction here causes Bergen to describe the "German Christian relationship to church doctrine" as "essentially paradoxical" (45). Notwithstanding, "German Christians took the assault on doctrine seriously" (45). These apparently contradictory claims become intelligible when we understand "doctrine" materially rather than formally, that is, in terms of the incarnational and redemptive content mentioned above, rather than as a merely formal appeal to revelation from above as authoritative. German Christians appealed to a formal revelation in creation in order authoritatively to limit sharply, even eliminate, the matter of the Christological and soteriological content of traditional Lutheranism in Germany.

That distinction is manifest in the German Christian Reinhold Krause's notorious address at the Sports Palace rally in November of 1933, when he called for "liberation from everything un-German in the worship service and the confessions—liberation from the Old Testament with its cheap Jewish morality of exchange and its stories of cattle traders and pimps" (145). Along such lines, other German Christian radicals at this time argued that today's Christian can learn freedom from the law better from Nietzsche than from Paul and thereby avoid "the dangers of being infected by dreaded Jewish-rabbinical doctrines" such as the "exaggerated emphasis on the crucified Christ" and the notion of "human sinfulness" (158)—the just mentioned material content of Christian doctrine. Such was the reaction against these attacks on the material content of Christian doctrine in the early thirties, however, that evasion of such direct theological confrontation between Nazified theology and the traditional doctrine quickly followed. German Christians henceforth sought to fight by "[e]mphasis on the cultural rather than doctrinal or ethical dimensions of the Christianity" (213), with the publication of revisionist editions of the Bible and hymnody (212). This cultural turn was justified on the grounds of an ideal *Volkskirche* (a "people's church") inclusive "of all those defined as true Germans" (163) over against the "pre-Constantinian 'Ghetto-'ideal of the Confessing Church" (225) gathered around true doctrine.

Interestingly, the *Volkskirche* is an ideal, as Bergen notes, that survived the war and the defeat of Nazism. Bergen quotes a veteran of the German Christian movement in 1951, "The German Christians . . . had always sought the people's church, demythologization of the gospel, and Christ alone," (225–26) echoing themes, albeit crudely, in Rudolph Bultmann's post-war theological profile, as we will discuss more thoroughly in Chapter 5. In this diffuse form, with the explicit racism scrubbed out, the German Christian ecclesial ideal not only survived but arguably triumphed (not only or exclusively in Germany!) in the latter twentieth century's ecclesiastical "three 'antis': anti-intellectualism, anticlericalism, and antilegalism" (173). Susannah Heschel's discussion of the post-War rehabilitation of Walter Grundmann and other Nazi sympathizers, as we shall note below, corroborates this thesis.

The Nazi Party for its part abandoned its early hopes for the German Christian Faith Movement to produce a united *Reichskirche* (Imperial Church) "coordinated" with Nazism: *Ein Volk, Ein Reich, Ein Führer* plus *Eine Kirche* (One People, One Empire, One Leader plus One Church). According to Scholder, Hitler only temporarily abandoned his own version of the Two Kingdoms doctrine publically to support Ludwig Müller in the church election for Imperial Bishop of the newly unified Protestants in the Third Reich. Disgusted with the "quarrelling parsons" in the Church Struggle that then broke out, Hitler returned to his previous stance of privatizing and depoliticizing religion.[21] By the mid-thirties a definite anti-Christian hardening within Nazism took place with the rise of figures like Heinrich Himmler and Martin Bormann. We will consider Hitler's own theology in Chapter 4. For present, it suffices to note that the then orphaned German Christian movement floundered, according to Bergen, not only by Hitler's abandonment of it but on the basis of its own internal contradiction of being

---

21. In the *Table Talk* dated August 29, 1942 Hitler commented: "Once only in my life have I been stupid enough to try to unite some twenty different sects under one head; and God, to whom be thanks, endowed my twenty Protestant bishops with such stupidity that I was saved from my own folly. If I had succeeded, I should now have two Popes on my back! And two blackmailers! I can easily deal with the seventeen Protestant Bishops who still exist—but it is only because I have the absolute power that I can do it." Trevor-Roper, ed., *Hitler's Table Talk 1941–1944*, 507; cf. also 393.

doctrinally anti-doctrinal. Not least of this root contradiction was the German Christian attempt to capture the sixteenth-century reformer,[22] Martin Luther, for its purposes. In German Christian hands, Luther—in fact a virtual pacifist, precisely so also in his notorious opposition to violent revolution at the time of the Peasants' Revolt[23]—became an emblem of machismo (75) in their quest for a "manly church." Such "references to Luther reveal the German Christian propensity to appropriate and transform elements of religious tradition to their own ends. As one critic of the movement observed, such manipulation created a 'new Luther,' a 'mirror image of their own fantasies and vanities'"(105).

JAMES STAYER'S *GERMAN SAVIOUR*

But such dishonest appropriation was a broader tendency of the time, a transgression not only committed by the German Christians, according to the probing study of James M. Stayer. Stayer discovered "three distinct schools [that] were in conflict: the Karl Holl School, which has subsequently been called the 'Luther Renaissance,' the Dialectical Theology [of Karl Barth], and the confessional Lutherans" i.e., Althaus and Elert (118). Roughly speaking, Holl's school, proceeding out of Harnack's camp of liberal historicism but prompted to seek new foundations after the catastrophe of World War I, rediscovered in the young Luther an emblem of the theocentric ethic of duty. The early "dialectical" Barth, by contrast, found in Luther's rediscovery of Paul the Apostle the never to be captured and domesticated "event" of God's Yes in the No by the sign of the Wholly Other given in the word of the crucified Messiah. In contrast to both of these, Althaus but especially Elert claimed Luther's virtual pantheism, the immanence of the hidden God who moves all things, leaving no one to be idle, but in this way fatefully binding each and every person to the terror of the concrete situation. All three of these positions shared the turn away from religious individualism to social awareness and responsibility (119). But each constructed a different Luther. Holl found in Luther a forerunner of a chastened Kantian liberalism. Barth found in Luther a forerunner of theological existence between the times. Althaus and Elert found in Luther a forerunner of conscientious national socialism.

Citing Bernd Moeller, Stayer thus notes how modern "Luther research had become 'one of the battlefields where contemporary theological schools air their differences'" (90). Althaus had complained that in both Holl and

22. Carter, "Martin Luther in the Third Reich."
23. For the argument here, see Hinlicky, *Beloved Community*, 337–43.

Barth "[t]heir own systematic insights get insinuated into their interpretation of Luther" (87), although, as we have seen, Althaus is not free from the same tendency. Perhaps nowhere was such self-deceived presentation "of the Reformer's writings as systematic theology yet claiming historical veracity" more egregious than in the case of Eric Vogelsang's 1933 essay, "Martin Luther's Struggle against the Jews," where the old Luther's foul diatribes against Jews from the end of his life reappeared now as forerunner of the "manifest" modern insight into "the evils of capitalism" (116). Stayer's thesis is that given "the background of war and defeat the academic enterprise of rehabilitating Luther became the search for a German saviour" (17). Methodologically, his probing investigation of the evidence and subtle analyses of it demands greater self-awareness among historians, especially in the field of theology where intellectual decisions about interpretation inevitably coalesce with personal religious investments (recall Bergen's acknowledgment in this regard). It also demands that theologians take responsibility for their appropriations of historical material from the tradition and not dodge responsibility by claiming only to represent objectively an authoritative voice from the past.[24] Theologians always select from the infinity of the data and in this way consciously or unconsciously shape the materials re-presented. Theologians today in the tradition of Luther surely should de-select his noxious ravings against the Jews (and the Pope and the peasants[25]), just as historians should want to contextualize those sixteenth-century ravings so that easy transferences into the present are rendered less possible and genuine insight into moral, not to mention theological, error from the past is made fruitful for today.

Substantively, Stayer's patient analysis of the anti-Barthian "mock-Lutheran common platform for Elert, Althaus, Hirsch and Gogarten" in "belief in a nationalist revelation through the law" (120) is a major advance in understanding the convoluted polemics (123) of these fateful times. Stayer additionally points out how Barth's position against these "Lutherans" is not a return to the pre-critical but "a thoroughly modern option" that just like the liberals" was "tied to no creed" (120) other than the infinite qualitative difference between God and humanity (as the confessionalists polemically pointed out against him). For the sake of clarity, let me note that I take this correct observation of Barth's modernity differently than does Stayer, or than as Forstman will take Bultmann's parallel continuity "with the much-maligned liberal theology of the pre-war era" (120). In my view the

---

24. Ibid., xviii-xix.

25. See the appendix, "The Problem of Demonization in Luther's Apocalyptic Theology," in ibid., 379–85.

positions of both Barth and Bultmann are not sufficiently postmodern, as I will argue in Chapter 5 by finding the way forward in Bonhoeffer. Interestingly, in the utilization just here of the facile "left-right" binary Stayer notes dependence on Ericksen (135).

RICHARD STEIGMANN-GALL'S *HOLY REICH*

We now turn to one of the most insightful and stimulating studies in the train of Ericksen's breakthrough, Richard Steigmann-Gall's *The Holy Reich* (cf. x; 5, fn 14). Steigmann-Gall takes a radically empirical approach to the evidence, eschewing any notions of theological normativity in terms of an essential doctrinal opposition between Christianity and Nazism. In his Introduction, Steigmann-Gall claims that a growing body of evidence disputes Karl Barth's 1943 claim that Christianity was separated "as by an abyss from the inherent godlessness of National Socialism" (4). He upholds in its place the historical-genealogical claim of the Nazi Ukrainian Gauleiter Erich Koch in 1949 "that the Nazi idea had to develop from a basic Prussian-Protestant attitude [*Grundhaltung*] and from Luther's unfinished Reformation" (2). While it is unlikely that Steigmann-Gall grasps the theological nuances of speaking of the "Prussian" theological tradition and an "unfinished" Reformation, he is nonetheless justified in exploring "the ways in which many leading Nazis [like Koch] in fact considered themselves Christians (among other things) and understood their movement (among other ways) within a Christian frame of reference" (3). This sheer and unprejudiced empiricism (reiterated in conclusion, 266) of examining all who in some way self-identified as Christian leads "with growing empirical certainty" to the conclusion "that many Christians of the day believed Nazism to be in some sense a Christian movement" (5).

The implications of this method and these results are far-reaching. Steigmann-Gall skewers the likes of John Conway, Klaus Scholder, and Doris Bergen, as in general the narrative of essential enmity between Christianity and Nazism that we witnessed in General Donovan's report, for employing the self-exculpating pretext that Christians who supported Nazism either "deceived themselves, or they were not truly Christian" (5). He singles out Doris Bergen especially for criticism: "only false-consciousness theory allows us to contend that millions of sincere Christians could create a non-Christian movement." Her analytical category of "canonicity" (i.e., the theological normativity of the canonical scriptures of Old and New Testament) "set[s] the bar sufficiently high to prohibit the German Christians from passing the test of true Christianity" (6). Ironically, as we shall see, with this kind of criticism Steigmann-Gall mirrors the very anti-theological theology that he otherwise—empirically and incisively—traces to the German Christians' roots in nineteenth-century liberal theology. Notwithstanding that irony of method, the empirical evidence he so gathers for the complicity of many who self-identified as Christians with Nazism leads to a thesis that is apparently diametrically opposed to General Donovan's. Rejecting "the intentionalists' 'Hitlercentric' interpretation of Nazism," which offloads "as much responsibility on as few people as possible," Steigmann-Gall uncovers the basis of support for Hitler in the "positive Christianity" commended in the Nazi Party platform (10). On this basis Steigmann-Gall argues through this impressive volume that "Nazism was not a result of a 'Death of God' in secularized society, but rather a radicalized and singularly horrific attempt to preserve God against secularized society" (12).

Fittingly, given the stakes of the issue involved here, this argument is as impressive as it is intellectually radical. It causes theologians a salutary discomfort to consider whether Nazism may be the product rather than the failure of civilization (Bauman, 261), just as Christianity "may be the source of some of the same darkness it abhors" (267). From the perspective of theology, certainly, Steigmann-Gall commits some mind-boggling howlers that might cause a theologically educated believer, Jewish or Christian, to close the book in dismay at his amateurism. For example, Steigmann-Gall regularly inveighs against the superstition of an "interventionist God of history," a "providential, active deity," a "supernatural religion instead of a religion of nature" (e.g., 21, 26, 36) without the slightest indication that we owe such conceptions of divinity to the salvation event of the Exodus of the Hebrews from Egyptian bondage and to the prophetic tradition in Israel that developed from this belief in the scriptural Lord of History. Likewise Steigmann-Gall crusades against "a dualistic understanding of human behavior hegemonic in Western, Christian civilizations . . . defending good by waging war against evil, fighting for God against the Devil, for German against Jew . . . [not for] the death of God, but the preservation of God" (261) with no cognizance of the sources of such "dualistic" views, for example, in the book of Joshua, or in the Jewish apocalyptic of the Second Temple period, as well as in Jesus, Paul, and John. Nor does Steigmann-Gall betray any capacity to distinguish Platonic, apocalyptic, and Gnostic "dualisms," nor any understanding how the Augustine's notion of original sin—genuinely "hegemonic" in Western Christian tradition and conceived in his struggle against Manichaeism—complicates any simplistic moral dualism of good and evil. Notwithstanding, Hitlerism functions in Steigmann-Gall's text as a moral absolute in history, the incarnation of evil, against which this very passionate and intelligent author wages total intellectual warfare.

Stunningly, however, Steigmann-Gall in his ignorance of the Bible and theology unwittingly mirrors the anti-dualistic demand for totality that animated his antagonists, the German Christians, who by a *Volkskirche*, absorbed into the State by a process of *Volkswerdung*, would overcome the distance and separation demanded by the Two Kingdoms doctrine, when taken as an iteration of the complex entanglement and yet conflict between Augustine's *civitas terrena* and the *civitas Dei*.

He is an historian, certainly not a theologian. These flaws, on the other hand, should not excuse theologians from taking Steigmann-Gall's discoveries even more seriously than he does or can do, that is to say, from taking them theologically. And here Steigmann-Gall has rendered a great service, though a word of caution previously spoken remains in order concerning what now follows. As we have already noted with regard to Martin Rade, not all liberal Protestants drew German Christian conclusions in the crises of modernity in the context of German desperation in the Weimar period, and it would be worthwhile to debate what the difference is between a Rade and these others. In any case, we are not speaking directly here of Schleiermacher, or Ritschl, or Harnack, or Troeltsch but of the appropriations made of these theologians by German Christians in the 1920s and 30s, just as was also the case in the appropriations of Luther that Stayer studied in Holl, Barth and Althaus-Elert.

Duly warned in this way, we may now consider the massive display of evidence from the primary sources that Steigmann-Gall uncovers how Nazi Christians repeatedly argued (confirming Doris Bergen's thesis) that "[w]hat 'Christianity achieves is not dogma, it does not seek the outward ecclesiastical form, but rather ethical principles . . . ,' the erection of a National Socialist Peoples' Community" (46); that "Positive Christians may have said little or nothing about the Augsburg Confession or other signifiers of theological orthodoxy, but they nonetheless regarded Christian social theories—'practical Christianity' as it was also known—as a linchpin of their worldview" (49); that "[o]nly by ignoring the intellectual precedents for these ideas can we argue that positive Christianity was an 'infection' of an otherwise pristine faith"—instead, "these ideas found expression among bona fide voices of *Kulturprotestantismus* before the Nazi Party ever existed" (50); that Catholic and confessional Lutheran separatism aside, "here again we see an aspect of Nazi belief that bears striking resemblance to the position of theologically liberal Protestantism dating back to the nineteenth century. In large measure, liberal Protestantism was directed against the Lutheran defense of the confessional school and the "Christian state" that defended it. Although liberal Protestants believed in the church as a community of believers within the state, they maintained that it would ultimately be absorbed by the state" (78); that Nazism thus offered an opportunity "to foster the cultural hegemony of liberal Protestantism in Germany by simply removing reference to confessionalism of any kind, be it Lutheran or Catholic" (80). One could continue in the vein for a very long time. From this line of argument, Steigmann-Gall writes by way of conclusion: "Liberal Protestantism is of particular importance in understanding the racial antisemitism the Nazis would perfect. It represented a Christian response to the theological challenges posed both by secular modernity and the perceived danger of the acculturated and assimilated German Jew. The attempt to meet this challenge came through a theological accommodation with science, one that still preserved the relevance of the gospels . . . Not only did racialistic antisemitism find a warmer reception among liberal Protestants than among confessional Lutherans, in many ways racialist antisemitism was born of the theological crisis that liberal Protestantism represented" (263).

If with due caution we grant the substance of this connection Steigmann-Gall makes between liberal theology as doctrinal Christianity in crisis and the appropriation of this crises in support for Nazism, the most challenging counter-evidence that Steigmann-Gall has to face comes to the surface in his final, fascinating chapter on the *gottgläubig*, literally, those believing in God, a technical term adopted by the Nazis for their own "unitarian," i.e., non-Christian in the sense of non-doctrinal, belief in a higher power not identified as the Father who sends the Son and the Spirit into the world for its salvation. Steigmann-Gall strives mightily to connect this phenomenon to its historically Christian antecedents, but has about as much success as any attempt to connect Deism to Trinitarianism might have. On the contrary, all the arguments for the thesis that by the mid-1930s Nazi elites had gained clarity about the post-Christian nature of their movement, resulting in the expulsion of pastors from the party and the prohibition of church membership for the SS, find important confirmation in the Gottgläubig creed.

Quoting Goebbels, "A *Volk* that has gone through four years of war and fifteen of Marxism can no longer muster the energy to follow theological hair-splitting. It wants to see an active Christianity, and sees it better embodied in something like Winter Relief than in the theological disputes of the so-called Confessing Front." Steigmann-Gall tries to tell us that Goebbels' comment "displays a consistent attitude: low regard for the churches and high regard for Christianity" (232). This comment is baffling indeed. What Goebbels, just like the liberal Protestants, holds in contempt is Christianity as church and theology. What Goebbels, just like the liberal Protestants, holds in high regards is humble service and works of mercy in service of society. Just this anti-doctrinal doctrine, as in the words of other Nazi voices Steigmann-Gall collects in this chapter, "is the positive Christian faith in the sense of Point 24 of the Party Program, but never the dogmatic beliefs of the confessions and other international sects falsified by the Jews" (242). The anti-doctrinal doctrine of the German Christians, namely "to reject the Old Testament, firmly defend the New Testament against attacks from the paganists, and [that] Jesus was an Aryan," (243) slides seamlessly into the mature stance of the elite Gottgläubig. As Hannah Arendt commented in a dramatic passage surely known to Steigmann-Gall, Eichmann "was in complete command of himself, nay, he was more: he was completely himself. Nothing could have demonstrated this more convincingly than the grotesque silliness of his last words. He began by stating emphatically that he was a *Gottgläubiger*, to express in common Nazi fashion that he was no Christian and did not believe in life after death . . ."[26]

SUSANNAH HESCHEL'S *ARYAN JESUS*

I shall return to Steigmann-Gall's most tendentious argument in this connection, namely, that Hitler's *Table Talks* have been edited, rather distorted in a profoundly antichristian direction by Martin Bormann (255) when I turn in Chapter 4 to the topic of Hitler's theology. In any event, what Steigmann-Gall has demonstrated for Christian theology, contrary perhaps to his own intention, is that "theological hair-splitting" matters, indeed, that it can be a matter of life and death. Consequently, the question of this chapter now becomes even more precise. Can we learn specifically what the liberal Protestant alternative to doctrinal theology was and how it played into the hands of Nazism? Susannah Heschel has asked and answered this question in a profoundly important study on a number of different levels.

The main focus of her investigation is the work of the biblical scholar Walter Grundmann and his Institute for the Study and Eradication of Jewish Influence on German Church Life. Grundmann, building on a number of liberal Protestant commonplaces—that both Jewish legalism/ritualism and Greek intellectualism had distorted the original message of Jesus, that doctrine divides but action unites, that ethical relevance to contemporary social and political struggles not metaphysical speculation helps today—found in the History of Religions School the intellectual alternative to traditional doctrinal theology. Critical study of the Gospels in this mode uncovered the fact that Jesus was a Galilean, not really born in Bethlehem, in fact not really a Jew at all but an Aryan, the bastard offspring of a Roman centurion. As Heschel describes it, "[t]he Galilean Jesus argument entered

26. Arendt, *Eichmann in Jersusalem*, 252.

the work of university theologians in the 1920s and '30s who were rejecting supernatural miracles and established Christian dogma in favor of a historical approach to scriptures, and many were influenced by the methods of the History of Religions school. As historians, they rejected the binding nature of church doctrine and viewed texts as products of cultural and religious beliefs of their era; the canonicity of texts was irrelevant to their weight as historical evidence for the circumstances of Christianity's origins" (58).

The implications of this new methodology in severing the canonical link of the Testaments were enormous. "History of Religions opened the possibility of a radically revised interpretation of Jesus' message that would see it not as fulfilling God's promises, as contained in the (Jewish) Old Testament, but reflecting ancient Near Eastern and Asian ideas, some of which were then claimed to be Aryan in origin" (202). Thus we see how it was possible that "History of Religions methods were championed as the way to recognize the unique religious message appropriate to the German race—and eliminate Jewish influence that had distorted it . . . since each *Volk* received the message of God in a distinctive way, religious texts such as the Old Testament could not be studied 'theologically,' that is, as the unmediated word of God with a message for all peoples" (225). Moreover, in just this anti-theological way, History of Religions could claim for itself the mantle of science in a stance of disinterested objectivity, unprejudiced by dogma. "Over time History of Religions became identified with the German Christian movement, which used it as cover to overturn church doctrine and discipline. German Christian-affiliated scholars championed its putatively objective approach to religion and sought to imbue it with racial theory" (225). In the hands of Grundmann and his Institute, the History of Religions model of religious studies envisioned a radical reform of the curriculum. "Old Testament would be replaced by a chair in the 'History of Religions in the Near East . . . ;' New Testament would be replaced by 'Study of the Gospels and the Origins of Christianity . . . ' placed in the context of Hellenism . . . Church history would be the history of Germanic piety, and religions of the East would be examined to find their 'Aryan religious element.' Systematic theology would be taught as 'reflection on the effective powers of the gospel for pious German life.'" Heschel comments immediately: "the proposal reversed the traditional systematic theology by making present-day experience the hermeneutical key to truth" (227) as opposed to the biblical gospel, taken as an external Word from God, telling of an event in time and space otherwise unknown to "present-day experience."

What in the background could have brought German Protestants to such a paradoxical self-cancellation of their tradition—Martin Luther, after all, made his living as a professor of Old Testament and had formed the modern German language by rendering its stories and poetry in his famed translation into early modern German directly from the Hebrew (no longer via the Vulgate or Septuagint)? Here Heschel argues a complex and interesting thesis on the relation of the traditional, religiously focused Christian anti-Judaism and the modern, racially focused Nazi anti-Semitism. The German Christian's "enthusiasm for Nazism," she argues, did not bring them to racism in general; rather, "their theological anti-Judaism brought them to support National Socialism because of its antisemitism" (200). As a result even the post-war "churches had difficulty distinguishing the Nazis' antisemitism from what they considered legitimate expressions of Christian theological anti-Judaism." With its "conservative theological base," even members of the Confessing Church "frequently shared with their former German Christian antagonists a sense that Judaism and even Jews were degenerate and posed a potential threat to the spiritual well-being of Germany" (277). As a result of this slippery slope from anti-Judaism to anti-Semitism, "[d]enazification was a failure . . . Clear evidence of antisemitism in published scholarly articles could be attributed to classic motifs of Christian theological anti-Judaism, rather than taken as evidence of Nazi sympathy" (244). Heschel can thus concur with arguments now familiar from Ericksen and Steigmann-Gall that the very distinction between theological anti-Judaism and racial anti-Semitism fosters "the myth that theologians did not contribute to the Nazi murder of the Jews . . . that Nazism represented an anti-Christian pagan revival" (286).

But Heschel's account of the specific proclivity of Christian theologians for finding affinity with Nazism is more precise than in Ericksen or Steigmann-Gall: "Theologians gravitated towards racism as a tool to modernize Christianity and to demonstrate that its principles were in accord with those of racial theory. In addition, they considered racial theory a tool to grant scientific legitimation to religion" (286). In short, then, both the liberal theological desire for accommodation to contemporary culture and scientific advances and the traditional anti-Judaism of conservative theology colluded: "The antisemitism of Christian theological literature was simply not recognized as antisemitic; it was more often seen as expressing historical or dogmatic [or biological] truths about Jews and Judaism" (278). While this observation is undoubtedly valid, it can only be secured theologically by Jewish and Christian theologians working together in dialogue, as I shall argue in Chapter 5 below. The truth of this contention may be indicated presently, however, in Heschel's willingness (like Steigmann-Gall's) to make theological criticisms of Christianity, something that is only possible on the presumed basis of its normative self-understanding.

For example, Heschel sharply judges Christian post-war self-exculpation this way. "Christian theology, with its self-definition as a religion of forgiveness based on divine moral principles higher than those of a court of law or democratic political system, was used to oppose harsh judgments of Nazi criminals and suppress the sort of thoroughgoing investigation of Nazi affinities that might have brought the downfall of Institute members who instead enjoyed flourishing postwar careers" (287). Theologically, I welcome this critical theological intervention, because it rightly challenges a subtle but very false (i.e., antinomian) understanding of Christianity as a "religion of forgiveness based on divine moral principles higher than those of a court of law . . ." Theological dialogue with living Judaism along these lines forces Christians to reflect far more rigorously and seriously about how they can proclaim good news in a still unredeemed world.[27] By the same token, however, Christian theology that dares yet to proclaim good news in a still unredeemed world has the corresponding freedom to ask of Jews for a proper understanding of Judaism, including Judaism's own ambivalent relations to Christianity, and to engage in theological debate about this as befits moral equals. Proper Jewish identity is of course no more a settled matter among Jews than Christian identity is among Christians.

There are certainly neuralgic issues here in need of airing. During the rise of Nazism Christian defenses of its Old Testament as scripture, hence of Israel's divine calling to be blessing to the nations, had to claim fulfillment in that son of Abraham who is the Son of God, hence had to assert painfully the claim of Paul, the Jewish apostle to the nations so hated by Nazis, that Jews of Judaism read these same scriptures with eyes veiled by their commitment to the finality and supremacy of the law of Moses (2 Cor 3:14–16). Ignoring this root Messianic divergence, Heschel's criticisms of von Rad, following Jon Levinson (214ff, 229), are among the least sophisticated, not to say least helpful passages in her excellent book. Similarly, as we shall see in Chapter 3, during this period those who defended the co-equal humanity of Jews with Germans were just those "evangelicals" who were engaged in the Christian mission to the Jews, therein believing them to be human beings capable of "conversion" as also believing baptism capable of tearing down the dividing walls of hostility and creating a new unity thicker than "blood." Jewish theologians can surely dissent from these Christian convictions, but they can no more attribute these convictions to anti-Semitism than they can attribute their dissent to them as anti-Gentilism. We both and

---

27. As I tried to say years ago in my not yet mature "A Lutheran Contribution to the Theology of Judaism."

together have to work theologically to "achieve disagreement" here, at the root of our historic divergence.

Heschel throws down such a welcome gauntlet when she concludes her study with a savage irony visited back on Christians, namely, that Nazis were simply imitating the Christian supersessionist teaching in regard to Judaism and now completing it: "National Socialism, in Hitler's mind, took up the antisemitism of Christianity but elevated it to a more intense level and transformed theory into action" (285, cf. 165). Just as Judaism was fulfilled and replaced by Christianity, now "Christianity receives fulfillment in National Socialism . . . " (195). This is of course a theological claim that we will test in Chapter 4. That Heschel's brand of critical history, debunking convenient and self-exculpatory myths, drives us afresh to theology is itself a mark of genuine progress. And such is the cumulative contribution of all the authors discussed in this chapter.

Chapter Two

The Peril of Conservative Apologetics

LUTHERANS ON THE DEFENSIVE

Without great care, as we maintained in the Introduction but learned especially from James Stayer in the previous chapter, neither academic historiography nor historical theology is preserved from a temptation built into its necessarily retrospective posture. Just because this exercise in the *studia humanitatis* is interested in its learning, and interested for itself, the inclination to fall into the retrospective fallacy is well nigh inescapable. This may occur in one of two ways. First, in order to secure "objective" results, one may evade responsibility for, or suppress awareness of, present-day appropriation of traditional material by disguising the historian's or the theological interpreter's narrative act as a pure representation of the past. The result of this pretended objectivity were it, as is impossible, successful, however, would be that we should have in principle to leave the past in the past from which we can draw no usable lessons for our contemporary human self-understanding. But in fact a present-day human self-understanding has not only motivated but informed the narrative construction of supposedly "objective" history. Or, second, one may renounce objectivity as a pretension in the name of the infinite moral passion of the human subject who, condemned to freedom, must judge the past and judge from no other perspective than the one occupied by itself in all its glorious particularity of the here and now. The result of this all-consuming existential subjectivity is that the past never gets a hearing on its own terms in critical dialogue with the present, as enabled by the empathetic listening, through the historical interpreter's articulation of its claim to truth. Then and only then can a critical disputation about truth and truthful judgment occur. But in existential subjectivism what starts out as an inquiry into others ends up constructing a mirror image of the inquirer.

The first version of the retrospective fallacy is the one generally, though not necessarily, committed by structuralists, who tend to dissolve the human subjects of the past into the transpersonal social forces that so powerfully play them. The second version is the one committed usually, though not necessarily, by intentionalists, who tend to underplay that causal nexus in which human subjectivity is ineluctably born, formed, and carried along. Either way we face here the Ying and Yang of Destiny and Freedom—a polarity or dialectic or illusion, as we may variously think, that plagues understanding in the humanities. There is a reason, much suppressed nowadays, for this perplexity. How we think about Destiny and Freedom is our tacit theology, uncritical or critical, implicit or explicit, as the case may be. "God" is how we connect destiny and freedom.

In this light, the study of Martin Luther and of the Lutheran theological tradition is a particular bone of contention in the historical and historical-theological interpretation of Hitler's theologians. As Stayer pointed out, Karl Barth in our period was still claiming Luther's mantle. His famous attacks on Luther and Lutheranism come after—indeed arise from—disillusionment at the stance adopted by Althaus and Elert (and others, especially erstwhile fellow dialectical theologian, Friedrich Gogarten, as Jack Forstman shows[1]) during the rise of Nazism. While there are already foretastes[2] of the later fireworks in Barth's criticism of the "New Reformation" Movement alongside the German Christian Faith Movement in 1933,[3] it is arguably the

---

1. Forstman, *Dark Times*, 160–78.

2. Most notably in the Feuerbach essay of 1926 (thanks to Michael DeJonge for this note, personal correspondence, 1/4/13). See Karl Barth, "Introduction" in Ludwig Feuerbach, *The Essence of Christianity* x–xxxii. See Hinlicky, "Luther's Atheism" in *The Devil's Whore*, 53–60.

3. While Barth praises this movement, naming Walter Künneth at its head, for opposing the Aryan Clause in the church (*Theological Existence*, 64), he sharply questions its "joyous assent to the New German State" (65). "Is not, or was not, the New Reformation Movement perhaps merely the successor of the old 'Mediation Theology' in its occasional, but very spasmodic battle waged against the old 'Liberals'?" (66). With this double-sided ambivalence in view, Barth makes the very critique he will later make of the confessional Lutherans: "They are not standing out as an opposition based on

case that Barth's mature political theology was shaped decisively by his specific dismay at the ambivalent stance of the "confessional Lutherans" in that they thought they could criticize the German Christian heresy spiritually but lend support to the Hitler regime politically. In interpreting this double perspective of the confessional Lutherans, Stayer even claims that the term, *Zweireichelehre* (the Two Kingdoms doctrine), originated in Barth's polemics as a term of abuse.

Historically this claim may be doubtful, but substantively it has some merit. One will not find the Two Kingdoms concept as such, for example, in Heinrich Schmid's late-nineteenth-century compendium of the classical doctrinal theology of the Lutheran church. Instead one finds the concept of Christendom with its three estates of church, domestic economy, and state — what in the course of the nineteenth century morphed into the so-called Orders of Creation.[4] Oswald Bayer even maintains that it is the teaching on the "three estates" by which Luther "interprets for his contemporaries the primeval biblical history in terms of a theology of creation, a theology of sin, and ethics for society . . ."[5] such that this "precludes a simple and schematic articulation of his ethics by evaluating something such as his teaching about the two realms." Indeed, it would be error to advocate that "the," (*n.b.*, not Luther's particular teaching, as will be made clear in Chapter 5, but supposedly) "*the* teaching about the two realms can be easily integrated with the teaching about the estates."[6]

---

principle according to a Church theology which can be taken seriously" (62-63), but merely as conservative apologists of the inherited ecclesiastical establishment. But the stand of theology on the church as hearer of the Word of God, not on the church as heir of a theological tradition no matter how venerable, i.e., as the supposed "authentic voice of Lutheranism," is the heart of the divergence between Barth and the latter day Lutherans. This root divergence is not as such about the Two Kingdoms doctrine which is the reason why Barth could tolerate the amendment of his Barmen Declaration draft in Thesis 5.

4. Schmid, *Doctrinal Theology of the Evangelical Lutheran Church*, 604-23.
5. Bayer, *Martin Luther's Theology*, 122.
6. Ibid., 126 (emphasis added). For a responsible American adaptation, see the now forgotten Lazareth, *Luther on the Christian Home* with the republication of its final chapter and new preface in *Lutheran Quarterly* (1993) 235-68; cf. also "The Redemption of the Body: Luther on Marriage," Chapter 6 in Hinlicky, *Beloved Community*, 179-220 and Lazareth, *Christians in Society*. The matter is vexing. For a recent defense of the Two Kingdoms doctrine as Luther's signal contribution to social ethics, see Wright, *Martin Luther's Understanding of God's Two Kingdoms*. I tend to side with Bayer as in *Beloved Community*, 357, if only because it proves so difficult to disentangle Luther's meaning from the Cartesian-Kantian dualism through which it is read, as we shall see in Chapter 5 below. See also the postwar work of the chastened Althaus, *The Ethics of Martin Luther*, especially 79-82, which still wants to put political sovereignty into positive analogy to the kingdom of God.

On the other hand, as far back as the final article of the Augsburg Confession distinguishing the spiritual rule of bishops by Word and Spirit from the coercive rule of magistrates by the Sword (the distinction which historical scholarship has identified as the starting point of the composition of the Augsburg Confession and the goal of the final text[7]), the distinction between the temporal-secular realm and the eternal-spiritual one was officially imprinted on Lutheranism by its chief doctrinal statement. But in broader historical view, this distinction was but a new iteration of Augustine's Two Cities or the Apostle's opposition between Adam and Christ or the dominical statement about giving to Caesar what is Caesar's and to God what is God's. The distinction served theoretically to identify and reject both idolatry in the spiritual realm and tyranny in the political that occurs when in politics temporal powers claim eternal right or duration or when in religion eternal powers are captured for temporal purposes of dominion, although, in the vicissitudes of German Lutheran history, the alliance of throne and altar as often as not undercut that essential theological service. After the war, Johannes Heckel, a church lawyer who was very actively involved in negotiations for the unification of the regional German churches (the *Landeskirchen*) in the would-be newly unified *Reichskirche* under National Socialism,[8] published a major study on the Two Kingdom's doctrine in which he famously described the confusion surrounding the concept of the Two Kingdoms a "labyrinth."[9] He advocated the apocalyptic opposition between God and the devil as the basic framework of Luther's teaching on the Two Kingdoms—in part, no doubt, in reaction to what had taken place under Hitler. But this apocalyptic scheme of an essential opposition between the Kingdoms seems to give little place for Christian social responsibility in the political realm. A generation later, Ulrich Duchrow[10] modified Heckel's scheme in order to endorse the political kingdom as God's work, where his will for justice and peace is to be accomplished. This amounted to a return to Althaus's early political theology, though now in the mood of 1968 rather than of 1933. In either case one wonders why any distinction between the power of the sword and the power of Word and Spirit is to be maintained at all. The topic is indeed a "labyrinth." We will return to it in Chapter 5.

For the present, the point of the foregoing is to indicate the danger even, if not especially in self-professed "conservative" theological apologetics, that

---

7. Mauer, *Historical Commentary on the Augsburg Confession*, 59–238.
8. Scholder, *Churches and the Third Reich*, I: 373–78.
9. Heckel, *Lex Charitatis*.
10. Duchrow, *Christenheit und Weltverantwortung*. For a responsible American appropriation, see Robert Benne, *The Paradoxical Vision*.

the thesis lives on in the antithesis. That is to say, in defending a position under hostile attack, the "conservative" unwittingly adopts the premises of the attacker and so comes to frame the questions under dispute from a perspective alien to the position allegedly being defended, as we saw in the last chapter how German Christians argued that they were and could be better Nazis than the neo-pagans. Consequently one is pressed by a newly though often unconsciously adopted frame of reference subtly to revise the original position until one's ballyhooed defense step by step is lead to a substantive capitulation. As Doris Bergen showed us in the last chapter, that substantive capitulation is readily visible in the quixotic endeavor of the German Christians to "coordinate" the legacy of Reformation theology in Germany with Nazism. It is less visible but surely just as operative, as Robert Ericksen argued, in Althaus's attempt as "mediation"—the same posture of systematic apologetics that Karl Barth criticized as the modus operandi of the New Reformation Movement. Systematically pursued, systematic apologetics systematically misleads.

In distinction from such systematic apologetics, there is both need and possibility of what George Lindbeck called "ad hoc apologetics,"[11] that is, an occasional and non-systematic disputation with opposing, even hostile claims that aims intellectually at tasks as modest as setting the record straight to tasks as ambitious as "achieving disagreement." Lindbeck rightly noted that in contrast to his ad hoc apologetics "Christian fellow travelers of both Nazism and Stalinism generally used liberal methodology to justify their positions."[12] For Lindbeck, the great alternative to systematic apologetics of the liberal-foundationalist sort would be a systematic theology that comprehensively redescribes our contested reality in distinctively Christian terms. But this impressive ambition for comprehensiveness may be distinguished from the limited endeavor of ad hoc apologetics which proceeds on a case by case basis in the work of theology as critical dogmatics.

Indeed, this kind of ad hoc apologetics is codified, even by name, in the Lutheran theological legacy by Philip Melanchthon's *Apology of the Augsburg Confession*. Interestingly, as we see in this classical case, ad hoc apologetics is not defensive in the sense of seeking vindication in a court of appeal other than the one internal to theology itself. Instead, it is a contention for the Pauline "truth of the gospel" (Gal 2:14; cf. Gal 1:7, 6:15-16). It disputes on the basis of the *Verbum externum* (external Word) under which all stand in order to clarify, to "achieve disagreement" with opponents for the sake of a

---

11. Lindbeck, *The Nature of Doctrine*, 113-24.
12. Ibid., 126.

public that is confused and divided by conflict.[13] The method here is logical, even "scholastic" disputation. The style here is irenic, howsoever passionate, not polemical bombast. It is correspondingly as wary of partisan defenses of the faith as of partisan attacks on it. There are limits to this kind of apologetics, to be sure, since it depends finally on the good will, intellectual integrity, and moral honesty of opponents.[14] Melanchthon classically expressed that limit with the exasperated lament, "The saying is certainly true that 'there is no defense against the malicious attacks of deceivers.' Nothing can be said so carefully that it can escape misrepresentation."[15] Malice opens up an abyss that neither philosophical hermeneutics nor theological reasoning can bridge. And malice appears in many subtle forms, indeed informs entire structures of existence. Since, as per the hypothesis of Reformation theology, we are all caught up in such sinful structures of malice and injustice, when theology is stopped short by an unbridgeable abyss of malice, as will sadly but predictably occur, it will want with Bonhoeffer (to mix metaphors) "to throw a stick into the spokes of the wheel." The question then becomes how to resist in ways that are appropriate to the gospel for which one contends theologically. Needless to say, this is a hugely controverted topic that we will touch upon in the conclusion of this chapter when we consider the more successful ad hoc apologetics of Uwe Siemon-Netto.

Short of passing into an apocalyptic state of resistance, however, ad hoc apologetics welcomes the vigorous critique of opponents as part and parcel of the normal work of critical dogmatics under the conviction that God can and does speak even through Balaam's ass (Num 22:28–30). Ad hoc apologetics can and does learn from critics because its modus operandi is the ever renewed theological search for the truth, not of Christians or of the church and its tradition in the first place, but of the gospel that creates both church and Christian and by which standard behavior, including thinking, which claims to be Christian or church must be tested (as in the classic case of Galatia, cited above). By the same token, then, ad hoc apologetics is no naive, utter openness to every wind of doctrine of the so-called free thinker.

---

13. See Hinlicky, "Process, Convergence, Declaration: Reflections on Doctrinal Dialogue."

14. On this see Vilhauer's Part IV, "When Ethical Conditions are Lacking," in *Gadamer's Ethics of Play*, 133–48. Walter Künneth put the point about the limits of theology theologically after the war: "The great world powers have destroyed the rule by force of National Socialism, and have become the instruments of God to carry out God's judgment on our people. We understand therefore the concern of the victors lest the spirit of National Socialism revive, and we understand their efforts to do everything they can to render impossible any resumption of National Socialism." Green, *Lutherans against Hitler*, 355. All subsequent page citations given in parentheses in the text.

15. Kolb and Wengert, eds., *The Book of Concord*, 174:2.

Theology is not philosophy. The theological subject arises as *creatura Verbi*. Theological thinking is freed thinking and thus committed and interested thinking. As mentioned, we will return to these crucial considerations in Chapter 5 under the heading of theological existence.

These reflections for the present bring us to the chief topic of this chapter, the danger of merely conservative apologetics. The conservative apologist is so convinced a priori of the adequacy of her own articulation of the truth of God, yet so unconscious of her historically conditioned formulations thereof, that criticism of the latter constitutes self-evident blasphemy against the former. Not at all tempted by systematic apologetics, the wagon-circling conservative apologist regards fair-minded engagement with the vigorous critique of opponents as dangerous and diabolical seduction to be cut short with the non-negotiable conversation-stopper, "God said it. I believe it. That settles it." To which, as the sainted Robert Bertram taught his students, the retort (of what I am calling here ad hoc apologetics, in that Bertram and Lindbeck were alike inspired by the same Melanchthon and his *Apology*) would be: "Ah yes, so it is written. God has evidently said this. But do you understand it? Understand it spiritually as the Spirit intends? Why then has God said this? What is the good reason God has said so? And is this Word from God that perchance you now understand actually addressed to you? How has that come about? Who are you? Account, human to human, for your access to this putative truth of God!" Understanding such as this may never be taken for granted; indeed such understanding is the hard and indispensable hermeneutical work of theology, *fides quarens intellectum*. Here "orthodoxy" is never a self-ascribed and achieved status but always a theological work in progress, an intention not an achievement, a status to be awarded not claimed by a Judge other than the theological subject herself.

Bertram, as noted in the previous chapter, in the midst of a late-in-life discovery of Dietrich Bonhoeffer, made a half-hearted defense of his beloved Werner Elert (not so much of Paul Althaus) from whom he had learned very much indeed. There is indeed much to be learned from Elert, who grappled with the Nietzschean revolution profoundly[16] and rightly saw, though unrighteously opposed under the circumstances, the subtle

---

16. Stayer, *German Saviour*, 82. As charitably and succinctly summarized by Stayer: "In their way, Elert and Althaus spoke up for the religious relevance of ethics, human freedom, and history, for the immanence of God, and for the life of Christ, as well as his death and resurrection, against the one-sided dogmatics of the Lutheran Renaissance and the Dialectical Theology" (95). These were almost precisely Bertram's concerns. For a charitable assessment, see Matthew Becker, "Werner Elert in Retrospect."

The Peril of Conservative Apologetics

Barthian tendencies of the Barmen Declaration.[17] It is important to bear firmly in mind that debates to this day about the confessional Lutherans' supposed middle way between the German Christian Faith Movement and Barth's Barmen Declaration in the name of the "intact," wholly Lutheran Landeskirchen of Hanover and the south of Germany that had not be "destroyed" by German Christians, are still filtered by the traumatic outcome of Hitlerism and the chain of guilt-laden recriminations from all sides that ensued after the war. Matthew D. Hockenos has aptly observed that the Protestants who supported "the Confessing Church in varying degrees . . . did not see eye-to-eye either theologically or politically. Appreciation for the widely divergent theological perspectives within the Protestant churches is crucial for understanding the conflicting and overlapping ways representatives of the Lutheran, Reformed, and United Protestant traditions in Germany grappled with the church's ambivalent relationship to Nazi policies . . . At the core of the [post-war] debate over the past conduct of churchmen in the Third Reich were theological issues . . . disagreements over key orthodox Lutheran doctrines: the doctrines of the two kingdoms, the law-gospel dualism, the doctrine of divine orders, and the theory of supersessionism. Churchmen were deliberating in the immediate postwar years on more than just their action or inaction in Hitler's Germany; they were coming to grips with the whole Lutheran theological and political tradition in Germany . . ."[18] We will take up Hockenos's account in some detail in Chapter 5 below. For the present, it suffices to take into account how fuel was added to this fire by the "failure of many churchmen after the war to acknowledge the church's mistakes." Especially "for the conservative Lutheran majority in the church" that failure consisted in minimizing the church's "vacillation between complacency and complicity" under Hitler while now advocating on behalf of the suffering of post-war Germans in seeming unconcern for Germany's many victims (8-9).

It is in this light that Bertram conceded that the "Dahlemites," (the party name of the Barthians, derived from Dahlem, the Berlin suburb where Niemöller was pastor), including Bonhoeffer, were "no doubt" right that in matters of doctrine and life the church alone is to judge and decide. But, Bertram asked in the name of the "intact" Lutheran churches in the 1930s, "must it win its independence at the cost of becoming exclusive and sectarian, no longer a church of the people?" We hear here an echo of the German Christian ideal of a *Volkskirche*, but now as one shared by the intact

---

17. Bertram, "Bonhoeffer's 'Battle(s),'" in Bertram, *A Time for Confessing*, 65-95. Subsequent citations in this chapter are given in parentheses in the text.

18. Hockenos, *A Church Divided*, 7-8. Subsequent citations in this chapter are given in parentheses in the text.

Lutherans. Continuing, as was Bertram's wont, in dialectical fashion he then asked: "But if a church of the people, also of the people's political aspirations?" (74). In Germany by the middle of the 1930s that would mean by a large majority the people's political aspirations under the Hitler regime for *Volkswerdung* and *Lebensraum*. Thus Bertram puts us on the horns of a dilemma: either a pure confessing church with loss of audience or an inclusive people's church with loss of the gospel. Such are the difficult questions that have persisted regarding the alternative between Barmen and the Ansbacher Ratschlag.[19] The question will be whether conservative apologetics can own up to this dilemma or whether it achieves its defense of the traditional position by suppressing it.

In what follows, I give major and careful attention to the remarkable contribution, flawed though it proves to be in the ways of merely conservative apologetics just discussed, of Lowell C. Green's *Lutherans against Hitler: The Untold Story*. It is not promising, to be sure, when Green flatly declares that Barth's Barmen Declaration "rejected the Lutheran distinction between Law and Gospel and the two governances" (164), when as we have just seen from Bertram's analysis that the dilemma posed by Barmen is one that attended all the parties, Lutherans too, that signed on to it. Indeed the addition of Thesis 5 at the Barmen Synod under the leadership of Lutheran Hans Asmussen affirming the state's divine institution makes a "responsible interpretation" of Barmen according to the Lutheran confessional tradition possible, according to Bertram. But Green will have none of this, as we shall see in painful detail. Nonetheless Green's book provides an invaluable source of information for the English-speaking world. Moreover, it gives the proverbial "other side of the story" than that given by the authors previously discussed in this book, and hence, its effect is to complicate their interpretations in helpful ways—helpful, that is, if our concern is actually to engage with the voices of the past in common concern for the Christian claim to truth manifestly botched during the rise of Nazism. It bears repeating, then, that for this book the concern in avoiding the retrospective fallacy to engage the past honestly has nothing to do with avoiding critique, even radical critique, but instead has to do with gaining precise critique that holds all, including us present-day interrogators, morally and intellectually accountable. We will find a better balance in this regard in a companion volume of conservative apologetics, Uwe Siemon-Netto's *The Fabricated*

---

19. Bertram noted how bemused Elert was at Barmen Thesis Five's acknowledgment of the "two kingdoms" in contradiction to Barmen Thesis One's "one Word of God" in "Bonhoeffer's 'Battle(s),'" 70. Of course, we know that Thesis Five was added to Barth's original text in order to win Lutheran support at Barmen.

Luther: Refuting Nazi Connections and Other Modern Myths[20] to which we will turn in the conclusion of this chapter to identify and articulate critically the clichéd cultural screen of Anglo-American interpreters, that is, of us who write and read this book. That will prepare us well for the investigation of our "liberal" filter in Chapter 3.

GREEN'S DEFENSE OF CONFESSIONAL LUTHERANISM

Green tells his reader straight-off in the Preface that he has found the "denunciation" of theologians like Elert and Althaus, under whom he studied in the postwar years, "intolerable," especially as made "by those living in an easy post-Hitler era . . . scolding those who had done their best in dark and cloudy times" (11). This personal animus animates Green entire book, though not without some measure of justification, as we have already seen in Chapter 1. Green is in any case duly wary of the retrospective fallacy, the lack "of a sense of the historical context": "Some writers [are] too quick to judge people from the past without proper attention to circumstances during the Third Reich . . . 'a totalitarian state, where all information was controlled by an evil government and where everyone was moved by fear'" (31). Green faults historians who thus fail 1) to consider "the historical context of the difficult times under Hitter"; who 2) "leav[e] out details prejudicial to [their] own interests; and 3) who "exhibit an accusatory style" that in fact mimics the tactics of political denunciation perfected by the Nazi (33). In short, "some historians persist in writing as though the men and women of that time possessed knowledge that was not available until after World War II" (322, fn. 45). All of this caution to judge as we would be judged is well taken. But in Green's book it leads at length to the overblown claim, as Green puts it in summation, that the confessional Lutheran churches, theologians and bishops by their rejection of the Barmen Synod and Karl Barth's theology "prevented the DEK [the Reichskirche] from swallowing up the Lutheran churches [the regional Landeskirchen] and provided a haven for the resistance. Hitler had found the point where he had to stop. From the theological faculty of the University of Erlangen came a steady stream of theological material to strengthen the German churches in their struggle against National Socialism" (324). Sadly, tendentious exaggeration such as this (as already established for us in Chapter 1) undermines confidence in

---

20. Siemon-Netto, *The Fabricated Luther*. All citations in this chapter hereafter given in the text by parentheses.

the many important mitigating facts and interpretative nuances Green otherwise brings to the table.

Let us here consider those mitigating facts and interpretative nuances. First and foremost, Green dates preliminary support for the National Socialist revolution by the confessional Lutherans to the so-called "time of appeasement" (56), roughly from 1933 to 1935, when Hitler put on a false face of humility to calm alarmed nerves beyond the borders and consolidate power domestically. "The general effect of Hitler's promises during his first year was to build trust in the minds of church leaders . . . [so that] by the time church leaders became aware . . . it was too late to resist. The dictator had become so firmly entrenched that they were powerless to head him off" (56–57). In this connection, Green cites Künneth's postwar observation about the 1936 Olympics in Berlin: "How could the great mass of the common folk see through this grandiose illusion and regard Hitler as a 'criminal' while the representatives of the Western powers so very apparently stood at his side?" (56).

Against this mitigating factor, of course, one could object that the persecution of communists and social democrats, the suspension of civil rights, and the boycott of Jewish businesses in the first days of Nazism should have belied Hitler's pretenses of moderation for theologians exercising critical discernment. Yet, in support of Green here, I would point out that even the infamous Night of the Long Knives, in which Hitler had arrested and executed the head of the SA Brownshirts, Ernst Röhm, along with other possible sources of opposition within the Nazi movement, had the opposite effect. It assured many of these church leaders that the moderate Hitler was eliminating the most radical and brutal elements within the "revolution" and thus bringing its initial wild excesses to an end. The illegal violence of this act could thus be written off as the bloodshed that accompanies the consolidation of any revolution. Moreover, Hitler in these days made a point of appearing pious, invoking God and Christianity regularly. In his suppression of social democracy, he abolished non-religious schools in Prussia and reinstituted religious education (even as the Hitler Youth program simultaneously began its systematic indoctrination of youth). Thus Green notes that almost "all of those who later opposed Hitler were his supporters in 1933 . . . They all wanted to believe Hitler, and the hoped for the best . . . and expressed an optimism that, at last, Germany was arising from its post-Versailles slump" (58).

Second, Green points to the cumulative effect of the totalitarian manipulation of information that began in and only increased from 1933. The relevance of this observation is that while those formed by education and experience prior to 1933 may be held more responsible for failing to see through Hitler's initial pretenses, the Nazi seizure of the cultural apparatus for the education of the young and its reinforcement with comprehensive propaganda in civil society largely succeeded in indoctrinating the younger generation in the worldview of racial warfare. If these youth would become the fanatical and willing executioners of the Führer's will after 1941, it is because they had been more or less comprehensively so formed since 1933. So Goldhagen's claim about willing executioners may be true, but trivial.[21] Third, Green points to the known devil. "Joseph Stalin had deliberately imposed famine and starvation in the Ukraine and elsewhere. Many of the Ukrainian peasants affected had close cultural and ethnic ties in Germany" (53) via the German colonies along the Volga River, the so-called Volga Germans. These three mitigating facts are factors that need to inform any precise judgment about the theological subjects who were seduced or confused by the rise of Nazism. We ought to be grateful to Green for drawing our attention to them. Hitler lied and deceived. Hitler succeeded in his lies and deceptions by the control of information. Hitler also succeeded in his lies and deceptions because Germans, especially German Protestants, were rightly informed and justifiably alarmed by the massive atrocities of Stalinism. The weighed this known evil of the present against unknown evils of the future in supporting National Socialism.

Having granted that achievement to Green, it must be said immediately that Green does his cause little good by indulging in the most egregiously partisan theological prejudices. Nowhere is this more evident than in his scapegoating of Calvinism (25), the Prussian Enlightenment of Absolutism and Militarism (28), the Prussian Union of Reformed and Lutheran churches (100) and above all the Swiss Reformed Karl Barth as the source of all "theocratic" error (13, 55) in contrast to the live-and-let-live bonhomie

---

21. In response to the simplistic and sensationalistic moralism of Goldhagen's *Hitler's Willing Executioners,* see not only the sober work of Browning, *Ordinary Men,* but the highly nuanced and sociologically and psychologically well-informed work of Neitzel and Welzer, *Soldaten,* especially 3–43. Aside from firm repudiation of the retrospective fallacy (13) Neitzel and Welzer helpfully introduce the *social a priori,* so to say, into their analysis terms of "frames of reference" and cognitive "paradigms": "Interpretive paradigms are especially central to how soliders in World War II experienced others, their own mission, their 'race,' Hitler and the Jews. Paradigms equip frames of reference with prefabricated interpretations according to which experiences can be sorted . . . If I interpret the killing of human beings as work, I do not categorized it as a crime and thereby normalize what I am doing" (18–19). But this social a priori is itself the product of indoctrination under the epistemic conditions of totalitarianism. The executioners were "willing" because they had first been bonded to the person of the Führer and thence indoctrinated to follow his will unconditionally. There are, let it be noted in passing, versions of Christian ethics that unnervingly parallel this pattern of bonding and obeying.

of the Lutheran doctrine of the Two Kingdoms (68, 74). There are, to be sure, genuine issues indicated in these topics, as our discussion of theological topics in Chapter 5 will take up. But the tenor and tone of Green's treatment of Christian theological alternatives to his "confessional Lutheranism" betrays the worst conceits of self-exculpating, wagon-circling conservative apologetics.

To document this claim, let us simply collect a series of statements Green makes about Karl Barth and put them on display. "Barth was sympathetic with the goals of Lenin and the Soviet Union. He was marked ideologically by theocratic ideas . . . " (50); the Dahlem Front of the Confessing Church Movement "became increasingly liberal and increasingly committed to the theology of Barth and the Barmen Declaration" (78); "Decisionism, existentialism, dialectical theology, and crisis theology are all words or phrases that characterize the theology of Karl Barth, the Barmen Declaration, and the Dahlem Front . . . " (100); "Ideological decisionism, irrationality, rejection of the Law-Gospel dialectic in favor of the Law as part of the Gospel, the relativization of the Law with resultant antinomianism, and the furtherance of one-kingdom political thought (theocracy) all diminished the differences between Barth and National Socialism" (102); Dietrich Bonhoeffer's and Herman Sasse's abortive Bethel Confession is said to reject sharply "Barth's socialistic opinion that the state must become the agent of bringing into fruition the kingdom of God on earth" (175); "Barth's beliefs engendered from a postplatonic dualism, which accounted material things as inferior and only spiritual things as good" (199); "In his refusal to acknowledge a natural knowledge of God, Barth had no room for such a theology of creation, and because of his rejection of Christian ethics as a separate theological discipline, Barth was unable to offer adequate arguments against the Nazi atrocities" (219; cf. 223); "Karl Barth wanted his religion to control the civil realm and Adolf Hitler wanted his political system to control the church" in some kind of symbiosis (225); the true-blue Lutherans refused to sign onto Barmen because they "could not simply barter their beliefs so they might bask in the warmth of Barthian approval" (231), while the theological aggressor, Barth, "was safe, secure, and prosperous in his Swiss professorship in Basel" (234).

One would think from Green that Barth had tutored Hitler in theology and Hitler Barth in politics! The crudity of these statements in their reckless combinations of ad hominem, innuendo, caricatures of opposing positions, and self-exculpating indignation do serious damage to Green's credibility both historically and theologically.

Were this treatment of Barth not bad enough, it pales in comparison to Green's equally tendentious treatment of the "confessional Lutherans" whom he would defend, as it seems, at any cost. In his account of the abortive Bethel Confession, he claims that "the position of Sasse and Bonhoeffer did not differ greatly from that of Althaus and Elert" (170), although the little difference, left in the dark by Green, was enough to see through Hitler's pretensions on the one side and to greet him enthusiastically on the other. Green can praise Hans Asmussen's prescient Altona Confession of 1932 for its Lutheranism, but criticize the same man for supporting the "Christocracy" of the Barmen Declaration (180), without any consideration of what in the interim led this Lutheran to participate constructively in the deliberations the Barmen free synod and support its declaration. When Asmussen argued for Barmen on the manifestly Lutheran basis that great danger lies in "seeking God without Christ," Green now has Asmussen by this argumentation replacing "a trinitarian concept with 'Christomonism' . . . and saying that whoever does not agree with the version of theology held by Barth and himself is guilty of a theology of human reason and good works." So the once Lutheran Asmussen went over to the dark side at Barmen, into "the footsteps of Barth" (181; Bonhoeffer gets the same treatment, 205).

No less tendentious are Green's apologies for Lutherans who actively or passively collaborated with the German Christians to keep ecclesiastical peace. When reporting how in the name of church-political neutrality Bishop Henrich Rendtorff of Mecklenburg-Schwerin did not critically rebuke the German Christian call within his region in December 1932 to expel half-Jews and Free Masons, Green asks defensively, "But who could foresee the inherent dangers at that time?" When Bishop Marahrens of Hanover added his signature to Nazi Church Minister Kerrl's "Five Basic Principles," a watered-down version of the Godesberg Declaration of spiritual support for Nazism, we are told that Marahrens signed "with great hesitation" and that the act "brought him much grief" when he was publicly rebuked by fellow Lutheran bishops Wurm and Meiser for breaking ranks (297). In any case, Kerrl's effort "to win the favor of Hitler for the churches" in this way failed because "Hitler was no longer interested in working with the churches; instead, he turned to sinister plans for the utter destruction of the churches following an anticipated German victory in World War II" (297)—a truth that we perhaps know after the fact, but which neither Kerrl nor Marahrens knew at the time.

We are cautioned that Elert's and Althaus's notorious Ansbach Memorandum "should be examined within its historical context" (241), while ascribing authorship not to Elert and Althaus but to the nefarious German Christian Hans Sommerer (240–41, and fn. 5) who, Green suggests, duped these faithful Lutherans. Indeed, we are reassured that there can be "no question that Elert and Althaus lacked a thorough knowledge of what

Hitler and Sommerer were up to when they worked with the Ansbach Circle in June 1934" and it was only "[f]uture events [that] revealed the mistake made by the Erlangen professors" (248), while in the meantime it was "their near desperation at the blunders of the Barmen Declaration that drove Elert and Althaus into the arms of the Ansbach Circle" (249). The "direct and incisive" Marburg Faculty Opinion against the Aryan Paragraph "on the basis of the Bible and the confessions of the church" is lauded, in gentle comparison to the reprehensible Erlangen Faculty Opinion of the same time on the same topic, although Green neglects to mention that the author of the Marburg statement was Rudolph Bultmann[22] (instead mentioning the signature of the dean, von Soden, 133). Only later in connection with a subsequent comment supporting an aspect of the Erlangen Opinion is Bultmann mentioned (142). While Sasse, then having joined the Erlangen Faculty, criticized Elert's complacency and naiveté, as Green mentions in a footnote (133, fn. 10), Green tells us that Elert and Althaus at this time "were without a clue regarding the dreadful racism that was about to break out in Germany" (134). Conceding the Erlangen Faculty's document's "ambivalence" in recognizing the "state's basic right to take statutory measures" in its "struggle for the renewal of our *Volk*" against "the threats placed upon its own life by an emancipated Judaism," Green implores the very thing that he has systematically denied to Barth and Barmen Declaration, namely, that we "need not try to justify but must try to understand" (138) by "considering the emotional turmoil of 1933." Not only did many "thoughtful Germans" like Elert and Althaus find that Hitler's "program contained much that was good alongside much that was questionable," not only did "the typical German church leader simply . . . not take the racial threats seriously," Green goes so far as to suggest a cunning Elert stratagem in the Erlangen Faculty document to toss some bones to careless Nazi readers at the beginning "as a smoke screen to deflect attention . . . from the clear statements that were yet to come" (138). Green can sharply judge the erstwhile dialectical theologian, Friedrich Gogarten's "final and fatal step" of saying that the law is given to us in our *Volkstum* (105), while passing over without comment exactly the same teaching by Elert and Althaus (e.g., 204, as the doctoral dissertation of Nathan Yoder has recently established beyond any reasonable doubt).[23]

---

22. Forstman, *Dark Times*, 230.

23. See Yoder, "*Ordnung*," 132–80, with the important qualification that for Althaus *Volk* is not conceptually reducible to race. The same, of course, can be said for Gogarten. They were primarily discussing a cultural, not a biological concept, ethnicity not race, insufficiently wary of the cooptation of their notion by Nazism. For a charitable assessment of Althaus, see Schwarz, "Paul Althaus (1888–1966)."

Yet Green can praise Elert's "new natural theology" that comes not "before faith but after faith and out of faith, and from no other faith than that which justifies us before God for the sake of Christ" even though, as Elert immediately continued, it is "precisely out of faith that we confess our being bound to Blood and Soil, because the same things apply to them which Luther said regarding the First Article of the Creed" (214). Elert means by this theological appropriation of a Nazi slogan, "Blood and Soil," earthliness, immanence, as Green further cites his words: "If the believing sinner remains earthly, i.e. still bound to Blood and Soil, then the church must preach the Law until the Judgment Day. If she does not do this, then also the Gospel will be spoken by her into empty air" (215). Green explains, "One's station in life is where God has placed one. The orders are not a system of rules or requirements, but they deal with facts, with things the way they are" (216). Green's praise of this move of Elert towards Barth's view that Christian theology can theologize about nature on the basis of faith in Jesus Christ but not found itself on an autonomous natural theology, of course, goes unnoticed and unremarked. Green does not even consider Barth's burning problem all the same of how is one to distinguish "in the way things are" what is the good creation of God and what is its corruption by sin and death, especially if one has here a professedly hidden God at work "in the law" who "places us" and indeed "binds us unconditionally" to the here and now without making any such discriminations. Green never raises this rather obvious—"Barthian"—objection to the thinking that in fact landed Elert and Althaus in the chorus of the theologians cheerleading Hitler in 1933 as the heaven-sent savior of the *Volk*.

In short, at every opportunity Green indulges his favored theologians with very charitable interpretations of a type that he systematically withholds from those unfavored, while favor and unfavor turn simply on his personal loyalties and "confessional pigheadedness," to use the exasperated term Barth used to describe Elert after reading his dogmatics in the 1950s.[24] The result is to perpetuate the heat to which he so rightly objected at the outset of his book and darken the light he otherwise could shed on our difficult topic. At this state, then, an exasperated reader might well wonder why she has been dragged so slowly and painfully through this slough of partisanship posing as history. The answer, in part, has been precisely to illustrate in living color the deep faults of conservative apologetics. But beneath the self-serving tendentiousness of Green's presentation, there are important contributions within it to be dug out that bear further consideration and are worthy of possible redemption. These are the appearances of two un-

---

24. Busch, *Karl Barth*, 429.

derstudied theologians, Sasse and Künneth, and of four theological topics: 1) theological existence, e) the Two Kingdoms doctrine as an alternative to theocracy, 3) the Christological divergence between Barth and Bonhoeffer, and 4) Zionism.

Herman Sasse is a theologian who was so dismayed at the cover-up of Nazi complicity after the war that he immigrated to Australia. From there, tragically, the memory of his courageous, insightful and genuinely Lutheran-confessional opposition to Hitlerism has been overshadowed by his opposition, late in life, to the ordination of women. Coming out of Prussia, with its traditions of militarism, enlightened absolutism, and theological unionism, Sasse wrote in 1945, as Green reports, that "the Prussian Union had for a long time been a political instrument of the state, that its theologians had been the spokesmen of an ideology of ecclesiastical subservience to the civil order, and that these theologians had thereby distorted the teaching of Luther" (38) on the import of the Two Kingdom's doctrine. Thus Sasse, according to Green, "supported the concept of a Confessional Lutheran church in Germany that would be international and ecumenical in character and would avoid the snares of nationalism" (68–69). This ecclesial stance would comport with a differentiation that puts Luther's sixteenth-century distinction between the reign of Christ and the reign of the devil in line with the legacy from Augustine of the conflict between the civitas Dei and civitas terrena, ultimately to be traced back to Paul the Apostle and Jewish apocalyptic. This differentiation of the Two Kingdoms would be sharply distinguished from the modern, Cartesian dualism of a public realm subject to law and reason and a private realm of religious feelings and intuitions that goes on to endorse such a public realm of law and reason as analogous to the Kingdom of God. The latter bifurcation of reality along ontological rather than apocalyptic lines—what Bonhoeffer criticized as thinking in terms of "two spheres"[25]—would go a long way towards explaining subservience to Nazism in the name of "the" Two Kingdoms doctrine when in fact there are multiple iterations of it in theological history; indeed, we shall see how Hitler himself adopts a modern version of the Two Kingdoms doctrine in Chapter 4.

In any event, Sasse's substantive critique of Nazi theology in the name of the Lutheran theological tradition was spot on, as Green reports, when already in 1932 "his trenchant disclosure that true Christianity, with its doctrine of original sin, was an unavoidable insult against the Nazi idolization of the Teutonic race" (126). Sasse therewith detected the fateful and eventually fatal inner ambivalence of the Nazi notion of *Volkswerdung*—a

---

25. Bonhoeffer, *Ethics*, 196–206.

kind of domestic colonialization—when he asked, "Can the masses again be melted down into a genuine *Volk* with an organic membership, or can they only be 'organized'. . ."? [Nazism] has continuously vacillated between an almost religious veneration of the *Volk* and a contempt for the 'masses,' which are both composed of the same people" (126). In response to the Prussian church's early adoption of the Aryan Paragraph, it was Sasse who clearly saw and clearly enunciated "that also the apostles of Jesus Christ, yes, the Lord himself, who was a son of David according to the flesh, would have to resign from the preaching office of the Prussian Church. This new decree separates the Prussian Church from all Christianity" (133). Sasse emerges from Green's pages as a theologian whose thinking and conduct during the rise of Nazism cries out for a sustained and detailed treatment.

The same may be said of Walter Künneth, though Nathan Yoder's recent doctoral dissertation fills some of the gap in English-speaking circles. It is particularly instructive for showing the difference between Althaus's and Künneth's interpretations of the orders of creation, since for Künneth the orders are eschatologically oriented.[26] In his post-war treatise, *Der grosse Abfall: Eine geschichtstheologische Untersuchung der Begegnung zwischen Nationalsozialismus und Christentums*, Künneth ascertained the Social Darwinism at the heart of Nazism. Unlike the accommodating German Christians, he saw that "popular Darwinism, 'a mixture of mythology and science,' had been applied to the concept of society and had yielded the notion that man was only an animal, that men should fight like beasts, and that society would be improved by the elimination of the weak . . . '" (106). He also saw how Nazism "took over certain concepts from Nietzsche . . . and Schopenhauer" (107), who was of course one of Nietzsche's original inspirations.[27] He identified five points of divergence: race, contempt for Jews, the new portrayal of Jesus as an Aryan, the tendency to oppose Christianity as church and dogma, and religious inwardness as opposed to the *Verbum externum* (108-9). Like Sasse, the virtually unknown in English language circles Künneth appears from these pages as a theologian under Hitler deserving of greater attention.

When we turn to theological issues raised in Green's account, we can briefly consider the first three of the four previously listed as we look forward to fuller discussion of them in Chapter 5. First, who is a theologian? How does theological subjectivity arise? From Chapter 1 we recall that Barth made this the fundamental issue in the sense of not buying the Nazi

---

26. Yoder, "*Ordnung*," 213-77.

27. On this see further Aschheim, *The Nietzsche Legacy in Germany 1890-1990*, a book to be discussed in Chapter 4.

claim to a *Wende*, a revolutionary turning point, instead staying with Paul's proclamation of Christ as the turning point of the ages. Hence, Barth wrote in 1933 in words stupidly, if not maliciously misunderstood ever since: "I endeavor to carry on theology, and only theology, now as previously, and as if nothing had happened . . . even in the Third Reich."[28] While we can expect no such appreciation of Barth from Green, Green does raise the question of theological existence several times in fashion that is worth noting. Green lifts up the first article of Asmussen's 1932 Altona Confession that "the church must not be used to achieve political purposes: 'Whoever places the proclamation of the church under the influence of political power thereby makes the political power into a religion that is hostile to Christianity'" (65, cf. 68). Pointing correctly to the legacy of Johann Gottlieb Fichte for the genesis of "political theology"—a highly ambiguous concept, also much employed by Klaus Scholder with a negative connotation (whom nonetheless Green excoriates for his "Barthianism")—Green cites the "wry formulation" of Elert against the confusions embedded in this concept: "political theology—or antipolitical theology, which is the same thing—and theological politics, or antitheological politics, which is also the same thing—lie together in today's struggle" (209). The confusion indicated here touches a nerve that still unsettles theology today where so much "constructive theology" is not only Calvin's factory of idols, but modernized, a factory of ideologies.

Second, Green is not wrong to urge that the right reading of the Two Kingdom's doctrine contains an objection to "theocracy," though his wooden, if not malicious, anti-Calvinism would hardly notice that the reign of the one God is the subject of Jesus's proclamation just as the righteousness of the one God who comes to reign is that of Paul's. The point then of the Two Kingdoms' distinction would be that the righteous Reign of God who was reconciling the world in Christ has dawned in the preaching of the gospel (in the very act of distinguishing itself from the law) and hence in the creation of the new human subjectivity of repentance and faith though its promised future has not yet fully arrived in cosmic breadth. In that case, the problem with "theocracy" is that of a realized eschatology that thinks faith, church, or even world has already arrived, that battle is already finished not merely begun. One may arguably dispute with Karl Barth about this, and even more so with the political Barthians who followed him, but one cannot without careful distinction attribute to Barth and the German Christians alike the "theocratic" ambition to absorb the church into politics (74). With Barth it is just the other way around, that politics should be the predicate of revelation, never vice versa. One especially cannot cram Barth and the

---

28. Barth, *Theological Existence To-day*, 9.

German Christians together as theocrats by forgetting historically the *cuius regio, eius religio* (whoever the ruler, his religion) settlement of the wars of religion that had determined the alliance of throne and altar for Lutherans as much as Reformed and Catholics. But Green is frequently forgetful in this way, for example in reporting how Erich Vogelsang, earnest Lutheran and pupil of Karl Holl, presented a paper "read by Hitler 'with great eagerness'" on "occasions in church history, when the state had intervened in churchly matters" (83), beginning with Martin Luther's own address to the nobility of the German nation for the reform of church and society! How "theocratic" is that?

If we can get past this partisan shell game, however, we may note how Green also lifts up Bonhoeffer's more apt retrieval of theological sense from the "labyrinth" of the Two Kingdoms doctrine when in the spring of 1933 he affirmed that the "church, primarily, cannot directly engage in political actions" on the grounds of possessing no particular competence in politics, yet the church "can and must ask the state ever and again whether it can justify its actions as a legitimate civil action, that is, as action in which law and order, not lawlessness and disorder, are created . . . " (131). This represents a proper understanding and use of the Two Kingdoms doctrine according to the Reformation distinction, as we will also see Rudolf Bultmann employing in our further discussion of this topic in Chapter 5.

The third theological topic that arises in the course of Green's study, which we will merely note here, comes in connection with Green's efforts to save Bonhoeffer for Lutheranism against the clutches of Barthianism. It concerns Christology, and the subtle way in which Barth and Bonhoeffer differ regarding the otherness of the external Word which both upheld over against German Christian "enthusiasm." Pointing to Barth's reformed legacy from Zwingli, Green announces his suspicion that behind Barth's theology lay "the doubt whether one could really say concerning the incarnation of Christ that 'the Word became flesh' (John 1:14) or whether one should alter the words to say that 'the Word assumed flesh'" (205). As Michael DeJonge has demonstrated in an incisive monograph,[29] Green is on to something here. Barth locates the otherness of the external Word of God in the transcendent divinity of the Logos, the so-called *extra Calvinisticum*. But Bonhoeffer locates this otherness in the Incarnate humanity, the unappealing face of the One abandoned by all to crucifixion, the so-called *genus apostelesmaticum*, so that only as such, as the Crucified, is Christ majestically present to and for his people under the paradoxical forms of the foolish

---

29. DeJonge, *Bonhoeffer's Theological Formation*, a book to be discussed in Chapter 5 below.

preaching of the cross and the bread and wine of the new covenant meal. This is a subtle but serious differentiation in their common front against German Christian enthusiasm and, what is ultimately the same, against the not so strange theology of Adolf Hitler, as we shall see in Chapter 4.

The fourth issue that Green raises in this book that is worthy of the most sensitive and careful consideration is his treatment of Uriel Tal's important investigation into those "Lutherans who opposed racial antisemitism, yet drew a common denominator between the Jew and the racist" (116, fn. 52). These Lutherans saw an irony in that the contemporary völkisch movements had sunk to the same racism that, as they held, had originated with the very Jews to whom they were ostensibly opposed. Green gives as an example from Tal's work Heinrich Frick, a theology professor from Giessen, "who 'warned German Jewry against both the völkisch [elements], including the Nazi movement, and the Zionists . . . Frick defined Jewish nationalism and Nazism as two movements which turned earthliness, this-worldliness and materialism into metaphysical entities, i.e., into religions." Accordingly Frick held that neither Zionists nor Nazis could tolerate the other in their midst, while Christians and humanists and emancipated Jews could see integration as integral to German integrity (117). This unsettling argument cannot but suggest that Zionism is a racism. As Green finally puts it, after making his own welcome affirmation that the Jews are a holy people separated to God (though one wonders how that is compatible with "confessional Lutheranism,") the "Lutheran authors who were cited by Tal sounded the warning that Germany must not fall prey to völkisch ideologies and racism, whether the roots were in Judaism or German nationalism . . . " (125). We will return to this volatile set of questions in Chapter five's discussion of the Christian theology of Israel.

SIEMON-NETTO'S CONSEQUENT CONSERVATIVISM

Green's contribution has all the virtues of a passionate intervention on behalf of a beloved tradition under hostile and sometimes unfair attack, yet all the vices of merely conservative apologetics that does not own up to the dilemmas which in the first place landed that tradition in difficulty. Uwe Simon-Netto largely avoids this trap, in part because he takes his point of departure from the insights of Richard Steigmann-Gall, whom we studied in Chapter 1. With Steigmann-Gall, Simon-Netto sees the background of Nazified Christianity in the progressive self-understanding of liberal Protestantism, quite in contrast to the theological conservatism of the Lutherans (52). This latter, according to Siemon-Netto, provided the real though latent and internalized basis for the political resistance that actually arose within Nazism, that is, in the military conspiracy to assassinate Hitler. In addition to adopting this point of departure in search of more precise judgments, Simon-Netto openly confesses that "reading the sickening and seemingly endless reams of the older Luther's anti-Jewish hyperbole has been one of the most exigent exercises during my research for this study" (52), even though Siemon-Netto knows, as the historian Johannes Wallmann has argued with some evidence, that the particular memory of Luther's ranting had less historical role to play in the genesis of Nazism than the antecedent racial anti-Semitism of the nineteenth century (51).[30]

Yet such historical mitigations do not get to the heart of the matter for Simon-Netto. His book is about a set of clichés that operate in the dominant discourse of the Anglo-American tradition (in which also this book is written and will be read). These clichés attained today's prominence through Walter Shirer's widely read *The Rise and the Fall of the Third Reich*, where Luther was identified as a "savage anti-Semite" whose "passion for political autocracy ensured a mindless provincial political absolutism, which reduced a vast majority of the German people to poverty, to horrible torpor and a demeaning subservience" (46). This popular image of Luther in the eyes of the American liberal is Simon-Netto's "fabricated" Luther that he sets out to dismantle step by step in his book. His first step in this deconstruction is an exposé of Shirer's plagiarism of Thomas Mann for the construction of this Luther cliché (46). The further details of this deconstruction need not here detain us, since we have already established with the help of James Stayer that the fabrication of a usable Luther in search of a modern savior has been a cottage industry among scholars. Simon-Netto sees the "fundamental flaw," i.e., the retrospective fallacy in the modern critics (but also, we may note, in the modern proponents) of Luther in that "they interpret his writings using twentieth- and twenty-first century presuppositions and perspectives, which tend to be anthropological and are not sufficiently aware of Luther's decidedly theocentric orientation" (67).

That is well said, but it is only cogent—not as a defense of indefensible things said or done by Luther—but rather as a retrieval of Christian

---

30. Wallmann, "The Reception of Luther's Writings on the Jews from the Reformation to the End of the 19th Century." Wallmann's thesis finds further corroboration in Dorothea Wendebourg's recent sketch of the way Jews, particularly in Germany, joined in Luther jubilees and celebrations in the nineteenth century in praise of Luther as a son of the Hebrew scriptures and forerunner of religious freedom, in "Jews Commemorating Luther in the Nineteenth Century." She draws two sage conclusions: "[I]n our dealing with the Reformation in general and Martin Luther in particular there is a way between blind hero-worship and indiscriminate condemnation. Second, history is not derivable . . ." (263).

meaning from Luther that transcends Luther. Equally that is only possible if and when one would appropriate Luther's Christian meaning, that is, as Siemon-Netto rightly identifies in this connection, his "theocentrism" as a modern political possibility rather than revising it in support of the anthropocentric politics of modernity. Such theocentrism as a modern political possibility consists in the eschatological conviction that the "real world" is the coming Reign of God, that this present age, this *saeculum*, this "secular" epoch of political sovereignty, is passing away though now Christians live in the overlap, at times antagonistic and at other times collaborative, of the Two Kingdoms. Otherwise, the implication is that we must find Luther's genuinely theocentric meaning in the past and leave it there. But in his book Simon-Netto defends the present relevance of the anti-utopian sense of Luther's version of Two Kingdoms doctrine as a distinction between the inevitably coercive power of the secular regime of this age as instituted by and thus subject to the divine law in contrast to the spiritual power claimed in the church in promising by Word and Spirit in free assembly from among the nations the coming of the saving reign of God (70, 102–3).

While Siemon-Netto also claims a right to resist violently, based more on the second generation reformer Flacius than on Luther himself, and to which he connects Bonhoeffer's decision to poke a stick into the spokes of the wheel (96) by joining the military conspiracy to assassinate Hitler, the cutting edge of Simon-Netto's study is to argue for two deeper implications of Luther's actual Two Kingdom's distinction: 1) the end of the ideal of Christendom (76) and therewith 2) the fittingness for the future of "spiritual resistance" as the form of political passion and action that accords with the gospel. He sees this resistance instantiated in the example of the Leipzig mayor, Karl Goerdeler, who died at the hands of the Nazis for his Christian convictions along these "Lutheran" lines (105–48).

In sum, Simon-Netto's conservative apologetic is less partisan, less self-exculpatory, more illuminating of the clichés that substitute for consequent thinking in complacent Anglo-American liberalism, and more helpful in suggesting a way forward for Christian theology after Christendom, after the end of that political ideal buried and sealed in the tomb beneath its countless victims at Auschwitz. It may be put it this way: if the Lutheran theological claim is not a set of ideas, like a philosophy, to be adopted as a worldview and used ideologically, but the rather the claim to the truth of God's coming reign of righteousness performed by the encounter with the crucified and risen Christ in Word and Sacrament, then the painful emptying of the churches in the course of modern German, more broadly Euro-American history, is not a loss of influence and relevance that can be corrected by realizing the ideal of a *Volkskirche*, since even upon the success of such an ideal an effective deChristianization would occur. In facing this, Simon-Netto has owned up to the dilemma that Bertram exposed and moved forward the broader argument of Christian theology after the catastrophe of Nazism. But that points not to a merely conservative defense of Luther or Lutheranism but forward to a reconstruction of Christianity after Christendom (even perhaps with some help from Luther).

While Siemon-Netto's version of conservative apologetics is more successful than Green's, it remains the case, then, that mere apologetics aimed at conserving the tradition is not satisfying, especially not so in view of the moral and spiritual catastrophe of Nazism. To be sure, Rubenstein's proclamation of the "death of God" and Steigmann-Gall's charge that theocentric resistance to secularism was the very cause of the death camps, seem to Christians like Green and Siemon-Netto to give the Nazis yet another—posthumous—victory. Perhaps, but the defensive argument that real Christianity, or the real Luther, or real Lutherans are not really to blame also gives Nazis a posthumous victory. The fact is that these Christians, who should have known better, really failed because of blind spots traceable to their retention of Christendom assumptions. In any case, Nazism was not stopped Christianly or theologically but by the secular alternatives of Russian Bolshevism and Western liberal capitalism that allied militarily against it. How does theology own up to this manifest limitation of its power? Certainly not by more earnest "political theology"! How can a Two Kingdoms theology help after Christendom? Rubenstein is broadly right that it is the religious element that makes the Holocaust singular, if we mean by that specifically the outcome of Christian anti-Judaism. Siemon-Netto is broadly right that the failure occurred religiously insofar as the clichéd thinking of liberals, and conservatives, and of this binary itself failed to test the spirits—and still fails. In the next two chapters we will try afresh to look and see, first, in the words of Theodore S. Hamerow, "why we watched," and second, what Hitler was not so strangely thinking about God, providence, and the destiny that he felt summoned to fulfill. In undertaking this study we are on the way to renewed theological work as critical dogmatics after Auschwitz, hence also after Christendom.

Chapter Three

Seeing How We Saw

OUR LIBERALISMS

In this chapter we will survey some lesser known but no less instructive contemporaneous witnesses of the rise of Nazism, all either from North America or speaking to North Americans, with one notable exception at the end. The purpose of this selection, as previously indicated, is not only to look at Christian theologians during the rise of Nazism to see what we can learn about theology from this laboratory, but in the process also to look at ourselves and see how we saw things. In this we may take our point of departure in an observation that Alasdair MacIntyre once made, namely, that we Americans are all liberals—"conservative liberals, liberal liberals and radical liberals,"[1] meaning that we all assume the metaphysical exaltation of the individual free agent, as in Locke and Jefferson, in defiance of our bodily embeddedness in natural processes and our social embeddedness in historical processes, not to mention our obligations to God in the covenant of creation as caretakers of one another and of the good earth for the sake of generations to come. The manifest contradictions of this philosophical transcendence of the reality of human being in nature and society under God then play out in the divergent and indeed rival strains of liberalism. Libertarians repudiate as oppressive the moral restraints of life together in community through the generations. "Liberals," as we use the term today, favor an ever expanding paternal-maternal State to protect individuals from

---

1. MacIntyre, *Whose Justice? Which Rationality?*, 392.

the consequences of their "free" but as often as not stupid and harmful choices. "Conservatives," as we use the term today, see that both freedom from the expectations of others and freedom from the natural consequences of our "free choices" are paid for by infinite economic expansion. Conservatives are thus most aware of the hidden presupposition in this whole kaleidoscope of shifting liberalisms in triumphant "capitalism," though they have no solution but more of the same.

The triumphant capitalism driving liberal democratic regimes is not capitalism in the Marxist sense of a definite, mercifully limited stage in a rational historical development preparing the way for socialism, but in the "savage" or "schizoid" sense that the commoditization of all things by the omnivorous market, once unleashed, cannot easily be caged again by any of the three contending liberalisms. It is an unsustainable juggernaut tending to global catastrophe, just as we liberals are its ideologues in the sense that our fierce intramural disputes never challenge this deep operating assumption but rather merely sustain the confusion. Bread and circuses distract attention from the root contradictions of modernity now gathering steam for a monumental explosion. As MacIntyre noted, "There is little place in such political systems for the criticism of the system itself, that is, for putting liberalism in question."[2] I want to argue in the end that what Barth called "theological existence today" is the little, fragile space within liberalism that can put the system as a whole into salutary question, that is, not to destroy but to redeem. To be clear politically, then, about this theological questioning of liberalism at which I aim: the point for this author is certainly not to retrieve communist or fascist alternatives, but to achieve a chastened liberalism along Niebuhrian lines,[3] in that only the democratic state, as also a morally ambiguous monopoly of coercive power like all the other versions of political sovereignty, has the power but also the moral authority to put the free market back into the marketplace and keep it there in defense of those things that should not be bought and sold. To hasten such chastening of our unreflective liberalisms before it is too late, however, is to remember as latent contemporary possibilities the fascist and communist alternatives in their full and critical force. I suspect that as the global crises of modernity unfold, this will happen anyway. But for us who would think self-critically that means facing once again, as did actors in the 1930s, the full spectrum of the horizon of possibilities against which we today still make our increasingly critical choices. Theologically, it is to rediscover as a result the cov-

---

2. Ibid.

3. As Reinhold Niebuhr argued exquisitely in his *The Irony of American History*. See also Hinlicky, "Luther and Liberalism," in *A Report from the Front Lines*.

enant of creation as the forgotten but necessary grounding of a future of responsible freedom, by which the intramural rivalries of our contending liberalisms are de-fanaticized. That is the goal of this chapter's examination of various American perceptions of Nazism's rise and of several attempts to speak to Americans about the impending danger—and of one witness, from outside of North America but embracing pluralism and democracy philosophically and theologically, who perceived well, warned presciently and suffered nobly.

Admittedly, such a survey is no foolproof method for avoiding the retrospective fallacy. Indeed it is by virtue of this author's hindsight that the following actors are selected for examination as examples of those who discerned the devil disguised as an angel of light that arose in Germany in the 1930s. Because of this act of selection, what follows cannot be comprehensive, only at best representative and thus illustrative. Moreover, witnesses of this sort are still subject to scrutiny. Discernment of what was to come may prove such witnesses to be right but for the wrong reasons (think of the "dogmatic Marxists" whom Tillich excoriated at the conclusion of his 1933 *The Socialist Decision*).[4] The seeming complacency and wishful thinking of others may prove them wrong but for understandable, even good reasons (think of the peace-loving appeasers and well-meaning non-interventionists of Great Britain and the USA up until 1939 and 1941 respectively). All the same, to hear such voices for the acknowledged purpose of contemporary theological appropriation is a useful exercise in the kind of hermeneutical enterprise to which history as studia humanitatis, and therewith as well historical theology, aspires. It is an open-ended act that invites others to enter the debate because "reconstructing what people did not or could not have known is one of the most difficult tasks of social science . . . we could describe this task as the 'liquification' of history, the conversion of facts back into possibilities."[5] It is in view of the horizon of possibilities actors faced that we can discern and more precisely judge the actions which they took, though this very "liquification" depends on our intervention, unfreezing the frozen past. Naturally that is subject to error and open to criticism. By the same token, however, this action in thinking makes us the more discerning of our own contemporary horizon of possibilities—and its potential constrictions of vision, even as we rightly subject past horizons to criticism for narrowness of scope and blind spots within.

The point, then, is neither to attain a mirror-image reproduction of *wie es eigentlich gewesen est* ("how it actually happened"—von Ranke's

---

4. Tillich, *Socialist Decision*, 124–26.
5. Neitzel and Welzer, *Soldaten*, 13.

impossible ideal of objectivity), nor to judge the past in mere confirmation of our morally superior present (when we know that this too is historically conditioned), but the theologically penitential self-examination of our common condition that is studia humanitatis at its best. With regard to Christian theology, which is the special topic of our investigations in this book, the question of discernment—of testing the spirits to see whether they are of God (1 John 4:1–3)—is central. Who was the true prophet who foresaw the bitter fruit sown during the rise of Nazism? Who was the false prophet who cried, "Peace! Peace!" when there was no peace? This is not a question about some ineffable inspiration or mystical intuition or religious experience, but a question of theological understanding, so far as the Holy Spirit is the Spirit of the Word incarnate and thus not an independent variable.[6] It is something that may be known, so far as history admits of knowledge. With this, moreover, the terms in which this author seeks and finds those discerning witnesses during the rise of Nazism and the criterion by which instructive cases are selected and weighed is acknowledged: the Verbum externum.[7]

Studies in this vein on the admirable roles played by notables like Karl Barth, Dietrich Bonhoeffer, and Martin Niemöller are abundant, as we have had occasion previously to note. Jack Forstman's compelling analysis, previously noted and to which we will attend in Chapter 5, most notably of the theological witness of Paul Tillich and Rudolph Bultmann on the one side, as also of Immanuel Hirsch and Friedrich Gogarten on the other, is available, not to mention all the lesser lights scrutinized after Ericksen's seminal study, as reviewed in Chapter 1 of this book. In the last chapter, we lifted up Herman Sasse and Walter Künneth as theologians meriting further attention. The latter half of this chapter introduces to this well trodden field the American novelist Kressman Taylor, whose 1942 novel *Until That Day*[8] disguised under fictional cover the first-hand testimony of German refugee Pastor Leopold W. Bernhard; the Euro-American Jewish intellectual Maurice Samuel, whose passionate and stunning appeal to American liberals to awake to their passive and underlying but all the same real religious sympathies with Nazism was published in his 1940 *The Great Hatred*;[9] and the unsung Slovak Lutheran philosopher-theologian-bishop and confessor

---

6. Morse, *Not Every Spirit*.

7. I am not imposing here a standard from outside the situation, but retrieving one from within it, namely, Dietrich Bonhoeffer and Herman Sasse's appeal to the *Verbum externum* against German Christian *Schwämerei*. See Hinlicky, "Verbum Externum."

8. Taylor, *Day of No Return* (orginally titled *Until That Day*). All page citations in this chapter are hereafter given in the text by parentheses.

9. Samuel, *The Great Hatred*. All page citations in this chapter are hereafter given in the text by parentheses.

of the faith, Samuel Štefan Osuský, whose prescient 1937 lecture to the assembled pastors of his church, "The Philosophy of Bolshevism, Fascism and Hitlerism," I have translated and placed into the Appendix of this book.[10]

By way of introduction to these theologically discerning witnesses during the rise of Nazism, we will take up in the next section of this chapter an essay that appeared in 1934, "Hitler and the German Church," in the *North American Review* by George J. Walmer.[11] So oriented, we turn further in examination of how we liberals saw what we saw with the aid of the instructive studies of Andrew Nagorski, *Hitlerland: American Eyewitnesses to the Nazi Rise to Power*[12] and of Theodore S. Hamerow, *Why We Watched: Europe, America and the Holocaust*.[13] This will not be an edifying experience. We will see how we saw in such a way that passivity, not to say paralysis, greeted the rise of Nazism. This serves to establish a context for understanding those few who both discerned the danger, so often invisible to others, and also how they were empowered by their discernment to act, even if action could only be the martyria of witness to truth in an overwhelming matrix of deception and self-deception.

FIRST IMPRESSIONS OF THE CHURCH STRUGGLE

George J. Walmer began his remarkable 1934 essay, interpreting the outbreak of the Church Struggle in Germany to the North American world, with the notice of a recent plebiscite in Germany on November 12, 1933 that had endorsed Hitler's policies by the massive margin of 40 million votes out of 43 million cast. Against this background of nigh-universal German approval for National Socialism's consolidation of power, Walmer writes, something "wholly unexpected" had occurred, which he characterized as a "successful rebellion among the clergy of the German Protestant Church against the attempt to fasten upon their necks the yoke of the German Christian movement sponsored by Adolf Hitler" (133). He further noted that this "rebellion" had occurred after the rest of the opposition—the "Social Democratic party, the Communist party, the trade unions, the semi-military republican *Reichsbanner*"—had one and all "vanished from the scene so completely that it now seems almost incredible that they once ranked among the most powerful organizations of their kind in the world" (133). Under the mandate for "coordination" with Nazi rule centrist parties

---

10. Samuel Štefan Osuský, "The Philosophy of Boshevism, Fascism and Hitlerism."
11. All page citations in this chapter are hereafter given in the text by parentheses.
12. All page citations in this chapter are hereafter given in the text by parentheses.
13. All page citations in this chapter are hereafter given in the text by parentheses.

and other traditional and nationalist parties had likewise "disbanded and their membership amalgamated with the National Socialist movement." The regional governments had been "subverted beneath the Nazi steam-roller. The civil service, university faculties and chess clubs had been purged of Liberals and Jews. The Roman Catholic Church had negotiated a concordat, pledging itself to abstain from all political activity" (133–34). Likewise, it had seemed, the Protestant heirs of Martin Luther and John Calvin "had been united into a single Reichskirche, under the jurisdiction of a bishop virtually appointed by Hitler, who is himself a nominal Roman Catholic" (134). Under these circumstances—so Walmer concluded his introductory paragraphs—how remarkable that "such an expression of open dissent has made itself felt and has wrung concessions from the Government!" (134).

We are in the realm of perceptions here. We are studying a knowledgeable American liberal, openly dismayed at the Nazi "methods which transformed the exercise of the franchise into a farcical perversion of democratic procedure . . . [sealing] the sweeping victory of the dictatorship on a scale unparalleled in the history of popular suffrage" (133). Hitler had come to power legally. Hitler's exploitation of the alleged "state of emergency" had now received massive popular endorsement. The program of *Gleichschaltung* had apparently achieved "finality." A scene of democratic self-destruction has unfolded "to the startled gaze of foreigners who could scarcely credit that such things were possible in a civilized nation" (134), among whom Walmer undoubtedly classifies also himself. The little opening of light in the gathering darkness now shed by the "[t]housands of Protestant pastors [who] have uncompromisingly announced their determination to combat the attempts of the German Christians to graft their new doctrines upon the Bible and the faith of Luther," therefore attracts his attention, just as it should come to the attention of all North American democrats, for it gives hope that the boasted "finality" of Gleichschaltung is not so settled a matter after all.

From here, Walmer went on in his essay to give Americans a remarkably apt description of the German Christian Faith Movement, as recent scholarship has discovered it anew, as seen in Chapter 1. Their agenda is "that the Christian Church in the Reich must be Germanized and purged of all false notions of the universality of human brotherhood." They carry "the theory and practice of antisemitism to a logical extreme from which most antisemites hitherto have shrunk" since those "of former days, while declaiming against the Jews, usually remained orthodox Christians in the theological sense, acknowledging the Bible as the Word of God." But for these new antisemites the "Jews are a racial group" and the Bible, especially the Old Testament, "stands forth as pre-eminently the product of Jewish genius." Endowed with "more logic and less scruple" than their ancestors in faith, the German Christians are a modern and modernizing movement; the have "absorbed enough of the higher criticism of the Bible to know that some scholars doubt that it is divinely inspired, and this has furnished them with a peg upon which to hang their argument" (134–35) for removing the Old Testament from the canon.

Walmer next contrasts this movement within the churches for a thoroughgoing Nazi revisionism of the inherited faith to the neo-pagan German Faith Movement outside the churches that draws on sources as diverse as Nietzsche, Hinduism, and the vague pantheism of certain German poets. Altogether, Walmer observes, "[m]any men, loosed from their orthodox spiritual moorings by the rationalistic interpretation of the Bible and hungering after some cause to which they can devote themselves, have taken refuge in the cult of religious nationalism which finds its ethical justification in an old paganism transformed into a modern pantheism" (136). In response to this outside pressure from the neo-pagans, there arose within the German Christian Faith Movement corresponding wings of radicals tending toward neo-paganism, under the leadership of figures like the Bishop of Brandenberg, Joachim Hossenfelder, and his subordinate, Reinhold Krause, and of moderates, under the leadership of the presiding bishop of the new *Reichskirch*, Ludwig Müller. The latter's "moderate" Nazification of Christian faith, Walmer reports, runs as follows: "We German Christians want to be Christians and proclaim the doctrines of our church after our own fashion. We cannot be a conglomeration of Christians and Nordic Pagans. Christianity did not emerge from Judaism but grew out of wars upon it. We must learn to view Christ after the German fashion" (137).

While to us today these shades in degrees of religious Nazification seem to make the proverbial distinction without a difference, they served Walmer as background against which to appreciate the "rebellion" of the Protestant pastors in the newly organizing Confessing Church, "the first sign of organized unrest in Germany since Hitler embarked upon his coordination policy" (137). His recounting of this complicated and to North Americans exotic history need not here detain us. What matters is that the North American liberal Walmer recognized and lifted up the political significance of the public assertion of the freedom of Christian proclamation, citing the clarion call of the embattled Bishop von Bodelschwingh, the figure at the head of the pastors' rebellion: "We want a young, live church, in which spiritual matters will be dealt with in a spiritual way and in which the proclamation of the Gospel remains free from all means of political force. The struggle for the free church of the Gospel goes further. It is at the same time the struggle for the soul and for the future of our people" (138).

Just this outbreak of unrest along just these "spiritual" lines rivaled the total claim of Nazism, according to Walmer, and so caused Hitler to retreat from a "frontal attack." As the Church Struggle now unfolded, it became increasingly clear to the broader church public, according to Walmer, that the German Christians "had with blatant effrontery attacked and derided the central tenets of Christianity . . . [leading to] the paganization of the eldest daughter of the Reformation and her complete severance from fellowship and communion with the Christian churches of the world" (139). In this protest the Confessing Church, "for the first time" since Hitler's ascension to power voiced, albeit "by implication," a theological condemnation of "Hitler's anti-Semitic policy. 'The Church of Jesus Christ,' declared a group of pastors at Breslau, 'is no community of blood but a community of the Holy Ghost . . . '" (139).

Hitler was forced to back-pedal. "The German Christian movement was known to have all the resources of the Government behind it. If it were openly flouted with impunity, it would do irreparable damage to Hitler's reputation as a strong man who is unerringly guided by God and to the prestige of the 'totalitarian' state which asserts the right to regulate even the thoughts of its citizens" (140). Hence, disillusioned at his premature grab for coordination of the churches through the German Christian Faith movement and the unified Reichskirche, Hitler reverted to his previous—if I may say so, "Two Kingdoms"—policy of strict separation of church and state/party. That retreat brings us to Walmer's present in 1934. He concluded that it remains to be seen what "will be the Nazis' ultimate attitude toward the question of coordinating the church . . . "(140), noting that "any fresh offensive on the religious front will probably be deferred until the regime has succeeded in consolidating itself more firmly . . . " Indeed, it is likely that Hitler "will make doubly sure of his ground before he again runs the risk of burning his fingers by grasping the live coals of cherished religious beliefs and traditions" (141).

In much Walmer's astute observation and skillful analysis of a complex contemporary event stands the test of time. But what is remarkable from the perspective of the present study is that the danger Walmer perceives in Nazi racialist anti-Semitism is not one of a driving, causal factor. The notion of an official adoption in the churches of Nazi anti-Semitic policies seems to him to be an entirely obvious "heresy" produced by a radical revision of traditional Christian orthodoxy as provoked by the emergence of neo-pagan rivals. Here anti-Semitism appears rather as a reflux of the pagan past, a reflex or byproduct of deviation from the self-evident script of progress towards democracy among those civilized nations, that is, nations with a progressive Christian self-understanding. Hitler in this view is turning back the clock. Just that, moreover, is why Walmer can see such hope in the pastors' protest as a political event. Indeed the awakening of an orthodox Protestant Christian remnant appears here as the sole, institutionally viable expression of dissent, even "rebellion" within the consolidating regime of Nazi totalitarianism.[14]

All of these perceptions are attributable to Walmer's liberal and democratic American perspective, where the iconic Luther (whose traditional anti-Semitism Walmer alludes to but does not name by name) still stood as liberal icon of the rights of conscience and the freedoms of assembly and association. Indeed, what is even more striking is the self-confidence with which Walmer speaks from this perspective, as if the very rise of Nazism on the ruins of Weimar's democratic self-destruction did not fundamentally challenge the liberal narrative of progress in tandem with civilizing, progressive Christianity, as if the rise of the Confessing Church would and therefore hopefully could return Germany to the normal (so he assumes) trajectory of progress towards civil rights, the rule of law, and popular sovereignty. Despite the foreboding expressed in conclusion, we know today that Walmer's hope against hope in the rebellion of the pastors was one that was realized at best only "spiritually," not "politically," that in fact the only institutionally significant political resistance arose later on in the ranks of the *Wehrmacht*. Likewise, just here, the otherwise "democratic" doctrine of the separation of church and state was used—by Hitler![15]—to defuse the "spiritual" protest of the pastors' rebellion and neutralize its "political" effect. Liberalism's "Two Kingdoms" doctrine of public and private realms assigned to state and church respectively was also Hitler's, who used it for anti-democratic purposes to suppress free exercise in the name of institutional separation. We will further analyze this set of problems in Chapter 5.

---

14. This a fact worthy of greater attention. As Joachim Remak, editor of *The Nazi Years: A Documentary History* commented, "The significant fact, however, was that the number of dissenters was greater in the churches than elsewhere, and that besides, the churches offered the one place where the dissenter might still have a chance to be heard" (97). At the same time, as Susannah Heschel notes, just because the church is, or has offered itself as, an institution with pretensions of being the soul or conscience of the nation, it deserves redoubled scrutiny in cases of failure in its own self-proclaimed vocation. Recent scholarship has done much to scrutinize other institutions of civil society under Hitler. Notable studies include Browning, *Ordinary Men*; Cornwell, *Hitler's Scientists*; Katz, ed., *Death by Design*; Rubenfeld, ed., *Medicine after the Holocaust*; and Pringle, *The Master Plan*.

15. Klaus Scholder makes this point repeatedly, as first described in his notable chapter, "Hitler's Basic Decision on Church Policy (1924–1928)," in *Churches and the Third Reich*, 88–98. The only exception to a modern Two Kingdoms policy he made, and from which he felt badly burned, was the intervention on behalf of Müller's election as Reichsbishop.

For the moment, this reflection on Walmer causes us further to reflect on the unspoken assumptions of our own liberalism. Intriguingly, we can trace out diverging "liberal liberal" and "conservative liberal" patterns of American perception during the rise of Nazism among the more secular American voices during the 1930s studied by Nagorski and Hamerow.

LIBERAL LIBERALS AND CONSERVATIVE LIBERALS ON THE RISE OF NAZISM

Andrew Nagorski's study of "the Americans [in Germany] who witnessed these events firsthand, how they perceived and reported them either as part of their jobs or as curious visitors, and what kind of impact their accounts had on their countrymen's views of Germany at the time" (3) is valuable because he scrupulously seeks to avoid the retrospective fallacy. "Through their experiences," Nagorski writes of his subjects, "I felt I was reliving this heavily dissected era with an intensity and immediacy that is often lacking elsewhere... history as seen by eyewitnesses without the benefit of knowing where these events would lead" (7). He thus emphasizes that the "unfolding of history only looks inevitable in retrospect" (4). By "letting those stories speak for themselves" our assessments of "where their moral compasses were on target or completely missing" can unfold "from their experiences, not from our knowledge based on the luxury of hindsight" (8). Although it is not part of Nagorski's intention as such, his study is valuable for the present inquiry because it reveals the philosophically liberal lenses worn by American observers of all stripes as well as the characteristic blind spots in those variously refracted lenses created by the contradictions between American ideology and American reality. Liberal liberals (hereafter, conventionally, liberals) and conservative liberals (hereafter, conventionally, conservatives) shared the Lockean-Jeffersonian narrative of historical progress by virtue of the emancipation of the sovereign self from economic, social, and religious constraints on individual freedom. This is a modern, emancipatory faith, akin in this respect to that of Nazism, in the native goodness of humanity that, set free from external constraints, is assuredly willing and able to achieve an historical good of universal significance.

The liberals are represented by William Shirer in Nagorski's narrative. Since we have already encountered him as the subject of Siemon-Netto's critique of clichéd thinking, they can be treated summarily in what follows and we will give correspondingly greater attention to those conservatives who were impressed and/or seduced by Nazism. This is a stance transparent to their own conservative awareness of the nagging contradictions between

American ideology and American experience, especially in the matter of race relations, and their corresponding fear of the known devil, Bolshevism. That is to say, conservatives feared Bolshevism above all because Bolshevism tellingly pointed to the American contradictions and hence the hypocrisies of its liberal apologists.

Already the military commander of American troops in postwar Germany in 1920, Major General Henry T. Allen dismissed German complaints about the presence of French African colonial troops occupying the Ruhr valley. He explained the German complaints by referring to America's own experience, "where the negro question is always capable of arousing feeling." Dismissing the German reports of sexual misconduct as race-baiting propaganda aimed at arousing anti-French feeling in the USA and sympathy for defeated Germany, he was willing in his official capacity to make an antifeminist smear, claiming "that many German women of loose character have openly made advances to the colored soldiers." Revealingly, he reminds his superiors in Washington that "the color line is not regarded either by the French or the Germans as we regard it in America: to keep the white race pure" (17). It is evident that the race question for a conservative like Allen was hardly an idle one and we can only imagine where the General's sympathies would have fallen in thirteen short years. The point, for the moment, was that this conservative explained away German behavior with reference to America's own contradictions between ideology and experience in race relations. In fact, eleven years later, Annetta Antona, a columnist for a Detroit paper, interviewed Hitler in December of 1931 and noted a large portrait of Detroit industrialist and anti-Semite Henry Ford hanging in the Nazi Party Headquarters in Munich. Asked about it, Hitler reportedly replied, "I regard Henry Ford as my inspiration" (60). As Nagorski notes, such episodes "are useful reminders that Germany was far from unique in harboring such sentiments in the 1920s" (61). But in the USA, these sentiments represented the profoundest contradictions in behavior to its vaunted creed and gave American conservatives, like Ford, grounds on which to view Hitler sympathetically.

Already in 1921 the first American correspondent to interview Adolf Hitler wrote of him as the "Mussolini of Teuton Crisis" (sic), offering in retrospect a remarkable picture of a conservative's Hitler: seeking reconciliation with France, wanting to avoid war and advocating "true socialism"—"the welfare of all the people, and not of one class at the expense of others" (21), a Hitler who as a result was drawing "followers even out of the inner communistic and socialistic circles . . . " (22). Karl Henry von Wiegland, "star reporter for the Hearst publications" (18), described Hitler as "man of the people," a "magnetic speaker having also exceptional organizing genius"

(21), and "one of the most interesting characters I have met in many months" (22). This classification of Hitler as a Germany First populist comports with American conservativism's contemporaneous inclination towards isolation and national unity as the ticket to peace and prosperity. Interestingly, just a few years later, Wiegland wrote insightfully on the postwar "Americanization of Europe," and the "decidedly schizophrenic attitude [of 'the average German'] toward the new money culture, mass production and mass entertainment, including a flood of American movies," (50) transforming "Germany into 'the United States of Europe'" (51). This conservative saw the "schizophrenia" in Germans in the same way he saw it in his native land: the wealth created by economic freedom also and necessarily erodes traditional forms of communal life, which is the cost of growth and social progress. Hitler himself in 1928 acknowledged that "the European, often without being conscious of it, applies American conditions as a standard for his own" (56). In this way and with some empirical support, Americans like Wiegland were able to apply their own "conservative" spin on a Germany that seemed rapidly to be adopting American categories for itself. But we should also notice how Hitler, cognizant of this phenomenon, does not claim it as his own.

Chiefly what conservatives perceived in the rise of Nazism was a bulwark against Bolshevism and in this, though from a different perspective, they did make genuine contact with Nazi thinking. Thus Captain Truman Smith, military attaché at the US Berlin embassy, reported on his interview with WW I General Erich Ludendorff, one of the founders of the Nazi Party, who demanded that "the Allies must support a strong German government capable of combating Marxism" (25). Conservatives could hear with approval Hitler's announced goal, in 1930, "to save Germany from being economically enslaved to foreign powers on the one hand and on the other hand from being utterly bolshevized and falling into disorganization and demoralization" (68). Years later, a young US Army officer, Albert C. Wedemeyer, spent the years 1936–38 as an American exchange student at the German War College; he recalled "constant lectures about the Bolshevik menace." A supporter at home of the America First movement, Wedemeyer acknowledged that he became "convinced that the German search for *Lebensraum* did not menace the Western World to anything like the same degree as the world-wide conspiracy centered in Moscow" (250). The conservative, more fully aware of the dependence of liberalism's progress on the untrammeled growth of the free market, saw the radical threat in communism to economic growth and accordingly minimized the Nazi threat. He regarded Nazism as a peculiarly German cultural adaptation, state capitalism or welfare capitalism on steroids, so to say, and as such a bulwark against Bolshevism, just as also Ludendorff and Hitler thought about themselves.

After exposure to the "new" Germany at the 1936 Olympics Anne Lindbergh, wife of aviator Charles, wrote disapprovingly of liberals' "strictly puritanical view at home that dictatorships are of necessity wrong, evil, unstable, and no good can come of them, combined with the funny-paper view of Hitler as a clown" (205). Such conservatives were increasingly open to the German rebuke of American liberalism's dismissive view of National Socialism: "You realize don't you that in Germany there is not a single unemployed, and no man that goes hungry in winter or freezes, and this is not so for any other country except Italy which is also under the state's direction?" (224). Thus even the liberal Ambassador Hugh Wilson repeatedly reported back to the State Department from the Berlin of the late 1930s that "Hitler enjoyed the active and passive support of most Germans and that it was wishful thinking to believe that his regime could collapse—or that the minority who opposed it could do anything to make that happen" (238). The wishful thinking of the liberals shipwrecked on the hard rock of the conservatives' insight into the peace, prosperity, and national unity that Hitler had brought and the popular support it acquired for him.

Of course, we know that that peace, prosperity, and national unity was only a mirage. Perhaps the most important contribution Nagorski's study makes is in showing how in the earliest years Hitler cultivated this mirage for his regime in constructing an image of humility, reasonableness, and moderation (as Hamerow will show us, this image extends even to the anti-Semitic policies). This inclined conservatives to regard the suspension of civil rights as a legitimate "state of exception" caused by an emergency or revolutionary situation. Goebbels's words from this time thus resonated: "Never before have the young men had so good a right to clean up the debris of the past . . . " (107). The Night of the Long Knives on June 30, 1934 was interpreted in this light. Hubert Renfro Knickerbacker, whom Nagorski notes had been "so perceptive in many of his earlier dispatches," reported as fact that "Röhm's Brownshirts had planned 'what would have been the most extraordinary massacre in modern political history'" (163). The erstwhile "perceptive" Knickerbocker had pointed out "how the Nazis were following the Bolshevik lead when it came to new forms of terror" (150). It was likewise Knickerbocker who early on in 1933 was urging newly arriving American journalists to take up *Mein Kampf* and read: "No American I know of has taken the trouble to read it seriously; but it's all there: his plan for the conquest of Europe" (133). This "astute" young journalist evidently now judged, as conservatives were wont, that fire must be fought with fire—or, rather, in the case of the Night of the Long Lives that Hitler's resort to fire had to mean that there really was a dangerous counter-revolutionary conspiracy about to alight that justified this extreme act of extra-judicial terrorism.

Pulitzer Prize-winning reporter Edgar Mowrer, a progressive who eventually published *Germany Puts the Clock Back* upon return to the USA, similarly committed to writing his judgment that "[s]ubjectively Adolf Hitler was, in my opinion, entirely sincere even in his self-contradictions" (100). As a liberal, Mowrer saw contradictions in Hitler's populist nationalism in the same way that he saw contradictions at home between the conservative's ideological summons to patriotism and unity and the bitter reality of the exploitation of the working class and the latter's self-defeating distraction and division by conservative race baiting. If conservatives projected their own awareness of the contradictions between American ideology and American reality, as for example in the matter of race relations, and found their own greater awareness of capitalism as the goose that lays the golden egg reflected and defended in Nazism's anti-Bolshevism, prescient American liberals like Mowrer and Shirer minimized the problem of Bolshevism. This underplaying of the precedent in state terrorism and pure treachery that Hitler found in Stalin, as per Knickerbocker's assessment mentioned above, is evident in Shirer's despondency over the Hitler-Stalin pact. As Nagorski reports, Shirer clearly saw that it virtually "invites Germany to go in and clean up Poland"—though notably, Shirer is not reported here to observe that it equally well invited the Soviet Union to occupy the Baltics and take its own thick cut out of Poland's soon to be bleeding carcass. As Nagorski comments: "While Shirer knew what [the pact] meant, he clearly didn't understand the Soviet leader as well as he did Hitler: 'That Stalin would play such crude power politics and also play into the hands of the Nazis overwhelms the rest of us'" (260)—a self-report that speaks volumes, not about Stalin, but about Shirer's hope in Stalin and the optic of American liberalism through which he consistently read events.

In September of 1938 at Nuremberg Hitler issued the following taunt to liberal critics in the West: "People in those democracies deplore the 'unspeakable cruelties' with which Germany... is trying to get rid of the Jewish element... Now that the complaints [against the Jews] have at last become very loud and our nation is no longer willing to let itself be further impoverished by those parasites, people are wailing about it. But they are not trying to solve the so-called problem once and for all by some constructive action on the part of those democratic countries. Quite the contrary, they inform us very coolly that there is of course no room [for Jews] over there... They offer no help, but, oh, the moralizing!" Hamerow places this quotation as an epigraph over Part One of his deeply insightful study (31). The taunt, as

Hamerow shows in a massive showcase of evidence, was not without merit. Conservatives in the West argued successfully against immigration that "wholesale readiness to accept the victims of foreign persecution inevitably acts as a standing invitation to any country that wishes to get rid of its Jewish elements to start persecuting them" (228), a thought notable in its underestimation of Nazi hatred and fanaticism. From the opposite direction a small but vocal cadre of liberals hammered FDR's immigration policy with increasing fervor as the world catapulted towards war: "Was there not an inconsistency between America's position in international affairs and its policy regarding the refugee problem?" (280). Indeed, yes, there was, just as Hitler taunted. All the same, "the undercurrent of antisemitism in the United States [that resisted admitting Jewish refugees] did not seem to diminish" as war approached; instead "it was growing stronger. Why?" (280).

What Hamerow reveals is that that undercurrent of anti-Semitism was no exclusive domain of the American conservatives. Predominant among liberals was the "suspicion that the diplomacy of the United States was being controlled by a clever and unscrupulous Jewish minority" (281) to lure the United States into a war on behalf of their oppressed brethren under Hitler. The parallel to this among conservatives was the fear was that Jews were using "the refugee problem as an instrument of subversion" (281), i.e., to bring a flood of Reds into the country. Only after the US became involved in the war did liberals shift ground and now accuse the Roosevelt administration as a veritable "accessor[y] to the crime and Hitler's guilt" (317) for not having earlier acted to stop the murdering. This trickle turned into a flood of after the fact moralizing, since in fact American conservatives and liberals alike had resisted war and/or immigration as policies that would have stopped Hitler or mitigated his anti-Semitic policies. Hamerow's depressing observation is that only long after the war, "when the full extent of the Nazi genocide was fully recognized," did recrimination over what more "should have been done to stop the extermination of European Jewry" (416) become possible.

In sum, there were according to Hamerow "real concerns, based on rational, reasonable calculations" (388) first in resisting war and immigration, then in holding together domestic and international coalitions to assure military victory over Germany. These calculations continuously frustrated any interventions against the unfolding Holocaust, even after it became known from 1941 on. He devotes an entire chapter to the question (389–420). For our purposes, it is a secondary matter whether Hamerow is right about this. More salient is his well-grounded claim that there "was an undercurrent of popular ethnic suspicion which had become almost traditional, not only in Eastern Europe, but farther to the west as well, on both sides of the Atlantic" (388). The Jewish Question, in other words, was alive and well also in the USA. Jewish leaders in America agreed. For example, Cyrus Adler, president of the Jewish Theological Seminary in New York, "opposed the economic boycott of German goods which militant Jewish organizations launched as soon as Hitler came to power. It would only alienate popular opinion in America without changing racist policy in Germany." Special pleading on behalf of Germany's Jews during the massive sufferings of the Great Depression, he feared, would give "the impression that in the face of the difficulties and misery of the world [Jews] wish to put themselves forward as the only real problem" (254, cf. on Stephen Wise, 269, 285).

Hamerow's comprehensive study is a disillusioning catalogue of such conflicted and paralyzing thinking among American liberals of both stripes. Its effect is to force the realization that once a Hitler comes to power, no good choices remain. He concludes, "Paradoxically, those who maintained that only victory on the battlefield could save the Jews were in essence right. The tragedy was that by the time victory came, so few Jews were left to save" (418, cf. 321, 353, 382, 385, 392). This is not at all a happy outcome. It is a tragic one philosophically, a sinful one theologically. We watched, that is, we let Hitler's well-signaled hatred happen and the Jews and others be murdered, because only counter-violence would stop him. And the will to counter-violence must overcome great inertia. Short of that neither liberalism's optimism that, being understood, Hitler could be made reasonable, nor conservativism's pessimism, not to say cynicism, that Hitler's fury represented the lesser evil in comparison to Stalin was able to do anything to stop the genocide. Once the violence began, both conservatives and liberals more or less converged in prioritizing military victory on unconditional terms by preserving the otherwise improbable alliance with Stalin. Practically, this outcome vindicates Ericksen's proverbial counsel that an ounce of prevention is worth a pound of cure. The best way to prevent another Holocaust is rigorously to remember what happened in all its agonizing tragedy and sin and to inculcate the liberal values of tolerance and human rights. Yet if Hamerow is right, even this good counsel is not good enough. Tolerance and human rights meet their limits in the face of organized malice. Stretched to the breaking point before this limit, tolerance and human rights sold out in the ways that we have seen American liberals and conservatives did during the rise of Nazism.

Tolerance and human rights are not good enough for two reasons, both theological. First, the so-called Jewish Question remains, for Jews as also for Christians and Muslims, together the predominant religious realities in the world. Second, the crisis of the Enlightenment remains, a crisis that Ericksen so rightly but also so ambiguously or rather inconsequently invoked in his study. We should indeed inculcate the liberal values of tolerance and human rights. But on what grounds and at what cost and with what consistency? With this latter we come indeed to Judaism's own Jewish Question about the vocation of Abraham's children to be the bearer of Torah values to the world and today the ambiguous relation of that calling to Zionism and the empirical reality of the modern State of Israel. Needless to say, this has also to do with Judaism's relation to her offspring, Christianity and Islam. These both are theological questions.

Hamerow can lend yet a little further help on the Jewish Question that remains for us today. The title of his book's first chapter is "The Siren Song of Emancipation." It teases out the unforeseen consequences of modernity for both Jews and Christians in Europe: "Whether as greedy capitalists or as rabble-rousing radicals, the [emancipated] Jews were increasingly seen as a threat to traditional social values and loyalties" (24) and it was consequently just "at this time that the 'Jewish question' became a subject of serious discussion in many works dealing with the future of European society and culture" (25). With the Jews, the Jewish Question came out of the ghetto and became the common question of modern Europeans discovering the Jews in their midst. This notice of the modernity of the emergence of the Jewish Question from beyond Judaism itself sheds light on the difficult distinction between traditional Christian anti-Judaism and modern secular-racist anti-Semitism. Hamerow explains the difference: "At a time when belief in Christianity was the chief cohesive force . . . members of the Jewish community were viewed as aliens, as perpetual outsiders," that is to say, as disruptive of social cohesion. When such belief in Christianity as the "chief cohesive force" had passed away, that is, after the decline and fall of European Christendom, the same Jews were found to disrupt cohesion in new, secular ways corresponding to the secular substitutes for the lost cohesion of Christianity in the new political religions.

Nor was this secular transition to anti-Semitism a fervid fantasy, the pure invention of bigotry. It is not without some basis in the reality that Judaism itself is both a people and a religion, such that this new anti-Semitism looks upon persistent Jewish peoplehood, or race, rather than outmoded religion, as the source of social disruption precisely in the context of modern liberation movements based upon the principle of ethnic group, i.e., "national" self-determination. What self-determining people can tolerate another self-determining people within it? Hamerow reports how the theological voice of American liberalism, the *Christian Century*, threw up its hands in 1938, baffled at the intractability of the "Jewish question" so posed. It urged every assistance to the victims of Hitlerism, above all urging readers to raise a loud voice of outrage at their treatment and so far as possible to advocate for the reception of refugees, limited and inadequate to the challenge as that would be. And it concluded, astonishingly as it seems to us today, that "if we seem skeptical of the practicality of many of the present proposals for mass deportation to far away and unoccupied territories [i.e., Madagascar], we shall rejoice if events prove that we were of too little faith" (235). Thus American liberals of the progressive Christian stripe joined in the hope for peaceful deportation as a morally viable even if impractical answer to the Jewish Question.

Hamerow's own blunt answer to the Jewish Question is that Hitler settled it in a "direct, effective, and lasting solution . . . All that was needed for its adoption was a ruthless ideology and a regime powerful enough, determined enough, and pitiless enough to embrace it" (235, cf. 469). Yet this not the whole truth. Try as Hitler did, the Jewish people as a people survived the Holocaust, though not in Europe. Out of the Holocaust, Zionism emerged as the dominant force for Jews. With the founding of the State of Israel, Zionism transposed the Jewish Question to a new key. Prima facie evidence that the Jewish Question in this way abides may be seen in Iranian president Ahmadinejad's taunt, identical in substance to Hitler's in 1938, that the "Zionist entity" should be dissolved, its stolen land returned to the native Palestinians, and the Jews returned to Europe whence they had been expelled by Hitler's would-be but failed "final" solution.[16] A host of volatile issues surfaces at this point. Centrally, is it adequate to reduce the "Jewish Question" to the ironies and/or failures of emancipation and of the European Enlightenment? Or is this at root a genuinely theological question, first for Jews, but also for Christians and Muslims, going all the way back to Israel's vocation of blessing to the nations? If so, how ever might we address it? The discussion of this question continues in Chapter 5 in the discussion of the Christian theology of Israel. For the remainder of this chapter, the ground is now prepared to look and see afresh how three witnesses, Taylor, Samuel, and Osuský, discerned the threat veiled in the rise of Nazism with neither conservative nor liberal eyes but ones discerning of Ericksen's double crisis of modernity.

KRESSMAN TAYLOR'S "BATTLE OF THE TITANS"

By the time of the publication of *Day of No Return* (published under the title, *Until that Day*) in 1942, Kressman Taylor was already known from her 1939 *Address Unknown*, a novel that sold fifty thousand copies and won

---

16. CNN Monday, April 24, 2006. Online: http://www.cnn.com/2006/WORLD/meast/04/24/iran.nuclear/index.html

from the *New York Times Book Review* the accolade: "This modern story is perfection itself. It is the most effective indictment of Nazism to appear in fiction" (10). As a result of her reputation, the FBI arranged a clandestine meeting with Pastor Leopold W. Bernhard, who had arrived in the USA in January of 1938 as a refugee from Nazi Germany (11). The result of this encounter was her fictionalized account—to protect the identity of Bernhard's family that had remained in Germany—of the young pastor's experiences in church and society during the rise of Nazism. Thus we have in her novel a layered account of a firsthand theological witness as filtered by an American from the time before Auschwitz.

"The Nazis had prepared a perfect plan," Taylor wrote by way of introduction. "By a subtle scheme that looked on the surface like co-operation they would take over the Lutheran church and use it to serve their purposes. They would disarm the churchmen and place their own men at the head of a united Church" (13). Taylor gave the name Karl Hoffman to her fictionalized representation of Bernhard, and portrayed this theological student, influenced by Barth and Brunner (290), as one who had in the previous six years garnered ". . . an inside view of one of the cleverest, the most subtle and measured of persecutions the Church of God has endured during the long centuries since it became a power in the world" (48, cf. 72, 126). By the seemingly positive step of an ecumenical union of Protestant churches (82, 84) Christianity's Nazification and subordination to the Third Reich was attempted. Reporting on this to an American audience is Taylor's purpose in the novel. But that is not all. Taylor also wanted to bear her own definite theological witness, as she explains in the original introduction to the book. And this is what makes her Christian perspective something other than those of the conservatives and liberals Nagorski and Hamerow have described for us. She wrote, "Because they were materialists the masters of Germany" increasingly "turned to attack this resistance with physical forces. They had all the power . . ." (14). But Karl Hoffmann/Leopold Bernhard "was never enslaved. He wears a man's dignity because his strength is fed by the Source from which men first drew their dignity and learned to walk with their heads uplifted. God is the strength of man" (15, cf. 265, 270).

Taylor articulates her faith in God as the paradoxical grasping of the mystery beyond the materialism that Nazism exemplifies for her (40). In either case, God or materialism, it is a faith which requires theological work to discern. As she puts it on the lips of Karl Hoffmann: "I had begun to see in that interplay between the lives of men on this earth which is essential to their existence in a society, that every man is of necessity a servant . . . the only choice left to him being the choice of a master" (46). At this juncture a genuine intersection of theology and politics occurs. Whose is the kingdom, the power and the glory? On the first page of the novel, Taylor's Hoffman expresses Bernhard's and Taylor's fundamental conviction: "I believe that the real battle of Titans is being waged not between military powers but between men's fundamental beliefs" (17, cf 285ff). This conviction, as we shall see in Chapter 5, determines the sense of the Two Kingdoms doctrine—or otherwise the Two Kingdoms doctrine becomes the tool of secular totalitarianism and metaphysical materialism pressing faith to an impotent preserve of personal inwardness in a public world dominated by force.

Taylor uses the novelistic genre to inform North Americans about the cultural particularities that shape the German context and the rise of Nazism. She stresses Hoffmann's "conservative" heritage in the sense of his family's preference for the old order of monarchy over the "disaster and disintegration" attending Weimar democracy (18). She has Hoffman's father, a traditional pastor, commenting early in the novel on the social unrest in the 1920s: "All this lawlessness is the result of the penetration of socialism. The Monarchy had its faults, but such a reign of criminality as we are living today, such widespread hunger, the breakdown of industry, such an abandonment of all morality, the depravity of officials, the looseness of the young people, could never have occurred under its strict forms" (22). Very much a "conservative" in this way, as we have learned from Siemon-Netto about the Prussian Junkers who conspired against Hitler, Hoffmann's father had the strength of character to slap a cigar from the mouth of a uniformed Nazi when his troops invaded the worship service, "Remember that you are in God's House!" (101). In the end, the old man resists the Nazi invasion of the church at mortal cost of his failing health, telling his concerned son, "It would be harder than death for me, Karl, to give up this fight while I can still do anything" (260)—and so he does, opposing in failing health to his death what he describes as the Nazi's attempt to "turn the people from the worship of God to the worship of the state" (261). In the elder Hoffmann's "conservative" thinking, monarchy was subject to the limitations of its divine institution. Its claim was not total or absolute. Just this made opposition to Nazism a genuinely "conservative" possibility.

Aside from this portrait of the "conservative" elder Pastor Hoffman's exemplary and ethically consistent conduct, much later in the story the younger Hoffmann reflects on the blindness of "German aristocrats" to the impending dangers: " . . . these people and hundreds like them made their correct appearances at church, yet were completely ignorant that the Church was fighting for its very life and that on the other hand a rival religion had arisen, preaching a harsh and cruel paganism and that their very sons were walking in the streets shouting its bombastic shibboleths" (176–77). The character Orlando von Schack, as we shall shortly see, is the novel's figure of this newly militant Nazi son of the aristocracy. But Taylor stresses the class blinders in which Hoffmann was raised, having him confess: "Hemmed in by a narrowness of social strata, blinded to the implications of the popular unrest, when the Nazi threat appeared we did not begin to understand it" (22). This class-based narrowness of the "conservatives" continued in the virtual segregation of the theological students, "excluded from the more active life of the University," taking little part in political discussions, uninterested in "the secular concerns of their fellows," and "forbidden by the Church to engage in dueling" (53)—though later this de facto isolation provided needed distance from the tyranny of the immediate and gave a certain basis for anti-Nazi militancy and resistance in the Confessing Church (103). Correspondingly in the novel it is the German Christian advocates of Nazification who array themselves against the "conservatives" in church: "Who is it who have done nothing to support the great ideal of National Socialism? The conservative churchmen" (91–93), though here the term "conservative" denotes orthodox Lutheran theology as opposed to the accommodating theology of the liberal Protestants, not nostalgia for the monarchy as such.

A number of real actors appear in the novel: the revered professor Hans Lietzmann (65ff, 84–87, 104, 107ff) who disappoints his students by finally supporting the Reichskirche, and the dauntless Martin Niemöller (117, 120–21, 129–30, 185, 243–46) who courageously leads the church's resistance to Nazification. But for the most part, Taylor introduces the doctrines of Nazism, and paints pictures of their social bases, in fictional characters. There is theological student Heinrich Gross, who introduces the Führerprinzip into the University Faculty of the Theology (63) and terminates debate with fellow theological students with the threat: "You cling to old, outmoded Christian doctrines. This is another day. We have the power now . . . From now on we will use force" (190). There is Hans Kraemer, one of those "small men whose ambitions are greater than their talents" (147). He is the German Christian pastor that comes to usurp the pulpit of the elder Pastor Hoffman after his arrest and internment in a concentration camp. His message too is directed against the "conservatives" now in jail: "Too many reactionaries have had their say in the Church and the true German religion has been stifled . . . Our first work is to get rid of the degrading and emasculating influence of the Jews . . . and work for the ideal of national honor and exalt the Nordic hero, and all who join it must be of pure Nordic descent" (148). The biblical calumny against the Jews from John 8 is put on his lips: "Ye are of your father the Devil . . . " (149). The swastika must be exchanged for the cross: "We have been deluded by the Crucifix into worshiping weakness" (154). There is the young Baron von Rauth, whom Hoffman meets while conscripted for service in a Labor Battalion, "a Nazi hotbed [where] men not only talked—they lived National Socialism" (247). The aristocrat von Rauth had suffered loss of status and impoverishment after democratization but now enjoyed a new prestige and purpose in the National Socialist movement. So he has become "a believer, in a really religious sense, a convert, a disciple of the new faith" (248). He assures Hoffmann that the "last enemy which National Socialism has to overcome is Christianity" (247). He claims that the Nazis have "over a thousand ministers in the concentration camps now" (247) and justifies this repression with the new creed: "We have only one savior and he is Adolf Hitler . . . Why should we allow anyone to teach [people] that they have a different Savior . . . ? The stupid Church has refused to go along with the new order. It has made itself the enemy of all progress" (249).

Through such character sketches Taylor made tangible to her American readers the "idealist" appeal of Hitlerism as progressive force, an appeal that she never tries to square with her own interpretation of Nazism as metaphysical materialism. Perhaps her meaning is that what was a calculating materialism for elite leaders was propagandized as a self-sacrificing idealism for followers, a quasi-Nietzschean division of roles and perspective between the leading Übermenschen and the herd that followed. We shall explore Hitler's theology with a distinction like this in Chapter 4 between a form of the Kantian ethic of duty for the followers and a Nietzschean ethic of mastery for the elite. In any case, Hitlerism appealed. There was not one of us, Hoffmann at one point tells, "who did not resent the ignominious position that had been forced upon our fatherland after the great war" (58). It is no wonder, he says, that so many turn to the dream of an integrated and organic society, "something more vigorous and understandable and wholesome in comparison to the stink they are living in. Hitler says he will give them a new Germany. Each man will work for his brother and all can believe again in their own goodness . . . " (61). The appeal of National Socialism lay also in such "purely socialist goals such as raising the standard of the working class, equal distribution of wealth, and so on. Even the methods . . . come from the socialist pattern. They are working toward a government-controlled economy" (78). Most profound, however, is Karl Hoffmann's increasing awareness of Nazism as a political religion[17] filling the spiritual void vacated by Christianity and the social cohesion it had once lent to European civilization. Nazism, Karl tells his father in the period after Hitler

---

17. The category of interpretation has been renewed of late by the incisive studies of Burleigh, especially his *The Third Reich*. See also his *Earthly Powers*. Similarly, though focused upon Fascist Italy, Emilio Gentile, "New Idols" and "Fascism as Political Religion."

has consolidated power, "isn't gaining force now as a political power; it is becoming a religion" (77).

This captivation of heart and mind by Nazism as a modern political religion is figured in the character of Orlando von Schack, Karl's childhood friend and classmate ne'er-do-well who had already as a teen been telling Karl, "you must read Nietzsche!" (37), all the while cynically spouting Social Darwinist bromides (38). But upon his conversion—"Now I have friends. Now I have a leader" (69)—Orlando comes to see the fascinating parallels in faith between himself and Karl. "You believe in salvation by the blood of Christ and I believe in salvation by the strong red stream that flows in all Aryans" (69). Hitler "is the center—the recreated hero of old . . . lifted above us, he will draw all men to him" (173). Seeing Orlando march in a uniformed parade of the SA, Karl sees "the people of Germany, my people, turning toward their future, and my friend was among them. I felt a great wishfulness to be a part of what I was seeing . . . I was lonely, lonelier than I had ever been in my life" (215). But in the course of the novel Orlando's newfound faith dies prematurely and this death of his idol takes Orlando's life with it. Disillusioned by the Night of Long Knives, Orlando commits suicide, leaving Karl a note, "I have been made a fool of—and there is nothing left. I am so alone. I do not want your religious immortality. I do not want to have to live any more in any form whatsoever" (228). By the device of a suicide note, Taylor through her Christian optic discerns a death-wish at the heart of Nazi nihilism that would see annihilation of one and all before owning up to sin in repentance and faith.

Thus we are shown the elder Pastor Hoffman before his church packed with SA troops boldly proclaiming the First Commandment and the *solus Christus* (140), requiring as these orthodox fundamentals do the doctrine of universal sinfulness and the universal need of salvation by the cross of the Messiah. Just this is what so profoundly and so precisely offends Nazism as a political religion: "The heroic German does not need to have his sins forgiven. He carries his salvation with him in the blood that God has sent coursing through his veins" (165). "Christianity with its morose teaching of sin is guilty of bringing immorality into the originally perfect German race" (192). Theologically, this precisely stated confrontation between Christian and Nazi theologies emerges as the dominant motif in Kressman's novel. Here too, before Auschwitz, the danger of Nazi anti-Semitism appeared as a byproduct of a more basic antinomy symbolized by the alternative, Cross or Swastika. Indeed, so things do appear when the confrontation is parsed from the perspective of Germany's classical Reformation theology.[18] That is

---

18. For this claim see the unsurpassed analysis of Oberman, *The Roots of Antisemitism*

certainly not how Nazis perceived it, however, for whom racialist anti-Semitism had the status of a foundational theological dogma, backed by cutting edge science, in which light religious ideologies were but the reflexes of various racial interests. If there is nothing but a confrontation here, Nazism as a philosophy of force wins—unless matched by counter-violence. Thus we next turn to another theological witness of the rise of Nazism to see how this confrontation appeared in the perspective of a most perceptive Jewish thinker who was scandalized by the imperceptiveness of America's liberals.

MAURICE SAMUEL'S "CHRISTOPHOBIA"

First published in October 1940, Maurice Samuel's *The Great Hatred* was occasioned by the "incapacity of the liberal world to pull itself together and rediscover a foothold from which to denounce the dread purposes behind Germany's ostensible demands" (150–51). Thus he is speaking to the same situation that Hamerow's research recovered for us, but particularly to its liberal religious expression, as for example in the *Christian Century*'s hoping against hope that some scheme to deport Europe's Jews to a far off and undeveloped land might yet meet Hitler's taunt and "ostensible demand" and thus save the world from war. Liberal churchman, Samuel tells us, have "trivialized antisemitism by reducing it to a vulgar political maneuver; they made no attempt to understand its deadly attractiveness, and therefore did not even begin to look for an explanation" beyond their own progressive belief in national self-determination. The deadly appeal of Nazi anti-Semitism on its own racialistic terms was reduced, in other words, to garden-variety ethnocentric prejudice and rivalry. It was not taken seriously in its obsessive ferocity. And this "fact that liberals and Churchmen saw not exceptional circumstances in that unique entrenchment, reveals where the debacle began" (164–65). "Why," he demands, "is antisemitism to be found in all countries, the 'haves' and the 'have-nots,' the sated and the unsated, those which were victorious in the first world war, those which were vanquished, those which remained neutral, and even those which were born or re-born of it?" (140) thus not so subtly implying its presence also among the American liberals to whom his book is addressed. Or again, "Why is anti-Semitic propaganda unique in character, differing altogether from the familiar literature of national hatreds and intolerances, and using demonology in place of the ordinary 'rational' lie?" (138). What is the religious secret of this demonology at work in anti-Semitism?

in the Age of Renaissance and Reformation.

The easy answer would be John 8. But Samuel does not take that route. Of course, neither does Samuel take Nazi racial thinking at face value. He wants critically to see through the appearance to the underlying reality. Thus he reads *Mein Kampf* rather than the Gospel of John and takes it seriously, although critically. He cites Hitler chapter and verse: "The Jewish doctrine of Marxism rejects the aristocratic principle in nature; instead of the eternal privilege of force and strength, it places the mass of numbers and dead weight . . . By warding off the Jews I am fighting for the Lord's work." Samuel immediately comments on this excerpt: "Very clearly then, what Hitler hates, in common with Nietzsche, whose hand lies heavy on the quoted passage, is fundamental Christianity . . . It does not matter that moral opposition to the Nazi-Fascist view of the human being is often without the specific Christian stamp. The unmistakable relationship is there. Nazism-Fascism says that man exists in and by virtue of the machine; Judaeo-Christianity says that a machine must exist for man, or must not exist at all. And everyone who takes this point of view allies himself ultimately with Judaeo-Christianity" (108–9). Thus Samuel brings a simple but normative theological principle to his analysis of the data.

Unlike, then, Steigmann-Gall, whose purely empirical study would take such statements at face value, Samuel claims with his normative principle to see through Hitler's religious rhetoric about doing the Lord's work in fighting against the Jews to an underlying doctrinal abyss dividing Nazism-Fascism and Judeo-Christianity. Several questions arise here at once. First, can Nazism-Fascism be doctrinally reduced to what Samuel calls, after his reading of Nietzsche, the "force philosophy"? Second, can Judaism and Christianity likewise be linked together doctrinally as the "anti-force philosophy"? Samuel takes both of these claims for granted. He even hopes, as suggested above in the conclusion to the discussion of Taylor, that "[t]oday we can hope for a dynamic juncture between Christianity and democracy . . . to convert democracy into a cause, rather than accept it as the incidental effect of economics" (196–97)—a hope that this author substantially identifies with in calling theologically for a chastened liberalism. But we cannot quite so glibly grant these premises to Samuel. Like empirical Christianity, empirical Judaism is a far more ambiguous a phenomenon than Samuel allows and their common cause is not obvious from history. Something of a theological purification is in order to sustain Samuel's claim that "Nazism-Fascism says that man exists in and by virtue of the machine; Judaeo-Christianity says that a machine must exist for man, or must not exist at all." We will return then to this topic in Chapter 5, for the moment accepting for the sake of the argument what are in fact contestable suppositions.

The surprising thesis that Samuel advances on the basis of these premises is that "Antisemitism is the expression of the concealed hatred of Christ and Christianity, rising to a new and catastrophic level in the western world" (36). Or again, "antisemitism is the conspiratorial, implacable campaign against Christ the Jew" (39). Here we have a post-emancipation Jewish appreciation for Jesus as also a son of the covenant, a true Jew and bearer of Torah values, who in this capacity has become the Christ of the gentile world. In Nazism, "Christ and Christianity are not attacked by name; but their significance must be destroyed from the earth, and the values they stand for must be discredited by the indirect method. And so the Jews are hated as the givers of Christ, but denounced as the killers of Christ" (139). Anticipating objection, Samuel continues, "If this sounds like a piece of amateurish psycho-analysis, I ask the reader to explain why it is the enemies of Christ, the believers in a force philosophy, who always emphasize with such bitterness the Jewish role in the death of Christ, while it is the friends of Christ, the believers in non-force, who emphasize the Jewish role in the bringing forth of Christ" (139–49). Laying down this challenge to his doubtless dumbfounded American liberal colleagues and churchmen, Samuel concludes his essay with the claim that the fundamental issue raised for us by the rise of Nazism is "the modern programmatic and total revulsion from Christ, which began more than half a century ago and is now reaching its climax, is not confined to any one country..." (140). "The fury of antisemitism is universal and inevitable because to destroy Christ and Christianity is the most important single idealistic objective of the force-philosophy... the longing for an amoral world" (142).

It is to be emphasized here that Samuel's reading of the religious secret of antisemitism as hatred of Christ is a Jewish one that views Christianity as Torah for the Gentiles. That overlaps, but is not identical with, Taylor's Hoffman/Bernhard neo-Reformation Christian orthodoxy. What these two have in common is a sharp critique of theological liberalism and its antinomianism. It is the Christian liberals who have objectively rejected Judeo-Christianity by accommodating to the utilitarianism and hedonism of modern "economic man," even as they deplore the social consequences of greed unleashed. This latter accounts for " ... an indigenous intellectual antisemitism, shared by most leftist groups with a mechanistic outlook on life" (199). It explains why "antisemitism, which among Christians has been the secret valve of anti-Christ feeling" (200) has its underlying hold, as Hamerow disclosed, among the American liberals to whom *The Great Hatred* was addressed (6).

Before Auschwitz

HOW ANOTHER SAW: OSUSKÝ'S 1937 WARNING[19]

At the conclusion of a notable lecture in 1937, that was printed before Auschwitz in 1940, Samuel Štefan Osuský laid down the stance that would predominate among the minority Lutheran Church during the First Slovak Republic, a puppet state created by Hitler after the dismemberment of Czechoslovakia. I cite from the conclusion of his "The Philosophy of Bolshevism, Fascism and Hitlerism":

> What can I say not only about Hitlerism but about the philosophy of all three of these tendencies? Democracy is on the defensive. These tendencies, according to their essence, are on the offensive. Our situation is not easy, but in short we must assert: in so far as Bolshevism is atheistic and materialistic, we cannot accept it from a religious standpoint; so far as Hitlerism is naturalistic, we cannot accept it from a Christian standpoint; so far as Fascism is Catholic, we cannot accept it from a Lutheran standpoint. I will not analyze the matter in greater detail. But I will point further to this: the method, terror, the denial of individual freedom, we cannot accept either as Christians or as Lutherans, and Hitlerism we cannot accept either as Slavs. I have expressed my astonishment at how anyone from the ranks of the Lutherans could agree with Fascism, and [with] no less astonishment do I express how anyone from the Slovak Lutherans could sympathize, preach and write sympathetically about the philosophy of Hitlerism.

This latter (individual, as it turns out) who sympathized with Hitlerism was a relatively rare but significant exception, as we will shortly note. I leave the study of this prescient lecture to the reader. It is provided in translation in the Appendix to this book. It is only necessary for the purposes of this chapter to note two features of the lecture salient to seeing how we saw the rise of Nazism, now by the prism of a comparable alternative. First, Osuský refused to play Fascism, Hitlerism and Bolshevism against one another as greater or lesser evils, but instead linked Christian faith in its Lutheran iteration to the defense of a multinational, i.e. Czech and Slovak, republic and its democratic institutions. In this way he also pastorally steeled his listeners for a time of testing about to descend on them. Second, in his discussion

---

19. The following is adapted from the Introduction to the publication of my translation of Osuský's lecture in *Pastoral Letter on the Jewish Question* (1942). This *Pastoral Letter on the Jewish Question*, co-signed by Osuský and Bishop Pavel Čobrda with the consent of the Church's General Presbyterium, was a remarkable and courageous act of witness.

of Hitlerism, Osuský dissected the arguments in *Mein Kampf* and, taking them with philosophical seriousness, subjected them to theological critique. That combination of intellectual virtues is what gives the lecture its exemplary standing and makes it an instance of theology as critical dogmatics. These two factors belong to themes that will inform Chapter 5 of this book in its exploration of theological topics. For the present, then, we conclude this chapter's inquiry into the perspectives by which we interpret the rise of Nazism by learning of an alternative to our North American liberalism, no less democratic in intention, that in fact proved to be prophetic. What follows for the remainder of this chapter provides the necessary context for understanding Osuský's lecture at an act of theological existence during the time of Nazism's rise to power.[20]

Born in 1888 in the district of Senica of Upper Hungary in the then Austrio-Hungarian Empire, Samuel Štefan Osuský lived until 1975. He studied in the Lutheran Lyceum in Bratislava and at the same church's theological seminary, then in Germany at Erlangen and Jena in 1914–1916. He was awarded the PhD from the Philosophical Faculty at Charles University in Prague in 1922. He already began to serve as vicar in 1911, then as pastor during the war years until 1919. He became an adjunct professor on the staff of the Lutheran Seminary in 1919, a regular professor in 1920 and a full professor in 1933, where he worked until the Communist purge of the Faculty in 1951 when he was prematurely retired. He spent his remaining years in the imposed silence of internal exile. Osuský was elected one of two bishops of the Slovak Lutheran Church in 1933 and served until 1946. He was imprisoned during the final year of the first Slovak Republic during the Slovak National Uprising for his opposition to the wartime Fascist government, whose inhumane treatment of the Jews, he, along with the leadership of his Church, had protested in a public letter in 1942 during the time of the first deportation of Slovak Jews to Auschwitz. Apart from responding to crises, Osuský's many-sided academic work was focused on gathering philosophical, historical, and scientific resources for education in support of faith in the modern world; he conceived of this theological work as "a service to the nation" (recalling here his multi-national "Czechoslovakism," as the Slovak Fascists disparagingly put it), lifting up the public contributions of Slovak Lutheran thinkers to the formation of the first Czechoslovak Republic and its renewal after 1945. This put him into conflict with the

---

20. In what follows I rely on Ušiak, "Evanjelická Cirkev a Slovenský Štát"; the doctoral dissertation of my former student, Žitňan, *Evanjelická Cirkev Augsburgského Vyznania na Slovensku v rockoch 1938–1945*; and Tóth, ed., *The Tragedy of the Slovak Jews*.

Political Catholicism of the 1930s and 1940s[21] as well as with the Stalinists who captured the government in 1948. He suffered as a confessor of the faith.

His 1937 lecture to the assembly of Slovak Lutheran pastors in the northern city of Ružemberok is of interest on several levels. First, it is a precious historical record of a Lutheran churchman and intellectual's prescient analysis of the cruel future about to unfold. Second, the lecture is not complex or arcane in its analysis but rather takes up the modern secular movements of Leninism, Fascism, and Nazism at face value as "philosophy" or "worldview" that entail such and such behavior. Using the limited resources available to him, Osuský's analysis shows the power of a straightforward theological critique of the pseudo-religions of the twentieth century from the perspective of theology in the tradition of Luther unhinged from the vicissitudes of German history and modern nationalism. Finally, while the contemporary reader has the luxury of knowing the outcome of the movements in which Osuský was personally immersed, his churchly and intellectual leadership in the midst of ominous times full of confusion speaks a word of rebuke across the decades. Can we imagine in America today a churchly theologian or a theologically and philosophically adept bishop giving a lecture on this level to pastors—one, moreover, which might display such probative value, let alone prove to be true?

Certainly there are non-theological factors which sharpened Osuský's perception. Lutherans were a minority within a minority in Slovakia, with a painful memory of persecution—a fact which (as in the well known case of the Huguenot village of Le Chambon in France) disposed them to be sympathetic with others suffering persecution. As a Slav who has read *Mein Kampf*, Osuský saw in black and white exactly what Hitler intended for him and his kind.[22] Yet Slovak fascists, including a handful of Lutherans, were blind to this,[23] and this blindness has an arguably theological explana-

---

21. Žitňan, *Evanjelická Cirkev*, gives this sample from Jozef Tiso, "a doctor of theology, a priest, and president of the republic," from a statement on August 9, 1940 justifying the racially motivated laws against the Jews: "... the argument is that I will not give the nation to perish for the sake of the Jewish community. For me the nation is more than Jews, howsoever many of them. And when I see that the nation could therefore suffer mortal damage, then I say according to Christianity: First for me, then for you." (146, my translation.)

22. On "intentionalism," such as Osuský might be charged with, see Dawidowicz, *War*, xvii–xxxiii and the discussion of this topic below in Chapter 4.

23. Žitňan's dissertation is especially helpful here in uncovering the role played by the Nazi sympathizer, B. Klimo, who was a member of Tiso's political party and sat on the State Council, yet was also the general superintendent of the Slovak Lutheran Church, a lay position (147).

tion which Osuský lays out for his reader. In any case, Osuský's theological commitment, via the Czechoslovak leader Tomaš Masaryk, to democratic governance and liberal principles, and his Christian, i.e., non-Marxist but rather "religious socialist" commitment via the Swiss Leonhard Ragaz (1868–1945),[24] cries out again across the decades for theologians who will not be, disillusioned by failing liberalisms, enchanted anew with the characteristic modern alternatives of fascism or communism in new guises.[25]

A further note on the immediate context of the lecture is helpful in underscoring the presuppositions of Reformation theology behind Osuský's analysis, which may be less visible in this particular text because of his practical decision, as noted at the beginning of the lecture, to lecture on political philosophy in keeping with his disciplinary specialization. Thus it helps to learn a little about his co-lecturers on the occasion of the November 22, 1937 gathering of the pastors. Dr. Ján Jamnický, professor of Pastoral Theology and Church Law, lectured on the "The Essence of Preaching the Word of God and the Contemporary Problem of Exegesis," in which he engaged knowledgably with Karl Barth's new summons to theological exegesis, but also refused to separate that from historical understanding. Appealing to the Luther rule of tentatio, oratio, meditatio, he connected scientific-historical exegesis with Luther's description of preaching in the church, where "nothing else will take place but that God will converse with us in His Word and we will converse with God in hymns and prayers."[26] Dr. Ján Beblavý, professor of Systematic Theology, lectured on the Faith and Order meeting that had taken place earlier that year in Edinburgh, interpreting its consensus statement on the doctrine of the church in a Lutheran way. Similar to Jamnický's acknowledgment of the new impulses coming from Barth, Beblavý claimed that the anti-doctrinal liberal theology[27] of the previous century had committed a great error in regarding the church as a human work. In this spirit, Beblavý called his auditors back to Luther's teaching about the church as the

---

24. Gluchmann, *Slovak Lutheran Social Ethics*, 58ff, 70ff.

25. At the conclusion of his study, Ericksen pointed to such non-theological factors (187): "We can best avoid the Nazi error by heavily stressing the values of the liberal, democratic tradition, humanitarianism and justice, and by conscientiously probing history with a view towards its significance for contemporary decision making." *Theologians under Hitler*, 191.

26. See Osuský, *Štyri Prednašky*, 11, my translation.

27. Beblavy's indictment—that the German Christians ranks were filled with liberal theologians—has been justified by recent historical research as we saw in Chapter 1. It is worth noting that the stooge theologians appointed by the Communist State to replace the purged faculty of Osuský and his colleagues after 1951 quite deliberately repudiated Barth in favor of the liberal methodology of Tillich's systematic apologetics for the task of "church in socialism."

creature of the Word: "The majority of German liberal theologians supporting the new regime have betrayed the church of Christ and entered into the service of German racism."[28] Pastor Juraj Struhárik lectured on the "Battle of the Spirit against the Flesh in the Church and in Church Life." Here he took up Luther's insight that the Pauline battle is not the Platonic-Stoic conflict between emotion and reason, but between the spirits of human self-reliance and of reliance on God. He applied this principle not just to the individual Christian but to the visible church in history as a field of battle: "the Church becomes flesh . . . by a collective divinization of the body, the blood . . ." so that "the chief virtue is the preservation of a pure race and the chief sin the mixing of races."[29] The appeal to Luther and the protest against the race theory-theology of die deutschen Christen thus characterized the lectures surrounding Osuský's that were presented on that day, forming with him a united theological front against the gathering storm of Hitlerism.

Osuský's worst fears came true. In 1939 Political Catholicism, seeing models created by Franco's Spain and Mussolini's Italy and foolishly overlooking the racist imperatives at the heart of Nazism to which he had pointed with philosophical seriousness in the lecture, took advantage of Hitler's dismemberment of Czechoslovakia to proclaim an independent Slovak Republic, allied with Nazi Germany. Its first president was a Catholic Priest, Josef Tiso, who had inherited the leadership from a deceased priest, Andrej Hlinka, at the helm of the nationalist Slovak People's Party. While the minority Lutherans under Osuský's leadership generally protested these developments, and eventually supported the uprising of the partisan movement in the summer of 1944, their anti-Fascism would not count for much after 1948, when the Communists invalidated the last democratic election results in Slovakia and proclaimed the dictatorship of the proletariat from Prague in the reunited Czechoslovakia. Having hung Tiso by the neck for his crimes, the Communists used the blunders and indeed crimes of Tiso and his Political Catholicism as a pretext for crushing independent church life in the darkest days of Stalinism in the early 1950s. Thus Osuský's multilateral predictions of disaster in the lecture would come true not once, but twice within fifteen years of its presentation. Among all the other crimes committed by Adolf Hitler, his giving anti-communism a bad name was not inconsiderable.

28. *Štyri Prednašky*, 74, my translation.
29. Ibid., 102.

Chapter Four

The Not So Strange Theology of Adolf Hitler

TAKING HITLER SERIOUSLY

H. R. Trevor-Roper, the English historian responsible for the publication in 1953 of Hitler's *Table Talks*, prefaced its publication with an essay claiming that Hitler "was a systematic thinker, and his mind is, to the historian, as important a problem as the mind of Bismarck or Lenin."[1] In Trevor-Roper's analysis, the systematic mind of Hitler was enthralled by "nature" with which he often "communed, but it was a hideous Nature, the devouring Nature whose cruelty justified his own; not a sociable pagan Nature of nymph-haunted woods and populated streams, but a romantic Wagnerian Nature of horrid Alps in whose intoxicating solitude he could best hatch his own equally violent and implacable interventions."[2] We will return at the end of this chapter to Trevor-Roper and the theology of Hitler revealed in the *Table Talks*. What matters to begin with is the claim—so counter-intuitive especially for American liberals of all kinds[3]—of method to Hitler's madness.

---

1. Trevor-Roper, ed., *Table Talk*, xxii
2. Ibid., xl–xli.
3. So according to the German-American Yale graduate, Ernst Hanfstaengel, Hitler once angrily rebuked his "bourgeois mentality" that "think[s] of everything in terms of trade . . . The most important consideration is that we should think alike in terms of policies and *Weltanschauung*." Hanfstaengel, *Hitler*, 135.

Before Auschwitz

At this juncture of our inquiry we thus come to a topic that is by no means obvious. Can we speak with Lucy Dawidowicz of "Hitler's system of beliefs"?[4] Can we dignify Hitler's National Socialist "worldview" with any kind of treatment that takes it seriously as a system of belief, as did Osuský, indeed as a coherent theology—so far as any theology can be coherent? If so, what would be the point? Given his monstrous behavior, what difference would that make? Do his beliefs finally matter when we can be done with such difficult and distracting questions—Hitler's theology—and simply judge his deeds as manifestly evil? Of course a judgment of a deed as evil expresses belief of one kind or another. While we can manage that more or less without resorting to theology, philosophically we do not really dodge the question involved here in that way. Thus if we can presume an affirmative answer to these preliminary questions, as is presupposed in this book, the question before us becomes more precise: how do his beliefs matter? This more precise question can perhaps be answered in as many ways as different people have been affected by Nazi beliefs. Certainly, for Christian theology knowledge of them would matter in offering precise insight into vulnerabilities that made Christian theologians open to Nazism on the one side and into those strengths that steeled resistance in others. Such insight would constitute progress in theological knowledge. The very exercise of "testing the spirits" speaks in the process to the theological sloth and intellectual lassitude that slid into seduction, self-deception, and support of the Third Reich in the majority of religious folk who had little taste for theology as critical dogmatics and swallowed whatever reservations they felt before the visible display of good deeds that the Führer had accomplished in the prewar years of the National Socialist revolution.

In the book of a generation ago that finally broke a taboo by seeing in Hitler and Stalin "parallel lives," Alan Bullock broached the question now before us: "Difficult though it may be to accept, I believe that the key to understanding both Stalin and Hitler is the recognition that they were entirely serious about their historic roles; it was certainly as much as anyone's life to question or mock them. Skeptical about the motives and claims of others, their cynicism stopped short of their own. They saw themselves, not as tyrants or evil men, but as leaders prepared to devote their entire lives to a higher cause, and entitled to call on others to do the same, so releasing in themselves and those who accepted their claim a perverted moral energy and self-confidence."[5] This positive sense of calling, not anti-Semitism as such which is rather its shadow side, went on to create Hitler's "willing ex-

---

4. Dawidowicz, *War*, 208.
5. Bullock, *Hitler and Stalin*, 381.

ecutioners" (Goldhagen), since this latter "higher cause" first created Hitler. And this latter gave Hitler what he himself viewed as a mystical or religious experience with the sense of divine calling to which he so often referred along with the specific theological articulation he made of it, including centrally of course his racialist anti-Semitism.

As generally what one is against is a function of what one is for, that is, theologically, that evil howsoever actual in the world is metaphysically a privation of the good, it is salient to recognize that the young Hitler had some kind of a "religious" experience,[6] "not a voluntary act but rather a visionary recognition," in Linz, Austria, in 1905 after the performance of the Wagnerian opera, *Rienzi*. The opera told the story of a thirteenth-century man of the people who led a rebellion against the aristocracy, only to be condemned by the Pope and finally defeated. Hitler's youthful friend, August Kubizek, who attended the performance with Hitler, related the "strange nocturnal experience" on "one of the solitary heights of the Freinberg mountain" that he witnessed Hitler undergo late that night on a post-performance hike. It was here "that his future life was decided." Hitler then spoke of a "special mission which one day would be entrusted to him"—perhaps reflecting Rienzi's dying words in the opera: "You will see Rienzi's return!" From that hour, Hitler referred back to this moment: "In this hour it began."[7] Kubizek reported that whenever Hitler "listened to Wagner's music he was a changed man . . . As if intoxicated by some hypnotic agent, he slipped into a state of ecstasy, and willingly let himself be carried away into the mystical universe which was more real to him than the actual workaday world . . . transported into the blissful regions of German antiquity, that ideal world which was the lofty goal for all his endeavors."[8] When Hitler and Kubizek were reunited many years later, they visited together the grave of Richard Wagner in Bayreuth, "this place," not literally Bayreuth but the place of Wagnerian

---

6. I should note here that holding to the *Verbum externum* against enthusiasm, I positively disbelieve "religious" experience and regard its use in theology as resort to a bogus category, as may be seen in my treatment of William James's classic text, *The Varieties of Religious Experience*, in *Beloved Community*, 17–30. Yet, reports of "religious experiences" are part of the data of history and this bogus category was available to Hitler, not least through Wagnerian opera and later his association with the Thule Society. No less an authority than Ian Kershaw contributed an Introduction to Kubizek's memoir and judged that despite errors in fact and chronology, it "rings true in the portrait of Hitler's personality and mentality." Kubizek, *The Young Hitler I Knew*, 14. Kubizek's account of Hitler's nocturnal experience certainly coheres with the sense of providential vocation that many commentators have remarked regarding Hitler's supreme self-confidence.

7. Kubizek, *Young Hitler*, 116–19.

8. Ibid., 188.

opera, "which was always the holiest for us both." So Hitler commented to him, recalling to Kubizek the "strange nocturnal experience" and concluding "with the unforgettable words, 'In that hour it began!'"[9]

The stakes in this inquiry into Hitler's theology are very great. Recalling Ericksen's double crisis of modernity, Hitler and Stalin (and Hiroshima) arguably represent what Alasdair MacIntyre has incisively analyzed as the failure of the Enlightenment project to secure a rational foundation for ethics,[10] referring to the same matrix of double crisis in which today we live and move and have our beings as Ericksen described. Not that the attempt was not made to secure ethics, or that non-rational foundations for ethics are not still claimed (as in Hitler's nocturnal experience), but that, in MacIntyre's judgment, rational grounding has failed. Our liberal values of tolerance and human rights, as passionately as we affirm them on the basis of history and our experience, go ungrounded rationally. They are, so far as we can know, nothing but the product of our particular cultural experience. And they are paid for in awkward truth by capitalism. A resort to "religious" experience makes perfect sense here as a response to this crisis and failure that is endemic to the contemporary West. It is in sorting out this complex and baffling stew of modernity and its crises that we are to look for and find the sources of Hitler's theology, a system of belief that led, in the vicissitude of events, to the Final Solution.

Michael Burleigh speaks pointedly of "the racially motivated criminality of the Nazi regime." He says that it "literally permeates [his] book, for no aspect of that past was untainted by it . . ." But just this focus on the criminal deeds of Nazi racism reflects, he claims, "epistemological advances in the study of history [which] have led to greater insights regarding [the Holocaust] than has been achieved by an approach based on the mere accumulation of archival 'facts,' . . . which explain little about the metaphysical motives behind the Nazi project."[11] Thus Burleigh portrays Nazism as a coherent, albeit repugnant set of racialistic ideas, a "secularized religion," a "counter-church with its own intolerant dogma, preachers, sacred rites and lofty idioms that offered total explanations of the past, present and future, while demanding unwavering dedication from its adherents."[12] The

9. Ibid., 256.

10. Enlightenment thought "reject[s] any teleological view of human nature, any view of man as having an essence which defines his true end . . . Since the whole point of ethics . . . is to enable man to pass from his present state to his true end . . . [these] moral philosophers engaged in what was an inevitably unsuccessful project." MacIntyre, *After Virtue*, 54–55.

11. Burleigh, *The Third Reich*, 811.

12. Ibid., 5. The passage continues, pointing to: " . . . the moral transformations

"metaphysical motive" in this "secularized religion" "parodied many of the eschatological and liturgical attributes of redemptive religions, while being fundamentally antagonistic towards the Churches: rivals, as the Nazis saw it, in the subtle, totalizing control of minds... In reality, [Hitler's] views were a mixture of materialist biology, a faux-Nietzschean contempt for core, as distinct from secondary, Christian values, and a visceral anti-clericalism."[13] In sum, he asks rhetorically, "For what else was the Führer than a messiah?"[14] Answering his own question, Burleigh cites the apostate Catholic's words from the *Table Talks*: "We lack a ritual. National Socialism must become the Germans' state religion. My party is my church."[15] In the same vein, Hitler asked how individuals can "grasp the extent of the total result of their innumerable personal sacrifices and their struggle for national socialist salvation?" And he answered that "once a year on the occasion of the general display of the Party [i.e., the Nuremberg Rally], they will stride forth as one from the modesty of their narrow existence to gaze upon and acknowledge the glory of the fight and the triumph!"[16] The "glory of the fight and the triumph" of becoming a *Volk* by the act of national will constitute the "metaphysical motive" of Nazism. At our own peril we fail to take this seriously.

THE IMMANENT STRUGGLE OF LIFE AGAINST LIFE

In years of teaching seminary students and undergraduates on the topics addressed in this book, in particular the mind and Adolf Hitler of his system of beliefs, I have used the following exercise to wedge apart and wedge open the dogmatisms closing our liberal minds (one of which dogmas is our supposed, principled lack of dogmatism!). Consider the following text from *Mein Kampf*, slightly edited:

> When man attempts to rebel against the iron logic of Nature, he comes into struggle with the principles to which he himself owes his existence as a man. And this attack must lead to his own doom. Here of course we encounter the objection . . .: "Man's role is to overcome Nature!" Millions thoughtlessly parrot this

---

Nazism was effecting, a concern almost absent from modern historical writing, with its social science notions of freedom from value judgments, as if morality is related to moralizing, rather than intrinsic to the human condition and philosophical reflection about it."

13. Ibid., 717.
14. Ibid., 210.
15. Cited in ibid., 113.
16. Ibid., 211.

> ... nonsense and end up by really imagining that they themselves represent a kind of conqueror of Nature; though in this they dispose of no other weapon than an idea ... But quite aside from the fact that man has never yet conquered Nature in anything, but at most has caught hold of and tried to lift one or another corner of her immense gigantic veil of eternal riddles and secrets, that in reality he invents nothing but only discovers everything, that he does not dominate Nature, but has only reason on the basis of his knowledge of various laws and secrets of Nature to be lord over those other livings things who lack this knowledge—quite aside from all this, an idea cannot overcome the preconditions for the development and being of humanity, because the idea itself depends only on man. Without human beings there is no human idea in the world, the idea as such is always conditioned by the presence of human beings and hence of all the laws which created the precondition for their existence. And not only that! ... All these ideas, which have nothing to do with cold logic as such, but represent only pure expressions of feeling, ethical conceptions, etc., are chained to the existence of men, to whose intellectual imagination and creative power they owe their existence ... At this point someone or another may laugh, but this planet once moved through the ether for millions of years without human beings and it can do so again someday if men forget that they owe their higher existence, not to the ideas of a few crazy ideologists, but to the knowledge and ruthless application of Nature's stern and rigid laws.[17]

The gross anti-Semitic slurs peppering the text as indicated by the ellipses would be a dead give-away. I have removed them from the text, not because they do not form part and parcel with Hitler's thinking in the passage, but, as argued above, because they are the shadow side of his positive intuition of reality. For the pedagogical purpose then of our seeing that intuition, then, the slurs are omitted to force the reader to think through Hitler's train of thought about the human place in the cosmos and the good to which it may and must aspire, later to see how it is that it comes to radical, racial, murderous anti-Semitism.

My first assignment is to give the students this edited text to analyze. The students are not told who the author is. They are told that they are to make a case for whether it was written by a supporter or opponent of the Holocaust. The typical result is that the preponderance of the students thinks that the author is a champion of an enlightened scientific worldview

---

17. Hitler, *Mein Kampf*, 287.

The Not So Strange Theology of Adolf Hitler

and so could not possibly have favored racial or religious intolerance. A minority discerns that the author has a view of reality in which violent struggle is scripted into the deepest nature of things and that this metaphysical violence could readily express itself in racial war as a sacred duty. What does the text in fact say?

In fact the text argues that all human ideas, especially ethical ideals such as equality and peace, are the late byproducts of natural selection and so cannot be turned back against the very law of evolution that had undergirded their production. If that turn of ethical ideas against life is made, it would destroy the natural, material basis of human life upon which those mental and emotional constructions of the ethical rest. The author pointedly rejects therefore the Kantian teaching of ethical idealism that "Man's role is to overcome Nature!" Nature for this author is the functional deity, to whose laws humanity submits for its own well-being. Indeed only human knowledge of Nature's "stern and rigid laws" provides any advantage to human beings, who thereby "lord over those other livings things who lack this knowledge." The author again returns to the fundamental point that ethical ideals like equality and peace "have nothing to do with cold logic as such, but represent only pure expressions of feeling." Such sentiments represent human aspirations, not natural laws, and so they have no cognitive weight or rational traction when it comes to human stewardship of the material basis of life. If this really real priority of nature and its laws over humanity with its mind and its ideals and sentiments is forgotten, misled human beings will come to violate natural law by insisting emotionally on utopian goods. They would thus demand the impossible. Acting on that would be disastrous. As a result, "this planet [which] once moved through the ether for millions of years without human beings . . . can do so again someday if men forget that they owe their higher existence, not to the ideas of a few crazy ideologists, but to the knowledge and ruthless application of Nature's stern and rigid laws."

The imperative of the Nazi biopolitical program of eugenics and euthanasia as political stewardship of the material basis of life—that is, the opening act of genocide[18]—is grounded in this indicative.

The author of this text is, in his own historical context, certainly no polished academic writer, but neither is he a dummy. His is not exactly learned prose, but it represents the autodidact's[19] adequate knowledge of a certain trajectory of German philosophy after Kant,[20] who had radically

---

18. Friedlander, *The Origins of Nazi Genocide*.
19. On this see Ryback, *Hitler's Private Library*, 49.
20. In the *Table Talks*, Hitler calls Kant, Schopenhauer, and Nietzsche the "greatest

juxtaposed the austere logical and ethical demands of practical reason to sensuous inclination and regarded rational obedience to the moral law of our higher nature as the exclusive source of moral value and human purpose. Such was Kant's attempt to ground ethics on reason instead of revelation. While this effort to free ethics from revealed religion succeeded in Kant, his attempt to ground ethics in practical reason shipwrecked on the impossible anthropological dualism between mind and body at the heart of Cartesian modernity as that recurs in his opposition of duty to inclination. Hitler stands in the wake of this wrecked and sinking ship of the redoubled crisis, not only the rational failure to secure ethics, as MacIntyre argued, but its regrounding in irrational drives discovered by the masters of suspicion. Ethics for Hitler becomes will, will guided by its intuition of Darwinian reality in Nature's laws and itself conferred by the Darwinian blood that courses through one's veins. As Alan Bullock specifies, "For his faith in the decisive power of the human will, Hitler could again draw on the teaching of German nineteenth-century thinkers, two in particular. The first was Schopenhauer, the author of *The World as Will and Idea*, from which his secretary says he could quote whole passages. The second was Nietzsche: he presented his collected works to Mussolini, 'that unparalleled statesman' whose March on Rome proved to Hitler that it was possible to reverse an historic decline. Hitler refused to recognize any difficulties as inherent in a problem. He saw only human incompetence and human ill will."[21] The author's polemic against ethical idealism is thus paradoxically related to Kant's deontological ethics, but in Hitler it is will rather than practical reason that provides the categorical imperative in that will is the expression in each of us of the entelechy of species preservation while acting on this imperative works purification and perfection in the contest of life forms. In this Hitler was typical of many post-Kantians from Feuerbach to Marx to Nietzsche for whom nature as the will to power, not the ethical idea, both expresses and instructs human behavior.

In this vein Hitler knows and applies the most up-to-date scientific speculations about the evolutionary process in the manner of contemporary Social Darwinists, e.g., Albert E. F. Schaeffle, "probably the most influential thinker to apply Darwinian thinking to ethical and social theory in the 1870s," according to Richard Weikart. He explains: "Schaeffle did not construe Darwinian struggle for existence as a brutal struggle among beasts or an amoral free for all, but on the contrary he argued that morality was

---

of our thinkers," especially Kant whose "theory of knowledge" first liberated us from "the dogmatic philosophy of the Church." Trevor-Roper, ed., *Table Talks*, 546–47.

21. Bullock, *Parallel Lives*, 374.

an essential element in the human struggle for existence. Like Darwin, he emphasized the collective struggle for existence among humans with tribe against tribe and nation against nation. Morality and law functioned to reduce conflict within societies, making those societies stronger than their neighboring societies and thus conferring a competitive advantage."[22] In just this way Hitler ominously but consistently refers in the conclusion of our passage from *Mein Kampf* to the "the knowledge and ruthless application of Nature's stern and rigid laws," that is, for the sake of moral order and the true health of the tribe. Ernst Nolte cites in this connection a Frenchman, Vacher de Lapouge, whose work on the Aryan race Hitler probably read. It contains the following pertinent text: "Every man is related to all men and all living creatures. Therefore there are no human rights any more than there are . . . rights of the armadillo." And Nolte comments: "As soon as man loses his right to be a separate entity in the image of God, he no longer has any more right than any other mammal. The idea of justice is in itself an illusion. Nothing exists but violence."[23] Lapouge thus "attacks Christian mercy, which inhibits the natural process of extermination of the unfit, and makes proposals as to how 'systematic selection' can be effected by means of certain injections."[24]

The point of the exercise with my students is twofold. First, when it comes to intelligent analysis of religious or philosophical views, many contemporary students are wanting in critical thinking skills—that which I take theology as critical dogmatics to be, thinking critically in the cultural domain of philosophy about matters of that final and inclusive Good for which people live, wittingly or not, by some act of initial faith. Students will indeed fervently aver to me that it does not matter what you believe, so long as you are sincere. The very good idea of civil tolerance over differing beliefs about the final and inclusive Good has come to mean for them a kind of uncritical acceptance of any and all possible beliefs. Such beliefs themselves, they think, make no difference that reason can critically discern, nor is there any rational way of settling differences between us about such beliefs. As a result, students descend into a night in which all cats are grey. They cannot see the veiled threat in our text in which Indifferent, if not Cruel Nature

---

22. Weikart, *From Darwin to Hitler*, 28. Weikart immediately contrasts Schlaeffle's influential interpretation of evolutionary ethics with that of Max Nordau, a "leading Zionist" with socialist sympathies who deviated from the Darwin-Schaeffle line to argue that "it was the human struggle against the environment, not a struggle among humans, which gave rise to society and thus morality" (29). In this difference we might detect the precise difference between national and international socialisms.

23. Nolte, *Three Faces of Fascism*, 280.

24. Ibid., 282.

with its stern laws is the operative deity and war for the survival of one's genetic population is the moral imperative of life itself. In fact, however, such metaphysics are not strange to most of them. Remove the Nazi brand name and such reasonings seem familiar, even reasonable. What they do see is the author's evident sincerity and resort to the cultural authority of natural science.

At this juncture I could read to them the following citation, which Timothy W. Ryback highlighted from Hitler's *Table Talks* in a fascinating article published in *The Atlantic Monthly* (later followed up by a monograph) entitled, "Hitler's Forgotten Library: The Man, His Books, and His Search for God." Hitler wrote: "Mind and soul ultimately return to the collective being of the world. If there is a God, then he gives us not only life but also consciousness and awareness. If I live my life according to my God-given insights, then I cannot go wrong, and even if I do, I know that I have acted in good faith."[25] For many of my uncritically "tolerant" students, there would be nothing here with which theologically to disagree. For them too, the mere sincerity of being true to your inner self guarantees that you can't go wrong when you act in good faith. My introductory exercise sometimes succeeds in shocking students out of the lazy complacency of uncritical tolerance of any and all theologies.[26] Sincerity does not count for much.[27] It is essential for students to grasp, as Ryback puts it, that "Hitler was the classic apostate. He rebelled against the classic theology in which he was born and bred, all the while seeking to fill the resulting spiritual void."[28]

A second purpose of the exercise is thus to expose students to the "modernism" of the Holocaust, "modernism" in the specific sense of resolutely embracing "Darwin's dangerous idea," as philosopher Daniel Dennett

---

25. Ryback, "Hitler's Forgotten Library: The Man, His Books, and His Search for God."

26. William James, who sustained a prescient, albeit subterranean polemic against the social Darwinism of Herbert Spencer through the pages of his *The Varieties of Religious Experience*, entertained the objection that if he "were to condemn a religion of human or animal sacrifice by virtue of . . . subjective sentiments . . ." he would be "setting up a theology" of his own: "To this extent, to the extent of disbelieving peremptorily in certain types of deity, I frankly confess that we must be theologians. If disbeliefs can be said to constitute a theology, then the prejudices, instincts, and common sense which I chose as our guides make theological partisans of us whenever they make certain beliefs abhorrent" (328). This concession to theology by the thinker who campaigned to replace theology with a science of religious experience, howsoever tongue in cheek, marks a felicitous inconsistency.

27. Ericksen comes to the same judgment in his conclusion about Gerhard Kittel, *Theologians under Hitler*, 75.

28. Rybeck, "Forgotten Library," 88.

put it.[29] In so far as students have thought at all about the sources of the Nazi genocide of the Jews, however, almost all are unaware of Hitler's modernism in matters of religion, nor of the fact, as we saw in Chapter 1, that the ranks of the Nazified German Christians were filled with theological modernists.[30] By this I mean the fact that Hitler regarded the Darwinian criticism of the West's antecedent religious traditions as decisive for their refutation and searched for a new, naturalistic theology guided by the root principle of natural selection, the immanent struggle of life against life. Hitler's new theology then would be firmly rational, based on science, with an articulate theological doctrine—not running around in the woods naked hugging trees and building bonfires, as he disdainfully mocked German neopagans. As Hitler famously remarked upon the publication of Alfred Rosenberg's myth-mongering *The Myth of the Twentieth Century*, "National Socialism is a cool and highly reasoned approach to reality based upon the greatest of scientific knowledge and its spiritual expression. As we opened the *Volk*'s heart to these teachings, and as we continue to do so at present, we have no desire of instilling in the *Volk* a mysticism that transcends the purpose and goals of our teachings."[31] So Hitler's theology, divine calling and all, intends to be revolutionary-modern, post-Christian, icily scientific in doctrine.

ARENDT AND THE FAILURE OF THE ETHICS OF DUTY

In this section and the next, we will dissect the paradoxical relationship of Hitler's theological program, as laid out in the cited passage from *Mein Kampf*, to modernity. On the one hand, Hitler inherits and indeed fanaticizes the ethic of duty. On the other hand, he replaces Kant's universal basis

---

29. Dennett, *Darwin's Dangerous Idea: Evolution and the Meanings of Life*: "What Darwin saw was that . . . the resulting process would *necessarily* lead in the direction of individuals in future generations who tended to be better equipped to deal with the problems of resource limitation that had been faced by the individuals of their parents' generation. This fundamental idea—Darwin's dangerous ideas, the idea that generates so much insight, turmoil, confusion, anxiety—is thus actually quite simple . . . This was Darwin's great idea, not the idea of evolution, but the idea of evolution by *natural selection* . . ." (41–42). Dennett argues that the *necessitarianism*—natural selection as an "algorithmic" process—is a universal acid eroding traditional notions of final purpose and so "dangerous" to our traditional groundings of moral order in natural purpose. But rightly understood, the collapse of final purpose in nature is liberating. We are freed by it to make our own meanings out of life.

30. Steigmann-Gall, *Holy Reich*, 263; Ericksen, *Theologians under Hitler*, 184–85; Heschel, *Aryan Jesus*, 69, 203, 272.

31. Cited in Burleigh, *Third Reich*, 253.

for duty in ideal humanity as the bearer of reason with the will to life, the preservation of one's species, that is, one's particular tribe in the competition for *Lebensraum*. How does this happen? How do you go from Kant's ethical idealism in 1790, not to mention the antecedent prophetic morality of the biblical tradition which had found new voice in the Protestant reformation,[32] to Hitler's "stern laws of nature" in 1923, not to mention his "ruthless application" of them following 1939? In the course then of a mere 130 years? A serious answer to this question must satisfy several conditions.

First, there is the test of historical specificity. Hitlerism is not too quickly to be subsumed, as we have seen, under vague notions such as conservatism, even fascism, least of all as the Marxist's last desperate reaction of the dying Capitalist Order. These clichés are derivatives of the Left-Right binary stemming from the French Revolution, though parsed differently on the Continent than in the iteration running from Locke through Jefferson to North Americans today. As an aside here, we might recall that Jefferson spent a term as ambassador to Revolutionary France where he witnessed the capture of Louis XVI: "though shocked at first by the random and savage character of the mob violence, he never questioned his belief in the essential rightness of the cause or the ultimate triumph of its progressive principles." Indeed, the experience of the French Revolution crystallized his own innovation within the Lockean tradition of the exalted individual in which otherwise he remained, namely, "*that the earth belongs in its usufruct to the living . . . that one generation is to another as one independent nation to another.*"[33] This revolutionary rupture of the covenant of creation—what British contemporary Edmund Burke called the "covenant of the generations"—Jefferson thereafter exported home and superimposed on incipient American politics, producing conservative liberals preserving the past and liberal liberals leaving it behind. But in any such schema, Hitler seems rather to be a liberal liberal. As we shall see, Hitler assumed for himself the very mantle of Napoleon—so little sense does the Left-Right binary in general, and its American iteration in particular, make of the historical specificity of Nazism. Rather, "the moral transformations it was effecting" (Burleigh) need to be explored in their unique historical particularity, which I am arguing is the dilemma posed for all of us in the Western tradition by the scientific discovery of Darwinian evolution, i.e., what Dennett has rightly, though from a normative viewpoint other than my own, called a dangerous idea. The dangerous idea is the notion, already enunciated by the pre-Socratic

---

32. For some evidence of this claim, see Steiger, *Jonas Propheta*, and this author's review of it in *Lutheran Quarterly*.

33. Ellis, *American Sphinx*, 130–1.

The Not So Strange Theology of Adolf Hitler

Heraclitus, that strife is the mother of all things. The fusion of Heraclitus's ancient antipode, Parmenides, and the Bible in Christian Platonism held instead that the peace of loving harmony, dogmatically depicted in the life of the holy Trinity of love, is the creative source, eternal being funding temporal becoming. This Christian Platonism intervened historically between Heraclitus and Darwin. With Darwin, however, the God of Christian Platonism culturally died, as Nietzsche announced, and his Dionysian vision of metaphysical warfare provided the new and catalytic idea for the particular stew Hitler eventually served.

In Hitler's own words from September 1941: "It was with feelings of pure idealism that I set out for the front in 1914. Then I saw men falling around me in thousands. Thus I learnt that life is a cruel struggle, and has no other object but the preservation of the species. The individual can disappear, provided there are other men to replace him."[34] Just as Dennett argues, and let me stress that I concur without at all questioning its scientific standing, Darwinian evolutionary theory signifies a real ethical dilemma and metaphysical challenge for all of us in the West who still depend, albeit parasitically, on the moral legacy of Christian Platonism with its notion of humanity as imago Dei (as did Jefferson himself in his immortal words from the Declaration about the equality and rights conferred on all by the Creator). By contrast, the gross reductions to rational, economic calculation, to which both liberal and Marxist historiography in their own way have inclined, explain very little of the uniquely Nazi "metaphysical motive" and thus they founder on the particularity of the evidence. We have to look at Hitler and his ideas and their appropriation and execution by his lieutenants to see what diagnosis they had made and what prognosis they were pursuing. Of course, in the process we have to dispute their bad science or false inferences and set the record straight on what science or nature can and cannot say. But only on this basis may we make apt judgments about the sources of Nazi philosophy.

Second, there is the test of moral agency. Crude and inconsequent as it appears and in some respects was, Nazism nevertheless formed a coherent philosophical idea, again in Burleigh's words: "an Aryan-Germanic mission to redeem Graeco-Roman civilization, to affirm a non-Jewish or de-orientalized Christianity and to lead the peoples into a 'new, splendid and light-filled future,' which only the Jews issuing from darkness could thwart. A mutant, racialized Christianity, divested of unGerman 'Jewish' elements, and purged of humanitarian sentimentality, that is sin, guilt, and pity, was a

---

34. Trevor-Roper, ed., *Table Talks*, 36.

very potent ideal indeed."³⁵ The test of moral agency requires that we treat Hitler and his executioners as human beings who conscientiously adopted this doctrine and acted in obedience to it. We to be sure judge this doctrine false and their obedience to it a crime. Indeed our moral agency turns on how we make this judgment against them. That is a matter of our own ideas, their truth and our integrity in applying them, holding them accountable as moral agents as we would hold ourselves.

Here one can vigorously agree with Hannah Arendt's conclusion in her *Eichmann in Jerusalem*, where she composed a rationale for Eichmann's death sentence that the Israeli judges should have delivered but shied from:

> You [i.e. Eichmann] said that you had never acted from base motives, that you had never had any inclination to kill anybody, that you had never hated Jews, and still that you could not have acted otherwise and that you did not feel guilty . . . your [personal] role in the Final Solution was an accident and that almost anybody could have taken your place, so that potentially almost all Germans are equally guilty . . . that where all, or almost all, are guilty, nobody is . . . Let us assume, for the sake of the argument, that it was nothing more than [accidental, personal] misfortune that made you a willing instrument in the organization of mass murder; there still remains the fact that you have carried out, and therefore actively supported, a policy of mass murder. For politics is not like the nursery; in politics obedience is support. And just as you supported and carried out a policy of not wanting to share the earth with Jewish people and the people of a number of other nations . . . we find that no one, that is, no member of the human race, can be expected to want to share the earth with you. This is the reason, and the only reason, you must hang.³⁶

In other words: subjective intention does not justify. Agency does not consist in authenticity nor is it justified by sincerity. Obedience to a false doctrine objectively implicates one in the falsehood believed. You are then responsible for what you believe, in whom you believe and consequently serve by your obedience. Ideas have consequences; rational human beings are obliged to think through ideas critically and lend a rational, not beastly or servile obedience to the imperatives entailed by the indicatives they hold

---

35. Burleigh, *Third Reich*, 14. The passage continues incisively: "In this sense, Nazism was neither simply science run riot, however much this definition suits critics of modern genetics, nor bastardized Christianity, however much this suits those who see Nazism simply as the outgrowth of Christian anti-Semitism."

36. Arendt, *Eichmann*, 278–79.

to. If the obedient doer of evil at another's command refuses to own his or her actions, "metaphysical motives" at all, then the community can and should impute guilt and demand a fit retribution.

Arendt's probing discussion of the moral guilt of those who obeyed, however, leads to a third criterion that must be satisfied to answer our question about the philosophical sources of the Final Solution, namely, that we distinguish—as the nature of the Nazi case with its Führerprinzip requires—between leaders and followers. Failure to observe this distinction leads to serious confusion. Prima facie the philosophical sources of mass obedience to Hitler and the sources of Hitler's own vision might well be diverse in origin. Part of the historically particular riddle of Nazism is how two such independent variables coalesced in the Final Solution. If we do not pay attention to this distinction, we fail to note the spell that Hitler's vision cast upon his obedient, indeed "willing executioners."[37] We instead dismiss Hitler's vision as manifestly bizarre and unworthy of rational adherence and so search instead for psychological or sociological or historical explanations of the freakish German obedience to it—a blind alley, which Arendt rightly repudiated in taking issue with the "assumption current in all modern legal systems that intent to do wrong is necessary for the commission of a crime."[38] Yet Arendt's account of the "banality of evil" in *Eichmann in Jerusalem* comes very close to committing the fallacy I am suggesting: overlooking the spell—nothing "banal" about it at all!—cast by the leader's vision which demanded and got unconditional obedience. Arendt gives this little credence. Her analysis leads to just this insight but stops in its tracks when it is reached.

Specifically and provocatively, Arendt analyzed Eichmann's claim that "he had lived his whole life according to Kant's moral precepts and especially according to a Kantian definition of duty . . . 'I meant by my remark about Kant that the principle of my will must always be such that it can become the principle of general laws . . .'" Eichmann to be sure ruefully acknowledged "that from the moment he was charged with carrying out the Final Solution he had ceased to live according to Kantian principles, that he had known it, and that he had consoled himself with the thought that he no longer 'was master of his own deeds,' that he was unable 'to change anything.'" But Arendt added, Eichmann "had not simply dismissed the Kantian formula as no longer applicable, but had distorted it to read: Act as if the principle of your actions were the same as that of the legislator or the law of the land . . . in Hans Frank's formulation of the 'categorical imperative in the Third

---

37. Neitzel and Welzer, *Soldaten*, 193–227.
38. Arendt, *Eichmann*, 277.

Reich'... 'Act in such a way that the Führer, if he knew your action, would approve it.'"[39] What would Hitler do? "In a world in which the word of the Führer is law," the law abiding citizen "not only obeyed orders but obeyed the law ... [Eichmann] ended by stressing alternately the virtues and vices of blind obedience, or the 'obedience of corpses,' *Kadavergehorsam*, as he himself called it."[40]

Arendt calls this a "distortion" of Kant's ethic, which assuredly from Kant's perspective it would have been. But also from a sincere Nazi's? In fact, Eichmann's personal sense of innocence derives precisely from his principled adherence to the Nazified categorical imperative: he "confessed his sins" when twice his feelings got in the way and he tried to save Jews.[41] He subverted Himmler's "corrupt" attempt to bargain with Jewish lives at the end of the war.[42] As Arendt herself rightly concludes: "the sad and very uncomfortable truth of the matter probably was that it was not his fanaticism but his conscience that prompted Eichmann to adopt his uncompromising attitude during the last year of the war."[43]

But is this a genuine alternative: either fanaticism or conscience? Can we not imagine a sincere Nazi, conscientiously doing his duty where duty is to do the Leader's will? Can we not see this in the world after Kant, in which the rational and hence putatively universal foundation for ethics has failed and the categorical imperative rather arises in an act of will and is validated by the obedience it acquires in the act? Arendt showed us that the Nazi Final Solution was the work by and large of bureaucrats like Eichmann, doing their routine bureaucratic duty conscientiously. The fatal philosophical weakness, in her view, lies at the door of the rationalistic ethics of duty, which suppressed all sympathy and fellow-feeling (what Kant called "inclination") for the sake of duty. This yields an ethic so formal in nature that it can be hijacked by a project as perverse as racist genocide. But then the question reverts: is an ethic that formal—so as to secure a rational and universal civilization—not defenseless when its particularistic pretensions are exposed and irrepressible "metaphysical motives" arising from the feelings that do reflect each one's particular embeddedness in nature and history then rush forward to fill the void, as articulated for us in some imperative to preserve or save or develop one's particular form of life? Was not just this

---

39. Ibid., 136.
40. Ibid., 135.
41. Ibid., 137.
42. Ibid., 145.
43. Ibid., 146.

evocation of feeling the "religious" spell cast by Adolf Hitler? Indeed, was not just such "religious" experience the spell that first put Hitler on his path?

As an aside, we may note here that one theologian-philosopher of the time thought so, Paul Tillich. He faulted the rationalism of his fellow Social Democrats for failing even to sense the profound religious appeal of what he called "the myth of origin" in fascism. He argued that the proper response to fascism was not the absolute rationalistic disdain for the symbols of the myth of origin in blood, soil and tribe, since in fact the proletariat also struggles in the name of these symbols of their bodily existence for human well-being and community against the savage reduction of them caused by wage labor and the monopolized economic calculations of the bourgeoisie. "Ontologically this means being is holy," Tillich wrote,[44] and fascism appeals because it pretends to reclaim and sanctify life profaned under the conditions of capitalism. Having no sense for this *basis in reality* of Hitler's spell, and misled by Kantian pretensions to enact the abstract universal, socialism was incapable of winning the hearts of the abused in the concrete and urgent case of Germany in 1933.

There is no doubt that the rationalistic, Kantian mistrust of "inclinations," i.e., fellow-feeling, sympathy, moral "sentiments," played a background role in Nazi obedience. Himmler notoriously consoled his *Einsatzgruppen*: "We had the moral right, we had the duty towards our people, to destroy this people that wanted to destroy us . . . [W]e have carried out this most difficult of tasks in the spirit of love for our people. And we have suffered no harm in our inner being, our soul, our character."[45] So also Goebbels: "A judicial sentence is being carried out against the Jews which is certainly barbaric, but which they have fully deserved . . . In these matters, one cannot let sentimentality prevail. If we did not defend ourselves against them, the Jews would exterminate us."[46] Examples could be multiplied of how Nazis had to battle their own human feelings as "sentimental," together with the pangs that remained from theistic or humanistic conscience. As philosopher Giorgio Agamben puts the point generally: there "is no reason to doubt that the 'humanitarian' considerations that led Hitler and Himmler to elaborate a euthanasia program immediately after their rise to power were in good faith . . ."[47] or for that matter led to the eventual construction of the death-factories. Once the decision to kill has been made on biopolitical grounds, a duty to kill humanely follows. The factory-efficient death camps

---

44. Tillich, *The Socialist Decision*, 17.
45. Cited in Burleigh, *Third Reich*, 661.
46. Ibid., 645.
47. Ibid., 140.

arose out of the demoralizing experience for the perpetrators watching day after day the death agonies of their victims by firing squad.[48]

All of these examples, however, beg an essential question, if we would think that thereby we have gotten to the philosophical bottom of Nazi obedience in a warped appropriation of the Kantian ethics of duty. Whether in religious or philosophical versions, the ethic of duty enjoins us to be a neighbor to those in need (e.g., Luke 10:25–37) or to treat others as bearers of reason whether they act rationally or not, since we belong under God or by virtue of our rational faculty to the same community. The Ought of duty is grounded in the Is of community: I owe myself to the community which has given me life. Thus Eichmann knew that he had departed from Kant at the precise point of excluding the Jews from the community of potentially rational agents and that the ground of this departure was the will of the Führer. What "will" was that which could cast such a spell, overruling both the religious and philosophical universalism of the antecedent tradition?

Hitler himself could appropriate the ethic of duty in most acute and pointed fashion: " . . . we are continually stirring the conscience of our *Volk* and making each of you once more aware that you should perceive yourself as a national comrade, and that you should make sacrifices! . . . We want to show the whole world and our *Volk* that we Germans regard the word 'community' not as a hollow phrase, but as something that for us really does entail an inner obligation."[49] Hitler's permutation was, so to say, Kantianism for the people, an ethic of dutiful obedience for the *Volk*. Of course, unlike either the Golden Rule of Jesus or the Categorical Imperative of Kant, "the exclusionary character of Nazi charity differed from Christian tenets, in which everyone was equal in the sight of God, and no one written off as hopeless . . . [it] deviated from both traditional conservative and progressive liberal outlooks, not least because the emphasis was on the collective well-being and the practice racially exclusionary."[50]

Corresponding to this was an ethic for the elite, preeminently the SS,[51] stemming from the Führer's "metaphysical motives." We know from August Kubizek's memoir how the young Hitler conceived of himself as an artist who would remake the world by the power of the will: " . . . with his whole overflowing heart he stood then in the ranks of the under-privileged. It was not sympathy in the ordinary sense which he felt for the disinherited. That

---

48. See the account of Himmler's visit to the Russian front to witness an "action" in Rhodes, *Masters of Death*, 152–53.
49. Burleigh, *Third Reich*, 223.
50. Ibid., 225.
51. Ibid., 194–97.

would not have been sufficient. He not only suffered with them, he lived for them and devoted all his thoughts to the salvation of those people from distress and poverty. No doubt, this ardent desire for a total reorganization of life was his personal response to his own fate, which had led him, step by step, into misery. Only by his noble and grandiose work, which as intended 'for everybody' and appealed 'to all' did he find again his inner equilibrium. What mattered to him was that the uprooted masses, who had become estranged from their own soil and their own people, should again settle down on firm ground"[52]—the "holy" ground of "being," as Tillich saw. With this observation, we turn from the question of the source of Nazi obedience to that of its vision in the mind of *der Führer*, Adolf Hitler.

NIETZSCHE NAZIFIED

Alan Bullock observed in this connection that "Nietzsche sums up this tradition ["of 'the powerful, embattled personality which imposes its demands upon the world and attempts to fashion it in its own image'"] in inimitable fashion. The future, he declared, belonged to the artist-politician, the political leader who was the artist in another medium . . ." He refers to Mussolini's boast, "'the masses are wax in my hands . . ., [taking Lenin as] an artist who has worked in men as others have worked in marble . . .' as a precedent. Kubizek confirms what Bullock reported about these sources inspiring the young Hitler: "As for philosophical works, he always had his Schopenhauer by him, later Nietzsche, too . . ."[53] Many passages in the *Table Talks* indicate an appropriation of Nietzsche as well.

This raises an interesting problem. Nietzsche was not a German nationalist, let alone a racist, least of all an anti-Semite.[54] His philosophical vision was profoundly individualist, not socialist but acerbically anti-socialist. How could such a thinker be a philosophical source of National Socialism—a name combining two values Nietzsche despised equally? Indeed a Nazi philosopher, Ernst Krieck, "caustically remarked: apart from the fact that Nietzsche was not a socialist, not a nationalist, and opposed to racial thinking, he could have been a leading National Socialist thinker! . . . What could this advocate of egoistic individualism possibly have in common with Nazi communitarianism or the goal of a völkisch organic racial totality?"[55] Yet even this criticism, Stephen Aschheim maintains, ". . . demonstrate[s] the

52. Kubizek, *Young Hitler*, 173.
53. Bullock, *Parallel Lives*, 181.
54. Aschheim, *The Nietzsche Legacy*, 338.
55. Cited by ibid., 253.

normative nature and centrality of that thinker as definitive of the Nazi order."[56] Counter-intuitive as it seems, a strong argument has been made for this thesis by Anscheim. Note well: It is not an argument about the justice of the Nazi appropriation of Nietzsche per se, but simply the massive fact of it.

Steven E. Aschheim in *The Nietzsche Legacy in Germany 1890-1990* amply documents the articulation of the rise of Nazism in Nietzschean categories as the antidote to decadence and nihilism: "in a spate of publications, nazism was variously depicted as the realization of the Nietzschean vision, as crucially inspired by it, or as thematically parallel. Had the master not called for the creation of a biologized, hierarchical, *Lebensphilosophie* society; the breeding of a higher, soldierly New Man unfettered by the resentment chains of traditional morality and an anti-life rationalist vision? Nazism was, after all, a regenerationist, postdemocratic, post-Christian social order where the weak, the decrepit and useless were to be legislated out of existence."[57] "For those [Nazis] interested in the fusion of Nietzsche and a right-wing politics of racial hygiene," Anscheim points out, "the differences [between Nietzsche and Hitler] were overwhelmed by the commonalities . . . [For them], Nietzsche was a powerful pioneer of race culture. It was he who had rediscovered biology for philosophy . . . His promoters highlighted Nietzsche's reassertion of instinct, his discovery of the body, and above all his naturalistic transvaluation in which the biological ethic replaced the moral one . . . [I]n his own way, he 'was the most acute antisemite that ever was: he was the most radical discoverer of the unholy role that Judaism played in the spiritual history of Europe.'"[58]

"Suitably adapted Nietzschean notions became a differentiated and integral part of Nazi self-definition . . . Nietzsche was made an integral part of Nazi ideological training . . ." Education, science, law, and medicine were as Nietzschified as Nazified: "Nietzschean illiberalism, antihumanism and a politicized *Lebensphilosophie* were placed at the center of the new educational philosophy . . . These notions applied also to revised conceptions of science and knowledge in general . . . Nietzsche . . . had demonstrated the tyranny of objectivity and the 'sick sovereignty' of smug, self-satisfied science. He had shown that there was no absolute truth, only the need to create one's own culture . . ." Nietzsche inspired a new jurisprudence as well.

56. Ibid., 255.

57. Ibid., 239.

58. Ibid., 244-45. The passage continues: "His demonstration that Christianity was the ultimate Jewish consequence and that it engendered the spread of Jewish blood poisoning made the Jews the most fateful people of world history. Through this road Nietzsche was brought to the race problem, opening the door to racial hygiene in an attempt to break the degeneration of a thousand years."

"Friedrich Mess's 1930 *Nietzsche: The Lawgiver* . . . provided the outlines for the desired post-Christian, post-Enlightenment, anti-Kantian society . . . The Nietzschean legal mode was designed to restore one to life, predicated on the non-Christian assumption of the innocence of being . . . [Law] was a dynamic instrument in the life of the *Volk* and an integral part of its biological and anthropological development . . . universal human law was both 'life-estranged and an unhistorical utopian conception.'" The same may be said of medicine: "no shortage of appropriate Nietzschean recommendations advocating what he called 'holy cruelty:' 'Life itself recognizes no solidarity, no "equal rights" between the healthy and the degenerate parts of an organism: one must excise the latter—or the whole will perish. Sympathy for decadents, equal rights for the ill-constituted—that would be the profoundest immorality, that would be antinature itself as morality' [cited from *The Will to Power*]."[59]

Anscheim recognizes, of course, that Nietzsche's biting contempt for anti-Semitism (Nietzsche once wrote: "I would simply have all antisemites shot!") clearly requires special explanation, not only for his own thesis but also for Nietzsche's Nazi appropriators. They argued that "Nietzsche had only opposed nineteenth-century forms of conventional [religious] and Christian anti-Semitism because he stood for a newer and far more radical form . . . [Anti-Semitism had been] limited to the confessional, economic, and social domains, overlooking the biological dimension . . ." In this way, Anscheim continues, Nietzsche "became a source for that radicalized drive designated by Uriel Tal as 'anti-Christian anti-Semitism.'"[60] No doubt this is true.

But what of the more significant objection, that Nietzsche is far too subtle and a significant a thinker to be guilty of this bowdlerization at the hands of Nazis? What are the differences that Nazi enthusiasts overlooked in their appropriation of the Nietzsche legacy that belie the Nazi claim to have found in him their philosophical source? It would take a lengthy study adequately to answer the question. But we can provide a few clues to an answer here. Rüdiger Safranski in his *Nietzsche: A Philosophical Biography* has provided a differentiated reflection on this problem that is useful for our purposes. In his zeal to overcome the metaphysical "beyond" (=Nolte's "transcendence") as a slander against this life, Safranski argues, Nietzsche at times fell victim to an inverse error, seeking a scientific "behind," so to

59. Ibid., 240–44.
60. Ibid., 252. The passage continues: "Perhaps the most extreme expression of this was Hans Eggert Schroder's 1937 *Nietzsche and Christianity* . . . Socrates the rationalist had destroyed the Dionysian essence . . . Plato's moral fanaticism had, after all, destroyed paganism. What was Christianity if not 'Platonism for the Volk'?" (251).

say, a reduction of human life to its physical apparatus (which he regarded, metaphysically, as finite matter in infinite motion). In his "positivist" stage, Nietzsche thus promoted a "grand disenchantment of nature by means of scientific knowledge [that] does away with the intentionality of a world that has a meaningful genesis and culmination and a goal-oriented process in the middle"; he "reduces [nature] to a universe of chains of causality that clash and become entangled and produce new causalities time and again."[61] In other words, he replaces an idealistic otherworldly metaphysics with a materialistic metaphysics of this world. Since human beings are nothing but nature at work in the form of "new causalities," for Nietzsche, we are moving 'beyond good and evil,' i.e., "praising and blaming human conduct [is] just as senseless as 'praising and blaming nature and necessity.'"[62] For this reason, Nietzsche opposed the optimistic spin placed on Darwinian evolution by figures like Herbert Spencer (even Darwin himself) and insisted instead on the daunting philosophical truth that "natural selection" represents nothing in the sense of design or purpose. Again in Safranski's words: "the truth of the organic is the inorganic ... Sentient life is an enormous error, an excrescence, a huge detour."[63] Nietzsche tried to communicate this disillusioning notion of dead matter in infinite random motion with his doctrine of "eternal recurrence": in the course of "infinite time, all possible constellations of matter and energy, and consequently all possible events pertaining to both the animate and inanimate realms, have already taken place, and they will recur ad infinitum."[64] (As an aside, it is interesting to note that Pierre Klossowski, the French scholar who worked to rescue Nietzsche from his Nazi appropriators, described Nietzsche's insight into the eternal return as his own breakthrough mystical or religious experience.[65])

Of course, as I just intimated, more than one critic has pointed out that if Nietzsche seriously intended this doctrine of the eternal recurrence as the truth behind the appearances, he is no less involved in metaphysics, indeed philosophical theology (Dionysius, not the Crucified!) than any of his Platonist or Christian opponents. Defenders of Nietzsche have replied that he meant eternal recurrence only as a thought-experiment, which clarifies for the individual strong enough the relationship to the ungraspable flux of reality, the chaos of becoming without intention or purpose. The

61. Safranski, *Nietzsche: A Philosophical Biography*, 175.
62. Ibid., 176.
63. Ibid., 226.
64. Ibid., 228.
65. Klossowski, *Nietzsche and the Vicious Circle*, 55–73.

experiment underscores the need for one's own existential decision about the meaning of one's life. Clarity comes, according to this reading, when "we accept and embrace the notion of an existence entirely determined by the law of nature without breaking down, and when the senselessness of absolute determinism no longer shocks us and we succeed in recognizing determinism without needing to turn fatalistic." This is what the *Übermensch* he speaks of really is: self-overcoming of the human-all-too-human weakness and resentment by a courageous because ungrounded willing of oneself in a free decision to be whatever one decides to be, all the while aware that "one force overpowers the other, absorbs it, disintegrates, is swallowed up by yet another force, and so on. It is meaningless, but dynamic, play of growth, enhancement, overpowering, and struggle."[66]

In this light, we may now see with real precision the evident affinity between Nietzsche (that is, in at least one stage, or according to one reading) and the Nazis: the positivist embrace of nature's stern and ruthless laws and further the mystical or religious embrace of them in a triumph of the will. But we can also now see the precise difference. The notorious text about the "blond beast," as Burleigh points out, was no indication of Nietzsche's hope for the future but his fear of the "return of the repressed" once the rationalistic and formalistic constraints of the Kantian ethic collapsed from "the tension which is caused by being closed in and fenced in by the peace of the community for so long."[67] Safranski analyzes the Nazi philosopher, Alfred Baeumler's 1931 *Nietzsche: The Philosopher and the Politician* in similar fashion. Baeumler argued that if we take Nietzsche's critique of "truth" seriously, there is only power. "People come into contact with one another, collide, disengage, and part ways in corporeal reality. Hostility culminating in war is truly the father of all things."[68] From this, Baeumler asserted that "we can learn from Nietzsche that there is no 'mankind,' but only concrete entities in a state of conflict with one another. These entities are 'a race, a people, a class.' Nietzsche [however], would not have used these terms."[69] This seems a nuanced judgment. Nietzsche's unrelenting search for truth with no comforting illusions led him to the doctrine of the eternal return. This may be read as the metaphysical basis of Darwinian natural selection. Being is a passing facade, becoming is all that is real. But Nietzsche regarded

66. Safranski, *Nietzsche*, 292. But there is ample evidence in the *Table Talks* for Hitler taking Nietzsche's teaching in this happy way as well, e.g., the statement in January, 1942, "The creative forces make their home in the bosom of the optimist. But faith is at the bottom of everything." Cf. *Table Talks*, 199, cf. 218, 238, 246, 297, 315.

67. Burleigh, *Third Reich*, 342.

68. Safranski, *Nietzsche*, 336.

69. Ibid., 337.

this insight into the deepest truth of nature as available only to the exceptional individual brave enough to face it. For such it would be liberation from false and conventional, but comforting, illusions of natural essence, law, and purpose. And yet, if he meant this insight seriously, metaphysically, as true insight into the ultimate nature of reality, he held onto the value of "truth" and in this way, like the Kant whom he despised, mastered the sublimity of nature with an act of intelligent human comprehension. Nietzsche, in my view, never thought himself out of the circle he was caught in here.

Be that as it may, if the metaphysics of eternal recurrence is the true interpretation of Darwinian natural selection, in turn the true scientific theory of the origin of species and descent of man, then there seems to be no reason why we cannot draw lessons from these truths that inform ethics and instruct duty in the fashion of taking evolution into our own hands. Beginning with Plato, it has been a long-standing habit of thought in the West to criticize conventional morality as artificial, arbitrary, unfounded, and otherwise oppressive by means of an appeal to the nature of things as uncovered by intelligent inquiry. In this respect, Nietzsche and Hitler following him, alike "moral revolutionaries," are at one with a deep impulse in the Western philosophical tradition: to attack conventional culture in the name of nature, i.e., one's theoretical grasp of nature. In this respect, Hitler no doubt appropriated a plausible reading of Nietzsche more or less coherently, projecting himself not as a member of the herd, but rather as an artistic creator of new values, freed from the old inhibitions of the Christian-Platonic synthesis or its secular restatement since Kant as ethical idealism. Hitler won for himself this right by his own unflinching insight into and embrace of nature's stern and ruthless laws. To this appropriation of Nietzsche Hitler added the "icily scientific" notions of *Blut und Boden*, the natural laws of racial evolution, as he found them proposed and debated in Darwinian literature. Nietzsche did not think racially and so far as we can see rejected such thinking. The question then seems to boil down to whether Hitler's addition of racialism is an alien distortion or the unfolding of an unforeseen consequence of Nietzsche's own thought, that is, if we take Nietzsche as the metaphysician of Darwinian natural selection.

In this regard, however, it seems important to underscore, as does Agamben, that we all as modern people face a dilemma here that is not foreign or strange after all. As John C. Greene pointed out, "The difficulty was that biology afforded no criteria for judging the progress of a creature like man. Survival was a precondition of progress, but it did not insure progress or define its essence. In the last analysis natural selection meant not the survival of the fittest but the survival of those who survived. Survival was a brute fact, not a moral victory."[70] Natural selection—a purely algorithmic process of alleles drifting in whatever direction the shifting tides of environmental conditions draw them—gives us no criteria by which to measure in any moral sense progress or regress, while any attempt to resolve morality into the laws of nature opens us to something very much akin to Nazism, which is biopolitically the bold and artistic endeavor to take evolution into our own hands. Hitler obviously came down on the latter side of this dilemma. Yet, as Richard Weikart has most impressively documented in his study *From Darwin to Hitler*, "many mainstream scientists, professors, and physicians—including those identifying with the political Left—upheld views about Darwinism and eugenics quite similar to Hitler's . . . Hitler's ideas derived ultimately from respectable scientists and scholars who were grappling with the implications of Darwinism for ethics and society."[71] After Darwin, appeal to nature in criticism of conventional morality typically denies "any possibility of divine intervention, heap[s] scorn on mind-body dualism, and reject[s] free will in favor of complete determinism . . . every feature of the cosmos, including the human mind, society, and morality, [can] be explained by natural cause and effect. Everything [is] thus subject to the ineluctable laws of nature. As a corollary to this, science became the arbiter of all truth. Not even ethics or morality [can] escape . . ."[72] Weikart gives us this list of metaphysical denials aimed at the antecedent tradition of Christian Platonism. This list of denials fairly begs for corresponding metaphysical affirmations. It is this latter that Hitler risked. Pragmatically, his beliefs were at length refuted as incoherent with many other beliefs we hold true—though at horrendous cost and without settling the crises that spawned them. Nor do any of us know how to make these divergent beliefs compatible with each other.

Where does this leave us? Contemporary natural science, of course, informs everything we can say in theology in the sense that in any age the best contemporary thinking about anything forms the horizon of possibilities in which we think, speak, and act. Rudolf Bultmann was right about this, even if he was not right in what he proposed to do about it. His subsequent program of demythologizing meant for theology a neo-docetism that robbed Jesus of his Jewishness and God of his Trinitarian being—draconian theological accommodations far from a redescription of our scientific worldview in Christian terms.[73] If this study is indicating that in theology we cannot

---

70. Greene, *The Death of Adam*, 335.
71. Weikart, *From Darwin to Hitler*, 8.
72. Ibid., 13.
73. On this critique of Bultmann, see below Chapter 5.

simply accommodate a secularist ethic founded on nature as intelligently understood on account of a justified fear of repeating the grisly evils of Hitler and lesser "social Darwinists," there are but two options. The first is the option that American pragmatism took and to which Reinhold Niebuhr responded theologically.[74] We can regard inquiry into absolute origins and ends as theological and dogmatic, too high for us to plumb, questions in their very asking that resolve into conundrums, the Kantian antinomies.[75] That is to say, the only possible objects of knowledge are specific changes and specific purposes that emerge in our experience as we find ourselves in the middle of things, ignorant of cosmic origins and ends. This is a skeptical but dynamic version of Kantianism that resolves itself in the triumph of instrumental reason, the perfectly progressive philosophy of liberal capitalism. Standing within it, Niebuhr waged a theological campaign of correction rather than see it subjected to the total critique of the competing political messianisms of fascism and communism. But after Hitler, and after Stalin, and after Hiroshima one has to wonder whether metaphysical hungers are so easily stilled, or renounced, whether the messianic question can simply be outlawed, outflanked, dismissed. That continues to be the posture of our increasingly desperate liberalism. To venture here into metaphysics, or messianism, with little alternative in sight, is the second option.[76] This is to subject our liberalism as a whole to theological critique, though not in the rival ways of fascism and communism. A further word on this will be given in the Conclusion to this book.

THE TRUTH IN THE INTENTIONALIST CASE

Historians of the Holocaust have in varying degrees divided themselves into so-called intentionalist and functionalist or structuralist schools. The former "line of thought accents the role of Hitler in initiating the mass murder of European Jewry, seeing a high degree of persistence, consistency, and orderly sequence in the Nazi anti-Jewish policy, directed from a very early

---

74. "Niebuhr was a liberal critic of liberalism, a household critic whose criticism went deeper than most and who did not hesitate to drawn the wisdom of *classical* conservativism in bringing out his own *liberal* reconstruction." Rice, *Reinhold Niebuhr and John Dewey*, 193. Cf. 210-15.

75. Kuklick, *A History of Philosophy in America, 1720-2000*, 179-97. See also the insightful study of Menand, *The Metaphysical Club*.

76. In Adkins and Hinlicky, *Rethinking Philosophy and Theology with Deleuze*, we have tried to take up this challenge of metaphysics after Darwin without sliding into Hitlerism and to raise the question how a crucified Messianism might arise under these epistemic conditions.

point to the goal of mass murder."[77] Functionalists on the other hand "present a picture of the Third Reich as a maze of competing power groups, rival bureaucracies, forceful personalities, and diametrically opposed interests engaged in ceaseless clashes with each other" from which the Holocaust emerged, as it were, "bit by bit"[78] rather than from some "blueprint" in Hitler's mind. Twenty years ago Michael R. Marrus surveyed this debate and tried to split the difference: "It seems useful, however, to understand Jewish policy in this period as evolving within a genocidal framework—extending beyond Jews to include the incurably ill, Soviet intelligentsia, prisoners of war, and others as well. In this fevered atmosphere, incredible as it may seem, an 'order' to send millions of people to their deaths may have been no more than a 'nod' from Hitler to one of his lieutenants."[79] Without denying the messiness of the evidence or the insights to be derived from analysis of the impersonal psychological, economic, social forces to which structuralists call attention, the truth of the intentional interpretation can be made more salient when latent ideas about moral agency and religious purpose are teased out and made explicit. In theology, freedom and destiny are so woven together that neither one exists without the other.

Lucy S. Dawidowicz's *The War against the Jews: 1933–45* is perhaps the classic statement of the intentionalist school of historical interpretation: "History begins in the minds of men and women," she maintains, "in the ideas they hold and in the decisions they make." Thus "Hitler had a general plan, not a detailed program, which he implemented in stages, as opportunities allowed."[80] This is evident in the fact that "hatred of the Jews was Hitler's central and most compelling belief [that] dominated his thought and his actions all his life . . . Hitler planned to murder the Jews in coordination with his plans to go to war for *Lebensraum* and to establish the Thousand Year Reich."[81] In her telling, Hitler's foreign policy was never an end in itself based on realistic geopolitical calculations, but always instrumental to the principles of racial war, a matter of "unwavering commitment to National Socialist ideology, and a strategy combining opportunism, expediency and improvisation."[82] Her historical claim is that "Hitler had embarked on an ideological war to achieve ideological/racial goals, but that to win that war

77. Marrus, *The Holocaust in History*, 35.
78. Ibid., 41.
79. Ibid., 46.
80. Dawidowicz, *War*, xxxi.
81. Ibid., xix. Kubizek substantiates this obsession from Hitler's teen years in Vienna, prior to World War I, including a report on a secret mission to a synagogue to observe a Jewish wedding. Kubizek, *Young Hitler*, 230–31.
82. Dawidowicz, *War*, 122–3.

he needed also to fight a conventional war." Her excruciating proof for this thesis is that "the rational interests of the latter [i.e. winning the conventional war] often were sacrificed to the racial imperatives of the ideological war."[83] Thus the conventional "war and the annihilation of the Jews were interdependent. The disorder of war would provide Hitler with the cover for the unchecked commission of murder."[84] Yet the connection Dawidowicz finds here between conventional war and genocide targeting primarily, if not exclusively the Jews, as we shall see, runs even deeper. It is to be found and made explicable in Hitler's theology.[85]

Structuralists resist this, in part, not because of their justified interest in the wave of history over those who ride it, but because it requires an act of imagination that many today find implausible on account of an associated contemporary secularism. This secularism consists in the doubts that one can be religiously motivated and that there is a method to the madness to be discerned by taking myth seriously, if not literally. "What's the Matter with Kansas?"[86] This doubt, this plausibility gap, is the basis of the deep objection to intentionalism, since, as we have learned from the deconstructionists, our ideas of self, subject, personhood, and agency are irredeemably theological. In coming to her claim, Dawidowicz not only treats her subject—Adolf Hitler—as a moral agent, but acknowledges that historians of the Holocaust also act as moral agents, making judgments of value in the very process of selecting and organizing data and placing it into an ordered narrative. Kant was right at least about this: we act *as if* we were moral agents, even if we can make no knowledgeable account of this agency but de facto rely upon the myth that we are made in the image and likeness of God (the bearers of reason, as Kant preferred). So also historians: the history that they narrate renders an account "not only of the battles and wars, elections and revolutions, intrigues and alliances, structures and systems, but above all of the ideas, ambitions and goals of the people who set events into motion." Functionalist or structuralist methods naturally can be helpful in setting the stage for such narrative; they can map out the landscape on which historical agents act and react to forces which oppose them. But a historiography in which the game merely plays us, not we the game—in which we are not genuine agents but purely patients, as it were, pawns of "the system"—cannot but in

---

83. Ibid., 184.

84. Ibid., 148.

85. As Dawidowicz herself indicates in her probing discussion of the *Blut und Boden* mythology which provided the basis of war for *Lebensraum*. See 102ff.

86. Frank, *What's the Matter with Kansas?*

the end make one and all, even the perpetrators, victims of those impersonal forces which supposedly drive us to act as we do.

"Because they use structures and functions to explain critical decisions made at historical junctures, structuralists cannot assign historical responsibility to their historical actors. They are consequently unable to make historical judgments"[87]—at least this holds where the vocation of history is and remains our human self-examination, *studia humanitatis*. The resistance is to acknowledging the power of the visions and expectations by which men live and act—as secularists, I am arguing, less than as structuralists—these thinkers think that men live by bread alone for the happiness of this world alone. In this way they misinterpret theology as illusion, and painting with this broad brush, they can no longer distinguish between good theology and bad, monstrous myth and salutary, worthy visions and demonic ones. To them it is all one, nothing but a grand mystification to be cleared up—with another set of mystifications (again, as the deconstructionists have shown us).

Dawidowicz, admittedly, does not engage in sufficient philosophic reflection to warrant her implicit notions of agency, action, and responsibility. She relies implicitly on the tradition of Judaism and the imago Dei tradition of scripture. By "moral agency" it is evident, however, that she means at least the capacity to recognize actions as one's own effects in the world, i.e., the reflective judgment to take, or to assign, ownership for some action or inaction.[88] History, from this perspective, is knowledge of the human past as human action or inaction in this moral, evaluative way that assign ownership to actions and failures to act and thus liability. So Dawidowicz acknowledges: "This is not a value-free book. The very subject matter of the Final Solution precludes neutrality. In writing about a nation that transgressed the commandment, 'Thou shalt not murder,' it is impossible to be what Charles Beard characterized as 'a neutral mirror.'"[89] But of course the commandment not to murder is grounded in the imago Dei notion (cf. Gen 9:6). Only so is it and can it be morally binding on human agents in history rather than a heteronymous imposition, as libertarians think it is. But this is theonomy, as living Judaism has always known.

---

87. Dawidowicz, *War*, xxxii.

88. I am presupposing here MacIntyre's critique of Nietzsche in the case of Paul DeMan in *Three Rival Versions of Moral Enquiry*: " . . . the genealogist faces grave difficulties in constructing a narrative of his or her past which would allow any acknowledgement in that past of a failure, let alone a guilty failure, which is also the failure of the same still-present self . . ." (213).

89. Dawidowicz, *War*, 22.

In order to make her claim of moral agency in the baffling case of Hitler's intention to exterminate Jewry, moreover, Dawidowicz finds herself not infrequently relying on peculiarly religious, or rather, biblical language. The German technical term, *Endlösung*, she writes, "reverberates with apocalyptic" tones, promising a "metahistorical programme devised with an eschatological perspective. It was part of a salvational ideology that envisioned the attainment of Heaven by bringing Hell on earth."[90] Consequently, as the shadow side of Hitler's millennialist or chiliastic vision the murder of the Jews was an end in itself, not a means to an end, undertaken for ideological—rather, for moral and religious reasons—not on practical or tactical or geopolitical calculations. This latter, that is with Rubenstein, this "religious element," is what makes the Holocaust "fundamentally different from all crimes that have existed in the past" and as such subversive of the "fundamental moral principles and every system of law that had governed, however imperfectly, human society for millennia."[91] Notice what happens with this resort to religious, or rather biblical, language to explain Hitler's motive: we have not the ordinary kind of moral conflict, between approved and disapproved behavior within a moral consensus, the ordinary disputes about the applicability of an agreed norm. Rather, we enter here into a radical conflict between opposing visions, differing visions of the Good and how we are to be included in it, and thus also of what counts as evil. This kind of conflict can aptly be called a "religious" conflict, since it is not about whether good will is owed to the neighbor but about who counts as a neighbor and why. With this resort to religious, indeed biblical, language to describe the Nazi targeting of the Jews, Dawidowicz thus claims for the Holocaust a virtual singularity in the particularity of Western history: a radical assault of a new morality against the antecedent one that she tacitly assumes from Judaism as universally applicable.

There has been much genocide in history. Structuralists very quickly dismiss singularities in history, just as I have criticized Ericksen's iconization of Hitler as a clear moral absolute, of evil to be sure, within history. Speaking of a singularity, rather than an absolute, however, is a matter of discerning historical particularity, of coming to precise judgments. If we were to argue against Dawidowicz that the Holocaust is only different in degree, not in kind, belonging to the general category of genocide, the objection would be true but trivial. It misses the historically particular dimension in the slide from Christian anti-Judaism to racial anti-Semitism, as already we pointed out in the Introduction to this book in agreement with Rubenstein, that

90. Ibid., 18.
91. Ibid., 19.

Hitler ultimately did attack the Jews for religious reasons, and that this final purpose for the final solution is singular in just this respect.

"To the Christian doctrine of the infinite significance of the individual human soul . . .," Hitler said in articulating this moral revolution and genocidal resolution, "I oppose with icy clarity the saving doctrine of nothingness and insignificance of the individual human being, and of his continued existence in the visible immortality of the nation."[92] Notice, Hitler's "icy" science is still said to be a "saving doctrine" and that his claim to the "greatest of scientific knowledge" is said to provide the basis of "spiritual expression." In Burleigh's insightful analysis: "While Nazism claimed scientific authority for its ideological mélange, it is essential to grasp that the allegedly scientific facts of blood, race and the reharmonization of mankind with nature were literally sanctified. The view that the 'supreme, fundamental value was Life, the perception of the Divine in an unceasing movement of Life,' had many consequences . . . Nature and Blood usurped God in eternity . . . Science was useful to bash Christianity over the head, but the science was heavily invested with religious properties."[93]

Even as the Soviet army closed in on Berlin, Hitler dictated these words on April 2, 1945 for his political Last Will and Testament: "Although trampled underfoot, the German people must try, in its helplessness, to respect the laws of *racist science* that we have given it. In a world whose *moral order* is more and more contaminated by the Jewish poison, a people immunized against it will finally regain its superiority. From this point of view, *eternal gratitude* will be owed to National Socialism because I exterminated the Jews in Germany and Central Europe."[94] Hitler lived and died a "prophet," self-proclaimed, of a set of religious convictions, engendered in his own strange nocturnal experience, about health and moral order, one that came to entail the "extermination of the Jews" as a matter of "eternal" significance. In just this way, Dawidowicz wrote in conclusion (notice the religious language):

> Anti-Semitism was the core of Hitler's system of beliefs and the central motivation for his policies. He believed himself to be the saviour who would bring redemption to the German people through the annihilation of the Jews, that people who embodied, in his eyes, the Satanic hosts. When he spoke or wrote about his "holy mission," he used words associated with chiliastic prophecy (not only in the millennial concept literally rendered

---

92. Cited in Burleigh, *Third Reich*, 256.
93. Ibid., 253–54.
94. Cited from Rhodes, *Masters of Death*, 256, emphasis added.

as the "Thousand Year Reich"), like "consecration," "salvation," "redemption," "resurrection," "God's will." The murder of the Jews, in his fantasies, was commanded by divine providence, and he was the chosen instrument for that task. He referred often to his "mission," but nowhere so explicitly as in *Mein Kampf*: "Hence today I believe that I am acting in accordance with the will of the Almighty Creator by defending myself against the Jew, I am fighting for the work of the Lord." From the moment he made his entrance on the historical stage until his death in a Berlin bunker, this sense of messianic mission never departed him, nor could any appeal to reason deflect him from pursing his murderous purpose.[95]

The parody of messianic-redemptive terms here—stolen ironically from the Jewish theological tradition itself—in this description of Hitler's theology is striking.

Let us pause to administer some antidote to this poison. The contemporary Jewish theologian Michael Wyschogrod, author of *Faith and the Holocaust*, provides a fittingly theological articulation of this enigma. He argues that only a traditional Jewish theological approach brings out the true significance of the Holocaust as an attack on the God of the Exodus, the God of Abraham, Isaac and Jacob, the God whom Jesus, a son of Israel and of the covenant, addressed as Abba, Father:

> The fate of Israel is of central concern because Israel is the elect people of God through whom God's redemptive work is done in the world. However tragic human suffering is on the human plane, what happens to Israel is directly tied to its role as that nation to which God attaches His name and through which He will redeem man. He who strikes Israel, therefore, engages himself in battle with God and it is for this reason that the history of Israel is the fulcrum of human history . . . We must learn to live with the knowledge that there is an abyss between belief and non-belief, that for non-belief Auschwitz is a member of a large and tragic class of human evil . . . For believing Israel, the Holocaust is not just another mass murder but, perhaps, the final circumcision of the people of God. But how else, except by the power of God, can anyone believe that? There is no salvation to be extracted from the Holocaust, no faltering Judaism can be revived by it, no new reason for the continuation of the Jewish people can be found in it. If there is hope after the Holocaust, it is because to those who believe, the voices of the Prophets

---

95. Dawidowicz, *War*, 208–9.

speak more loudly than did Hitler, and because the divine promise sweeps over the crematoria and silences the voices of Auschwitz.[96]

Wyschograd's sober affirmation of living Judaism's faith in the biblical God in spite of —rather, in defiance of—Hitler's theology of Cruel Divine Nature belongs under what Emil Fackenheim has called the 614th Commandment: "Thou shalt not grant to Hitler posthumous victories."[97] That applies above all in theology—also, in our judging of Hitler's theology.

NOLTE'S HITLER-AGAINST-TRANSCENDENCE

Nolte's book, *The Three Faces of Fascism*, was a richly documented and philosophically insightful examination of the spiritual basis of French, Italian, and German fascism. It preceded the *Historikerstreit* and the unfortunate statements that Nolte made under the sting of neo-Marxist ad hominem denunciation of his person. Specifically, Nolte argued that Friedrich Nietzsche's unrelenting attack on the biblical tradition of Judaism—as the wellspring of a poisonous slave morality—represents the philosophical basis of fascism.[98] The specifically racial, anti-Semitic turn of Hitler's Nazi brand of fascism cannot be laid at the door of Nietzsche, even if the fundamentally anti-Judaic themes and categories of fascism might be, i.e., the view of reality in which violence is scripted into the deepest, divine nature of things. For Hitler, as for fascism in general, war is the means to test and to verify one's own existence. In *Mein Kampf*, Hitler had written that "nature has given life to her creatures for the purpose of eternal struggle to ensure a rising evolution rather than a general putrefaction."[99]

96. Cited from Morgan, *A Holocaust Reader*, 170–71.

97. Cited in Telushkin, *Jewish Literacy*, 421–22. In dependence on these ideas, I published after my first visit to Auschwitz the meditative lecture I presented to the group of Christian pilgrims I was leading, "What Hope after Holocaust?"

98. "Nietzsche is not in any obvious sense the spiritual father of fascism; but he was the first to give voice to that spiritual focal point toward which all fascism must gravitate: the assault on practical and theoretical transcendence, for the sake of a 'more beautiful' form of 'life . . .' Many decades in advance, Nietzsche provided the politically radical anti-Marxism of fascism with its original spiritual image . . ." Nolte, *Three Faces*, 445. Similarly: "With not immediate relevance to the political events of the day, the Nietzschean doctrine, which alone permitted the equation of socialism, liberalism and traditional conservatism, was adopted and developed by a circle of fascistoid authors: the doctrine of the revolt of the slaves and of the impoverishment of life though Judeo-Christian resentment" (Ibid., 7). Kubizek confirms the young Hitler's obsession with art remaking life, *Young Hitler*, 96ff., 162ff. et passim.

99. Nolte, *Three Faces*, 419.

Nolte makes note of a remarkable fact in this connection. Hitler had hoped in retirement to devote his energies to a new Nazi theology; to cite the *Table Talks* directly, in December of 1941 Hitler started off the evening's conversation with the revelation: "The war will be over one day. I shall then consider that my life's final task will be to solve the religious problem. Only then will the life of the German native be guaranteed once and for all." This refers both to the retribution he planned to take on the churches but also to the religious future, as Hitler makes clear in going on in the same talk to mock the Christian "story. God creates the conditions for sin. Later on He succeeds, with the help of the Devil, in causing man to sin. Then He employs a virgin to bring into the world a son, who, by His death, will redeem humanity!"[100] Hitler regards this retelling of the Christian myth of redemption as so manifestly absurd that it required no further comment. Hitler here appears as one of those "modern men" of whom Rudolf Bultmann was almost simultaneously writing in his famous essay on demythologization: "To this extent the kerygma is incredible to modern man, for he is convinced that the mythical view of the world is obsolete." This is so because "all thinking today is shaped by modern science."[101]

Enter Hitler the post-Christian theologian. As Nolte comments: "this is the heart of [Hitler's] religious message, to which he wanted to devote all his time after the victory: 'Unconditional submission to the divine law of existence,' devout regard for the 'fundamental necessity of the rule of nature.'" To this new theology, Nolte posed an obvious question. "But why preach what is self-evident? Does 'nature' perhaps have an enemy that one must go to her defense? . . . [Hitler answered:] 'Man alone, of all living creatures, attempts to transgress the laws of nature.'"[102] This human attempt at ethical transcendence over nature—in fact an illusion, but in reality a transgression against nature that undermines life itself—is the religious enemy Hitler sees in religious Judaism and philosophical idealism as well as in the Christian "story." In the end, Nolte argued that fascism comes down to a rejection of the human project of liberty, "transcendence," as he philosophically calls it, in the name of the sheer chaos of life in all its amoral diversity and brilliant splendor of immanent change, conflict, becoming. If this interpretation is correct, Nolte concluded, "it should wipe out the impression that Hitler was a rather incomprehensible accident in the history of Germany and Europe. It becomes clear that he was possessed by 'something' and that

---

100. Trevor-Roper, ed., *Table Talk*, 110–11. This mocking of Christian dogma recurs frequently, cf. 258.

101. Rudolf Bultmann and Five Critics, *Kerygma and Myth*, 3.

102. Nolte, *Three Faces*, 420.

this 'something' was in no sense casual or trivial. . . . [Hitler's 'possession' was] the most desperate assault ever made upon the human being and the transcendence within him."[103]

By "transcendence," Nolte explains more precisely, is meant "the distinction between a finite and an eternal existence"[104] by which man reaches out "beyond that which exists [to] perceive something 'better' and hence exert a critique on that which is." Against such transcendence, fascism represents "the glorification of this [present] reality, with all its terrors, wars, exploitation, and affirmation of the here and now . . . [so that it will] cease to be possible to transcend them toward a goal, toward a 'beyond.'"[105] Or again: " . . . the power of 'antinature' fills Hitler with dread: it is this 'going beyond' in human nature which is capable of transforming the essence of human order and relation—transcendence . . ."[106] The metaphysical hatred of transcendence accounts for the remarkable fact that Hitler could connect the rival dynamisms of Wall Street capitalism and Moscow bolshevism and Christianity together as one huge Jewish plot. For all their rivalry, liberal democratic capitalism, Marxism, and Christianity each in its own way call for the negation of what is in favor of what could yet be, the realization of freedom in making the existing world new into a paradise fit for human joy. Of course, the three have very different, irreconcilably different visions of the Good and the way by which the Good comes and how we are to be included. But for Hitler that difference is beside the point: each of these three rivals is a version of this same project. Democratic capitalism, Marxism, and Christianity are three rival versions of transcendence. It is this very transcendence of natural life in all natural, immanent, violent, glorious strife which Hitler opposes—an opposition that is theologically deep.

Nolte discusses in this light a remarkable passage from Hitler's *Table Talks*.[107] "Hitler presents an emphatic interpretation of the Exodus from Egypt which he claims is entirely original. By quoting from Isaiah 9:2 and 3, and Exodus 12:38, he explains this mass migration as the result of a revolutionary and murderous assault of the Jews on the ruling class of Egypt. 'Just as among us,' the Jews were able to win over the lower classes ('the

---

103. Ibid., 424–25.
104. Ibid., 431.
105. Ibid., 443.
106. Ibid., 420.
107. Steigmann-Gall casts doubt on the reliability of the *Table Talks*, in his *Holy Reich*, 252–59, though he ends up with an unconvincing "re-reading" of the same source. This takes place in his book's least successful, final chapter, in which the author tries to anticipate and reject the considerable mass of material indicating that the Nazi *Endlösung* would turn on normative Christianity after victory in war.

rabble') by dint of humanitarian phrases and the slogan 'Proletarians of the world, unite'; the slaying of the first born was supposed to be the signal of the beginning of the revolution, but at the last moment the revolution was prevented by those Egyptians who had remained 'nationalistic,' and it had then been finally thwarted by the expulsion of the Jews and the 'rabble.' Consequently Moses was the first leader of bolshevism." Nolte observes that "the claim that Christianity [too] was a form of bolshevism was something not even Hitler at the height of his power ever dared to express [publicly] in so many words. Nevertheless, it is the central thesis of Hitler's *Table Talk*." Like many other modernists in theology, Hitler believes that Christianity went wrong with St. Paul. In his view, Paul "re-Judaized" the life affirming message of the Aryan Christ. Paul "goes to the Greeks, to the Romans," Hitler rambles. "And he takes them his 'Christianity.' Something which can unhinge the Roman Empire. All men are equal! Fraternity! Pacificism! No more dignity! And the Jew triumphed . . ."[108] In another statement: "Christianity was an early form of bolshevism, bolshevism an offspring of Christianity—and both were inventions of the Jew for the purpose of disrupting society . . . to destroy the pre-eminence of the white race in the world."[109] If this is what Hitler's theology in its anti-Semitism stood against—the project of human transcendence, true liberty, Judaism's messianic aspiration for the kingdom of God, the Beloved Community—what did it stand for?

NAPOLEON'S MANTLE

Hitler thought of himself as eminently modern, indeed as heir of Napoleon in bringing the revolution to the masses on the scientific-racial basis that his predecessors yet lacked and on account of which they had failed. That is why he dreamed in victorious retirement of settle the religious question theologically. Steigmann-Gall, however, is skeptical of Trevor-Roper's claim about Hitler's anti-Christian theology in the *Table Talks* and discounts in varying degrees the authenticity of this source.[110] As we have already in this study drawn widely from the *Table Talks*, that is, quite beyond any possible doctoring of passages opining negatively on Christianity, the weight of the evidence presented is broadly based, coherent, and thus indisputable in its theological implications. Steigmann-Gall points out that Trevor-Roper's handling of the materials has been called into question as insufficiently critical of the sifting of Hitler's views through the biases of the fiercely

---

108. Nolte, *Three Faces*, 331.

109. Ibid., 407.

110. Steigmann-Gall, *Holy Reich*, 254–59.

anti-Christian Martin Bormann, who had arranged for their recording and preservation.[111] Nonetheless Steigmann-Gall is still willing to use the *Table Talks* as a source of information, on the basis of which he makes the manifestly misleading (or deeply confused) statement: "Hitler gave no indication that he ceased believing in an active, providential God in favor of the rationalist, watch-maker God typical of theistic thought."[112] In fact this admirer of Frederick the Great and Napoleon very much identified with the Deistic critique of the Christian tradition by the Enlightenment *philosophes*. His belief in Providence (or Fate or Destiny) while religious was Stoic and pantheistic in background, not biblical or Augustinian. Unlike the Bible, Hitler might have read the *Meditations* of Marcus Aurelius with pleasure. Such significant theological distinctions are lost on Steigmann-Gall. But let us look and see.

"It would be better to speak of Constantine the traitor and Julian the Loyal than of Constantine the Great and Julian the Apostate."[113] For the "great ambition of the parson clique is, and always has been, to undermine the power of the State" (472).There is a direct confrontation between the Crucifier and the Crucified that, thanks to the secular Enlightenment, has been renewed and taken up afresh in National Socialism. Hitler repeatedly echoes in this vein the Enlightenment's self-serving critique of Christian intolerance. "Near Würzburg, there are villages where literally all the women were burned. We know of judges of the Court of Inquisition who gloried in having had twenty to thirty thousand 'witches' burned . . . One cannot succeed in conceiving how much cruelty, ignominy and falsehood the intrusion

---

111. Carrier, "Hitler's Table Talk: Troubling Finds." Carrier actually concedes that "Hitler did criticize priests and the Church and certain Christian dogmas quite a bit, but so do god-fearing Christians." This concession is quite enough for the purposes of this inquiry, which does not need to deny that Hitler may have in some way self-identified as a Christian or that Bormann may have tweaked the record in an anti-Christian direction. But the Nietzschean tropes suffuse Hitler's discourse vastly beyond the *Table Talks*; hence minimally the *Talks* can be used judiciously where they are corroborated by other sources. In this regard, we could turn to *Hitler's Second Book* to ground our claims about Hitler's theology or metaphysical motives, particularly in the second chapter, "Fighting, Not Industry, Secures Life" (16–28) and third, "Race, Conflict, and Power" (29–37). Ryback has an excellent discussion of this unpublished work, of which he says "Here the tone is notably measured, thoughtful, analytical. We find Hitler articulating his view on existence more thoroughly and completely than anywhere else in his published writings, speeches, or monologues. We see him seeking to stitch together his eclectic accumulated knowledge into a philosophical framework . . . " *Private Library*, 90.

112. Steigmann-Gall, *Holy Reich*, 255.

113. Trevor-Roper, ed., *Table Talk*, 193. In following paragraphs page numbers for citations from the *Table Talks* are given in parentheses.

of Christianity has spelt for this world of ours" (219). This thought recurs regularly: "Christianity promulgates its inconsistent dogmas and imposes them by force. Such a religion carries within it intolerance and persecution. It's the bloodiest conceivable" (244). "Here," says Hitler, "Christianity sets the example. What could be more fanatical, more exclusive, and more intolerant than this religion which bases everything on the love of the one and only God whom it revealed?" (298). Hitler tells his audience that he "believes in truth," that "in the long run, truth must be victorious. It's probable that, as regards religion, we are about to enter an era of tolerance . . . I shall never come personally to terms with the Christian lie . . . But I shall feel I'm in my proper place if, on some sort of Olympus, I shall be in the company of the most enlightened spirits of all times" (259). Hitler knows about and invokes the Christian persecution of the pagan philosophers and the destruction of their books in ancient Alexandria (425), and evokes nostalgia for the *convivencia* of Muslim Spain (458, 504).

Hitler spells out his claim to believe in truth by endorsing state support for untrammeled scientific research: "Research must remain free and unfettered by State restriction. The facts which it establishes represent Truth, and Truth is never evil." It was in the same talk that Hitler knowingly invoked Kant's Copernican revolution in philosophy (546). He there gives a respectable account of scientific method when he declares that "science must not take on a dogmatic air, and it must always avoid running away when faced with difficulties." This continual progress of scientific inquiry is sharply contrasted in the same discourse with "these abortions in cassocks" and their "superstitions maintained by the Church. Christianity . . . the worst of the regressions that mankind can ever have undergone . . . " On the same evening, Hitler concluded by telling how he turned away from "contemplating the grimacing face of a man crucified" and from the age of fourteen "felt liberated from the superstition that the priests used to teach . . . the miracle of the eucharist" (244–6).[114] "Reason alone must have the last word" (540). But reason is not religiously indifferent. It claims sovereignty. It arraigns itself against the lie. If "one believes that truth is the indispensable foundation, then conscience bids one intervene in the name of truth, and

---

114. "Religion draws all the profit that can be drawn from the fact that science postulates the search for, and not the certain knowledge of, the truth . . . science does not claim to know the essence of things. When science finds that it has to revise one or another notion that it had believed to be definitive, at once religion gloats . . . [but] it is in the nature of science to behave itself thus. For if it decided to assume a dogmatic air, it would itself become a church . . . True piety is the characteristic of the being who is aware of his weakness and ignorance. Whoever sees God only in the oak or in a tabernacle, instead of seeing Him everywhere, is not truly pious." Trevor-Roper, ed., *Table Talk*, 66.

exterminate the lie... Just as the pyres for heretics have been suppressed, so all these by-products of ignorance and bad faith will have to be eliminated in turn" (231).

Corresponding to his passion for truth, reason, science, enlightenment, and religious tolerance is Hitler's socialism. "I would regard it as a crime to have sacrificed the lives of German soldiers simply for the conquest of natural riches to be exploited in capitalist style" (199). National Socialism has three revolutionary objectives: first, "breaking down the partitions between classes"; second, "creating a standard of living such that poorest will be assured of a decent existence"; and third, seeing that the "benefits of civilization become common property." Certainly, this "imperils the privileges of the owning classes... for liberty, in their view, is the right of those who have power to continue to exercise it." We "can't, in fact, bridge the gap that exists between the rich and poor merely with the consolations of religion ... I certainly wouldn't choose to sing Hallelujahs until the end of time" (254). While Hitler endorses personal property and economic initiative in the name of incentivizing family growth and economic vitality, National Socialism is "distinctly opposed to property in the form of anonymous participation in societies of shareholders"—that is, capitalism—that does no other work than speculative investing, when such gains "belong by right to the nation, which alone can draw a legitimate profit from them" (274–75). Hitler ascribes to depraved Judaism "the fixing of prices... on the laws of supply and demand—factors, that is to say, which have nothing to do with the intrinsic value of an article" (283). Thus, he boasts, the success so far of the Third Reich is "due in no small measure to the fact that the State has progressively assumed more and more control... to defeat private interests and carry national interests triumphantly to their goal" (422). Socialism organizes life so that it flourishes: "Without organization—that is to say, without compulsion—and, consequently, without sacrifice on the parts of individuals, nothing can work properly. Organized life offers the spectacle of a perpetual renunciation of individuals of a part of their liberty." That leads Hitler to make note of Napoleon's greatest error, one that he himself has not repeated, when Napoleon renounced the title, "First Consul," in exchange for "Emperor." So, Hitler continues, Napoleon denied his former comrades, the Jacobins, and alienated countless "partisans who saw in him the personification of the moral resurrection that the French Revolution was to bring" (288–89). The wise leadership of organized life by the enlightened despot entails that "law is not an end in itself. Its function is to maintain public order, without which there can be neither civilization nor progress. All means used to this end are justifiable. The law must be neither harsh nor lenient. But is must adapt itself to the ends for whose benefit it has been created" (484). The reformatory principle of the Napoleonic Code could not have been better stated.

HITLER'S NOT SO STRANGE THEOLOGY

Donning, then, the Napoleonic mantle,[115] Hitler the theologian drew the consequence: no synthesis of National Socialism and Christianity would be possible,[116] since Christianity was dying away anyway (48, 191), in its final "somersaults" (254, though Hitler announced repeatedly his intention to finish it off by settling accounts with the churches after the war, 230, 260, 310, 417–19, 472). In the words of Otto Dietrich, Hitler's press chief and one of the few witnesses to his suicide, "Hitler was convinced that Christianity was outmoded and dying. He thought he could speed up its death by systematic education of German youth. Christianity would be replaced, he thought, by a new heroic, racial idea of God."[117] Thus synthesis was impossible, since Christianity unnaturally opposed the principle of natural selection, the mechanism by which life evolves and renews itself in generating new forms from the death of old ones. "The law of selection justifies this incessant struggle, by allowing the survival of the fittest. Christianity is a rebellion against natural law, a protest against nature" (41).

From this perspective Hitler sketches the contours of his new theology. "One may ask whether the disappearance of Christianity would entail the disappearance of belief in God. That is not to be desired . . . " Perhaps thinking back upon his own 1905 mountain-top experience, Hitler asks, "Why should we destroy this wonderful power . . . of incarnating the feeling for the divine that is within them?" (49). Hitler distinguishes himself this way from the Bolsheviks, who "were entitled to attack their priests, but they had no right to assail the idea of a supreme force." Bolshevik atheism is as arrogant as the superstition of the priest (68). What is needed is humility before the ineffable. "I know nothing of the Other World, and I have the honesty to admit it . . . I don't dream of imposing my philosophy on a village girl . . . The essential thing, really, is that man should know his salvation consists in the effort that each person makes to understand Providence and accept the

---

115. Hanfstaengel offered this explanation: " . . . under Goebbel's prompting [Hitler] came to appreciate the risks and restrictions which a coalition with these traditional forces would entail [under the model of Frederick the Great, Hitler's previous 'historical hero'], his allegiance subtly shifted. For this time on, Napoleon emerged more and more as his model." *Hitler*, 207.

116. Trevor-Roper, ed., *Table Talks*, 112. Citations hereafter from the *Table Talk* given in parentheses in the text.

117. Dietrich, *The Hitler I Knew*, 129.

laws of nature" (96). Providence—that is, not God in himself but God as manifest in his creative works, hence God as known by scientific insight into the principle of natural selection in the contest of life—this gives our duty and our way to salvation. "I believe that Providence gives the victory to the man who knows how to use the brains nature has given him . . . 'God helps those who help themselves!'" This struggle for life is divinely given for the best. "Providence has endowed living creatures with a limitless fecundity; but she has not put in their reach, without the need for effort on their part, all the food they need. All that is right and very proper, for it is the struggle for existence that produces the selection of the fittest" (104). In just this way, for Hitler, "It's impossible to escape the problem of God" (127). We meet it in the very struggle for survival that defines real life on the earth: the "conviction that, by obeying the voice of duty, one is working for the preservation of the species, helps one to take the gravest decisions" (104). "If I can accept a divine Commandment," Hitler adds a few evenings later, "it's this one: 'Thou shalt preserve the species'" (109).

The "appeal to the most recent results of racial research contributed much to the persuasive power of the völkisch idea. In contrast to pre-scientific views of the world, it seemed legitimated as objective knowledge."[118] So Klaus Scholder observed in his brief yet incisive chapter that located the young Adolf Hitler in the religious world of the Pan-Germans of the Thule Society.[119] "Hitler, too, entered the völkisch-religious circle of ideas when in September he joined the German Workers Party,"[120] where he came under the tutelage of the founder, Dietrich Eckhart, who considered himself to be "both a defender and renewer of Christianity."[121] Scholder finds a "remarkable testimony to Hitler's accord with religious-völkisch ideas" in the draft of a speech Hitler sketched at the age of thirty, where he affirmed the idea of race as key, and by this key would extract from the Bible what agreed with National Socialism and disgard the rest. By this device, the young Hitler was able to declare that "my Christian feelings point me to my Lord and

---

118. Scholder, *Churches and the Third Reich*, 75.

119. Ibid., 74–87. See Goodrick-Clarke, *The Occult Roots of Nazism: Secret Aryan Cults and Their Influence on Nazi Ideology*. Despite the sensationalist title, this is a sober study that finds the neo-Gnostic dualism of the Aryan cults to be "the granite foundation of Hitler's political outlook on life" (198). Similarly, Luhrssen, *Hammer of the Gods: The Thule Society and the Birth of Nazism* speaks of a "primieval gnosis" symbolized by the swastika (40). Both authors trace the active influence of Aryan occultism into the upper echelon of Nazism in Hess, Rosenberger, and Himmler.

120. Scholder, *Churches and the Third Reich*, 84.

121. Ibid., 83.

Savior as a fighter" in the battle against the perfidious Jews.[122] Where Hitler departed from these origins is only, but significantly, in his adoption of a Two Kingdoms doctrine on account of his insight that "the triumph of these ideas could not be attained through the development of a völkisch religion, but only through the organization of a political party."[123]

In an extended discussion in *Mein Kampf*, Hitler explained this apparent departure from his tutelage under Eckhart. Tactically, the focus on religion did not adequately appreciate "the importance of the social problem" and this neglect "cost it the truly militant mass of the people"; its quixotic "struggle against the Catholic Church made it impossible" to gain ground with "small and middle circles" and alienated important allies. Hence, without renouncing his *völkisch* religious convictions, which remain as the norm by which religious beliefs that are alien to the nation are to be identified, Hitler announced: "Political parties have nothing to do with religious problems as long as these are not alien to the nation, undermining the morals and ethics of the race; just as religion cannot be amalgamated with the scheming of the political parties."[124] According to Scholder, this modern version of the Two Kingdoms doctrine—the State claims the public realm, religion the domain of inwardness—consistently informed Hitler's church policy for the rest of his days, with the single exception of his intervention on behalf of Ludwig Müller's candidacy as Reich bishop (about which Hitler expresses regret in the *Table Talks*[125]). In both ways—the scientific critique of historical Christian doctrine in the religious-völkisch movement and this public/private version of the Two Kingdoms doctrine—Adolf Hitler was an exemplary modernist theologian. These theological ideas are not so strange after all. What Nietzsche celebrated as the *amor fati* from the moment of his experience of the Eternal Return, Hitler likewise embraced in his night vision as the role of Rienzi now made his own destiny, donning Napoleon's mantle. Steigmann-Gall has thoroughly misread the text on this crucial point. Hitler embraced the rationalist, watch-maker God typical of deistic (not "theistic") thought whose stern and ruthless law he discovered anew in Darwinian natural selection. In this way, Hitler renounced the God identified by biblical narrative. This too is typically "modern." Years ago when I began to lecture on this topic, I titled my presentation the "strange theology of Adolf Hitler." I have come to see, however, that his theology plays familiar chords within modernity and that it is not so strange after all.

122. Ibid., 86.
123. Ibid., 87.
124. *Mein Kampf*, 116–17.
125. Trevor-Roper, ed., *Table Talks*, 393, 507.

Chapter Five

Contested Topics in Theology

REFILTERING THE FILTER

The time has now come to try and make good on the promise of learning something for Christian theology from its wretched performance, by and large, during the rise of Nazism. To come to this, however, requires overcoming yet one final barrier that must occupy us for the next number of pages. That barrier is a cycle of acrimony within theology that was only too happy to hide itself from scrutiny beneath the presumption of vindication expressed in General Donovan's report. In reality, the outcome of the German Church struggle in the aftermath of the war was a miserable business. And this miserable mélange of blame, denial, and recrimination on all sides constitutes a convoluted filter, conscious and unconscious, through which the theological issues at stake have been and continue to be read. This filter must be refiltered before reconstruction in theology can begin.

The abstract doctrinal prejudgment among the Western allies, as we saw reflected in General Donovan's OSS report, assumed the doctrinal integrity and ethical solidity of the Confessing Church. Because of the desperate need to find new German leadership supposedly untainted by the Nazi past for the task of democratic reconstruction, and because the rapidly accelerating Cold War forced a realignment among social and political forces, the process of de-Nazification in the church was superficial.

It was even actively subverted by stellar representatives of the Confessing Church such as Martin Niemöller. As Matthew D. Hockenos puts it, "The overwhelming majority in the Confessing church wanted to rid the church of its worst German Christian elements, welcome the rest back into the fold, and end recrimination."[1] This too was Niemöller's motivation, as Heschel notes.[2] To the extent that they succeeded in the first two tasks, however, they suppressed recrimination rather than ending it. And at length it surfaced in convoluted ways. Lack of truth compounded theological confusion and the lack of reconciliation based on truth permitted selective and self-exculpating memories to prevail. Theology is in debt to historians like Ericksen, Steigmann-Gall, Bergen, and Heschel, who have reopened the matter for more searching examination, even if in some respects their work perpetuates the web of deception and self-deception.[3] In part, as we have seen, that is a matter of better history, hermeneutically more sophisticated history. But chiefly it is a matter of solving theological problems theologically. What should have been learned theologically from the failures, as from the laggard resistance, was swallowed up in a vortex of polemic and recrimination and confusion that continues, barely beneath the surface of scholarship, to the present day.

Indeed, it is not an exaggeration to say with Hockenos, as he put it in his 2004 study, that already in 1934 the resolve of the pro-Barmen Declaration Dahlemites to withhold cooperation from the Reich church under Müller created a de facto schism not only with the German Christians but that it "also caused a rupture between radicals and conservatives in the Confessing church" itself (29), the latter being "conservative Lutherans" of the "intact" regional churches in Hanover and the south. From that point on "[e]ach side adopted a different ecclesiastical course: conservatives in the intact churches concerned themselves with safe guarding their church functions and continually demonstrated a willingness to compromise with the German Christians and the state in order to achieve this; Dahlemites in the destroyed churches, many of whom had lost their positions, demonstrated a greater degree of independence . . ." (31). The "destroyed" churches refer to those regional churches where the German Christians had gained power, predominantly the large region of the old Prussian Union in contrast to the "intact" churches where the Lutheran establishment held firm against German Christian takeover.

---

1. Hockenos, *Church Divided*, 38. Hereafter page numbers for citations are given in the text in parentheses.
2. Heschel, *Aryan Jesus*, 276.
3. Ericksen, "Hiding the Nazi Past."

Hockenos's book provides a wealth of valuable information about the fallout of the de facto schism within the Confessing Church from after the war but it must be read with jaundiced eyes. In significant ways, Hockenos imposes on the conflict the by now familiar contemporary North American progressive/reactionary binary. This framing sheds heat but little light. Indeed, it perpetuates the cycle of recrimination with an account remarkably tendentious, polemical in spirit, and ultimately inconsequent. In reaction one might feel driven into the arms of Lowell C. Green's conservative apologetics. That would indeed be an unfortunate outcome, as we have seen in Chapter 2. Rather that vicious cycle of denial and recrimination and moral one-up-manship is the one that we are trying to break out of in this book, as we have affirmed repeatedly, not to excuse but to judge more precisely and truly. That would yield true progress, historically and theologically.

The conclusion toward which Hockenos polemicizes his way is that, after the war, continued "adherence to conservative Lutheran theology and traditions obstructed the process of evaluating critically the church's conservative nationalism and antisemitism . . . Rather, the new beginning [conservatives] sought meant confessing and repenting before God, restoring the established regional church authorities, renewing ecumenical ties, supporting a law-abiding conservative government, and ultimately, rechristianizing the German people" (172). The vagaries embedded in this conclusion are perplexing. On the face of it one has to wonder just what was wrong about repentance for failures under Nazism, repudiation of the Nazi-sponsored united *Reichkirche* and return to the principle of subsidiarity in regional church governance, rejection of the German Christian Sonderweg by return to the ecumenical movement, support for a new liberal democratic regime, capitalism too, in the western two-thirds of occupied Germany, and calling the German people back to Christian faith, even in its "Lutheran" iteration, after their toxic embrace of National Socialism—all this as part and parcel of coming to terms with the legacy of idolatrous nationalism and its lethal anti-Semitism. One wonders what makes this embrace of popular, not party, sovereignty, the rule of law and civil rights "conservative" in the highly charged and contemptuous way that Hockenos uses the term.

But the moral of the story for Hockenos consists in "coming to terms with the absence of a progressive political ethic" of "responsibility to both kingdoms, earthly and the spiritual" and in this way "break[ing] forever the alliance between throne and altar" (174). Thus Hockenos faults the "conservative Lutheran" Two Kingdoms doctrine in a rhetorical thunderbolt in which he fails to recognize how in the same breath he himself advocates Christian social responsibility also for the "earthly" kingdom. This, unfortunately, is typical. Inconsequence of this sort saturates his book. His concluding charge is that what was missing among the "conservative Lutherans" was the will "to examine thoroughly how the acceptance of political conservatism and orthodox Lutheran theology provided the motivation for churchmen to support many of Hitler's objectives" (176). This might pass for an arguable thesis, though not a conclusive word in demonstration, if one substituted the word, "pretext" for "motivation" in it, and if one contextualized the claim by acknowledgment of the reserve in the "orthodox Lutheran" support of Nazism in the "intact" churches in comparison to the enthusiastic embrace of it in Protestant liberalism that prevailed in the Union churches and indeed aided and abetted their "destruction," as we have seen in the preceding chapters.

A serious self-critique of the Lutheran theological tradition is indeed called for that penetrates to the contradictions embedded in its founding. I myself have written one.[4] In addition, a more searching ecumenical examination of the "anti-Judaism" that is taken for granted in the very distinction between anti-Judaism and anti-Semitism is required of theology today. But this calls for a surgeon's scalpel, not the broad axe that Hockenos cavalierly swings in sweeping jagged strokes. As it stands these words above written in conclusion amount to half-truths. One would think that there really had been no significant theological difference between the German Christians and the orthodox Lutherans, or for that matter that chastened liberal theologians did not also rally in support of postwar Western democratization, or that the postwar "political Barthianism" into which the Dahlemites evolved did not counter-rally in support of the Soviet tyranny newly imposed on the eastern third of conquered Germany. We will return to Hockenos's thesis shortly.

But it is helpful first to note by contrast how much more insightful and precise is the work of Doris Bergen, of which we took note of in Chapter 1, especially in regard to the German Christians and their postwar fate. In a concluding analysis entitled, "Amnesia, Defiance, Repentance," Bergen describes a postwar Church that evinces "a sobering degree of continuity" with the German Christian past in its conception of an anti-doctrinal people's church, even as just this postwar consensus "reveal[s] the acute challenge of genuine contrition"[5] in an anti-doctrinal people's church in which ecclesial accountability to the Christian truth claim is in principle rejected. Thus according to Bergen, in this milieu defiant and outspoken German Christians from the Nazi era were able to deny that anti-Semitism had been any part of

---

4. Hinlicky, *Paths Not Taken: Theology from Luther through Leibniz*. See also, "Staying Lutheran in the Changing Church(es)."

5. Bergen, *Twisted Cross*, 218.

Contested Topics in Theology

their own patriotic purposes. They were able to attribute Hitler's crimes to some quirk of his own tragically "divided soul" and even willing to question whether the Holocaust was factually established and not instead an exaggeration of the victorious enemy's war propaganda. In all these ways they were enabled to continue in the rhetorical staples of National Socialism. A sullen silence fell over the majority from the German Christian past. Even where there was a kind of objective acknowledgment of the role they had played in support of racial hatred in manifest contradiction to normative Christianity, it was compromised by pleas of personal innocence. All this was permitted and passed over in the name of "reconciliation." Significantly for church and theology, Bergen reports that "[m]any German Christian clergy discovered that their postwar parishioners shared their hostility or at least indifference towards the concept of right belief." These expressed dissatisfaction with the postwar church's emphasis on doctrine, attributed to the influence of Barth's neo-orthodoxy. This they described as a "defection from the Lutheran understanding of the 'church' to a pre-Constantinian 'Ghetto-' ideal of the Confessing Church." Indeed they eventually prevailed in this contention for a *Volkskirche*. Echoing the outbreak in theology of the postwar Barth-Bultmann divergence, former German Christians reclaimed their liberal Protestant heritage in a new key, asserting what they had always been seeking was a "people's church, demythologization of the gospel, and Christ alone."[6] This list, incidentally, provides a sampling of some of the controverted theological topics to be discussed in the latter half of this chapter.

Less helpfully than Bergen and in some ways even contrary to the thrust of her analysis, Robert Ericksen has made a number of reductive interventions since publication of his book, increasingly strident in tone —with the stridency in direct proportion to a seeming abandonment of his earlier caution in respect to the retrospective fallacy.[7] In his contribution to *Betrayal*, a collection of studies he co-edited with Susannah Heschel, Ericksen returned to the case of Gerhard Kittel's "unabashed" support to the bitter end of Hitler's supposedly "defensive actions" against the "menace of the Jews," a support Ericksen finds "hard to fathom," but in the end lays

---

6. Ibid., 225–26.

7. By this I mean the self-evidence with which Ericksen stands on present perspective of "what we now condemn"—as if we today were not disputing precisely about *why* we condemn what *now* appears damnable. Ericksen, "Christians in the Nazi Era: A Problematic Story" and "Emerging from the Legacy?: Protestant Churches and the Shoah" (359–82). The sleight of hand here permits Ericksen's unwarranted (recall his existential "leap") North American progressivism free rhetorical play, unexposed to rational justification as apt to the situation under historical scutiny.

rather vaguely to the feet of "the Christian tradition['s] long history of abuse of Jews and Judaism" going back to Matthew 23 and John 8.[8] The entirely vague continuity between Christian anti-Judaism and Nazi anti-Semitism thus implied so overwhelms the manifest discontinuities that Ericksen challenges the very viability of the distinction. He suspects that "insistence on the fine points of differentiation" between anti-Judaism and anti-Semitism "has primarily served an apologetic purpose."[9]

Given the gravity of the Nazi crime, Ericksen is surely right to object to apologetics when apology and self-examination are instead required. Doubtless for some, even many in the aftermath of the Holocaust the distinction has so served in whole or in part. But it may also serve other purposes. Probing its hidden assumptions may reveal inadequacies in Christian understanding that advance theological knowledge. Methodologically, as we introduced at the outset of this study, the theology of the gospel is as often subverted by it partisan defenders as it is misrepresented in the hostile attacks of open enemies. Getting to the truth of the gospel is the arduous and unfinished task of theology that has to keep learning from experience, thus also in this case. In just what ways a Christian theology which claims the legacy of the Hebrew scriptures as its own "Old Testament"—just this claim, bear in mind, is what was disputed by the German Christians—can or must be "anti-Judaic" is a difficult but pressing theological problem today. It cannot just be dissolved with the wave of a wand. From the beginning Judaism and Christianity have diverged Christologically, and thus also, ecclesiologically. That is a painful divergence at the root of things, since Judaism and Christianity alike derive the messianic motif of a renewed people of God from the scriptures of Israel. Achieving disagreement about this root divergence is exactly how after Auschwitz Jews and Christians can grow together in friendship, if not yet a common life before God that both expect at the end of days.

This divergence is a theological problem still today not least of all because, as Heschel, Bergen, Steigmann-Gall, and Ericksen have demonstrated,

---

8. Ericksen and Heschel, *Betrayal*, 36–37. Ericksen here also acknowledges that "the widely admired theological heritage of the nineteenth century" was at the very least "vulnerable to the interpretations extracted by Althaus, Hirsch, and Kittel" (38). This minimal account of liability borders on the very sin of apologetic history on behalf of contemporary "progressivism" that Ericksen rightly objects to in "conservatives."

9. Ericksen, "Emerging," 366. Apologetics gives the "impression of dissimulation and it fails to encourage a hard-edged, analytic realism upon which reassessment might take place" (376). I am in the deepest agreement with Ericksen on this point. We disagree about what kind of reassessment might take place in that he intervenes in theological debates without participating in them as a theologian (378–81), which is to say that he argues in bad faith.

Contested Topics in Theology

as a matter of historical fact the slide into Nazism did occur along the slippery slope of this putative distinction between anti-Judaism and anti-Semitism. At the same time, this slide occurred under specific theological and extra-theological circumstances, as analyzed in the previous chapters of this book. Thus these historians have opened up a problem for theology, but they have not gotten to the bottom of it, since in principle only theology can get to the bottom of a problem like this. In that case historians too are welcome to enter the disputation but here they must argue honestly as theologians or philosophers, as Jews and as Christians, and not hide behind the facade of scientific history and disinterested objectivity, emerging in lightning bolts to make piecemeal interventions that amount to moralizing pontifications. Under those conditions, the admittedly problematized distinction between anti-Judaism and anti-Semitism is and must be one of those controverted topics that falls under this chapter's agenda.

But before we tackle such topics, we need further to dismantle and reconstruct the inherited filter. A deconstruction of Hockenos's study serves this purpose, albeit painfully. Hockenos begins well where Bergen and Ericksen leave off, describing the "failure of many churchmen after the war to acknowledge the church's mistakes" in sufficiently precise and concrete ways. Especially "for the conservative Lutheran majority in the church" this failure meant, according to Hockenos, minimizing the church's "vacillation between complacency and complicity" during Nazism, all the while shamelessly advocating for the suffering post-war Germans to the neglect of the multitude of Germany's victims and their rather more massive and more innocent sufferings. All this must be conceded to Hockenos. Indeed, the truth here attested forms the starting point for the inquiry of this book.

But from here he further claims that "[f]ollowing the war these clergymen defended their conservative nationalist politics and in some cases their Christian-based antisemitism as well" (9) with the "myths of victimization, ignorance, and resistance" (10).[10] Here a truth that Ericksen and Heschel had laboriously established passes into a truism, a cliché. Hockenos in this way and throughout his book plays up the nationalism and downplays the socialism in National Socialism and its "conservative" sympathizers. Denying with an apodictic certainty any valid distinction between religious anti-Judaism and racial anti-Semitism, and assuming under the pejorative,

---

10. Hockenos, *Church Divided*, wants to demystify the Church Struggle (20–22) and see it for what it really was: "occasional critiques by a small group of churchmen against particular state policies, such as the Nazi euthanasia program and, most importantly, Nazi church policy... [C]onservatives, especially in the south German churches, showed a willingness to work alongside the more reputable churchmen in the German Christian movement" (16).

"myth," that "victimization, ignorance, and resistance" played no part in the church's behavior during the rise of Nazism, Hockenos constantly argues by means of such innuendo. As we will see, however, he cannot honestly sustain these global judgments and must constantly sneak in concessions to historical reality that on examination vitiate the force of the innuendo. This is the telling sign of a scholar who has not mastered his material but is forever forcing it into a Procrustean bed.

On the other hand, Hockenos rightly emphasizes that "at the core of the postwar debate over the past conduct of churchmen in the Third Reich were [and still are] theological issues . . . disagreements over key orthodox Lutheran doctrines: the doctrines of the two kingdoms, the law-gospel dualism, the doctrine of divine orders, and the theory of supersessionism. Churchmen were deliberating in the immediate postwar years on more than just their action or inaction in Hitler's Germany; they were coming to grips with the whole Lutheran theological and political tradition in Germany . . ." Accordingly, Hockenos "stresses the importance of theology, especially certain Lutheran tenets such as the doctrine of two kingdoms" (13). These contentions about the centrality of theology are apt, even though Hockenos takes as granted the allegation of one of the parties in the dispute about the "conservative" sense and the "Lutheran" vintage of the disputed doctrines, that is to say, as if the later Karl Barth's exasperated polemics from 1939 onward were a fair, adequate, and still useful description of the issues attending the de facto theological schism in the Confessing Church. As a result of this partisanship which begs all the questions that in fact are in dispute, Hockenos commits in the process not a few theological howlers.[11]

---

11. Hockenos's contention in *Church Divided* is that the conservative Lutherans "quite rightly perceived that the Barmen declaration challenged four of the conservative Lutherans' most sacred tenets: the law-gospel dialectic, the order of creation or divine orders, natural revelation, and the orthodox Lutheran understanding of Martin Luther's doctrine of the two kingdoms" (23), as if this laundry list formed a seamless garment. Hockenos claims that it was Barmen theses 1, 2, and 5 (!) that caused "the greatest alarm among Lutheran conservatives" (24), although this claim is not based on any exegesis of Barmen. Althaus, Elert, Gogarten, Hirsch, Asmussen, Bonhoeffer, and Sasse are lumped together as alike "conservative Lutherans," though Paul Tillich and Emil Brunner would side with them against what Bonhoeffer later called Barth's quasi-fundamentalist "positivism of revelation." At the time of Barmen, Barth was seeking Lutheran support and agreed to the introduction of the Two Kingdoms doctrine in thesis 5. At this time and later, Barth continued to find the source of the German Christian theology in nineteenth-century liberalism (25) while, in today's perspective, it is not difficult to see that his polemic against Martin Luther and his error on gospel and law is directed, not against the historical Martin Luther, but against those two who so boldly claimed his mantle, Althaus and Elert. It was much later, in 1939, that Barth "maintained that conservative Lutheranism paved the way for the paganism of the German Christians . . . 'Martin Luther's error on the relation between law and gospel . . . [which]

Be that as it may, I am accentuating here Hockenos's correct focus on the theological nature of the disputes, not his prejudicial construction of these disputes by means of innuendo by means of which he finds, or rather takes for granted, the later Barth's allegation of continuity between the "mainstream Protestant theology" of the "conservative Lutherans" and the "nationalism, antisemitism, and anticommunism at the heart of the German Christian movement..." (16). But the lamentable result of this partisanship is that Hockenos fails to recognize the real abortion that occurred in the post-war years when German church life had to be reorganized, namely, how the postwar establishment of the *Volkskirche* model could and did succeed at the expense of the Confessing Church's rediscovery of theology as public confession of the truth of the gospel. In its place these years saw a new anti-doctrinal alliance with the erstwhile German Christians returning to the Protestant liberalism from which they came, a synthesis forged by the existentialist followers of Rudolf Bultmann. These latter now laid claim to the authentic though chastened voice of Lutheranism in radicalizing the doctrine of justification as the demythologized, existentialist "decision of faith" over against the discredited over-beliefs of the Elert-Althaus Ansbach Memorandum as well as Barth's "neo-orthodoxy." But we are getting ahead of the story.

Returning then to Hockenos, it is a revealing exercise to consider the concessions he repeatedly makes in back-handed fashion to the evidence of historical reality that on examination is actually quite subversive of his thesis. Here is a somewhat eclectic but illustrative listing. We are told that even Karl Barth, his Reformed theology notwithstanding, "failed to see the link between his Christian convictions and political behavior" in 1933 (173). On the other hand, even though Niemöller in 1945 argued that the church was guilty because it should have known better, Hockenos writes, "obviously, the real blame lay with the Nazis, and the church could not have

has established, confirmed and idealized the natural paganism of the German people, instead of limiting and restraining it'" (57). Hockenos takes the claims of Elert and Althaus and their Ansbach Memorandum at face value, and does not bother himself at all with justified unease at Barmen's apodictic style and apparently Christomonistic features (26). Hockenos minimizes the evidence from Hans Asmussen's collaboration at Barmen that is contrary to his thesis (28, cf. Asmussen's drafting of the letter to Hitler in June 1936 rejecting racism and violence in the name of the First Commandment, 32). The tone of argument throughout is highly prejudicial, e.g., "But after the defeat of the Nazis, Asmussen began a transformation toward a more conservative position ... [he] believed, in good Lutheran fashion, that the church should confess its sins before God and then get on with business as usual" (48). I am second to none among Lutheran theologians willing to defend Karl Barth and to fault the likes of Althaus and Elert, but Hockenos's tendentious posturing obscures rather than illuminates any honest discussion of Barmen's strengths and weaknesses.

foreseen in 1933 or 1934 what would take place from 1941 to 1945" (68). Rather than betraying secret Lutheran nostalgia for monarchy and lingering anti-Semitism, Hans Asmussen's reasoning about the postwar reluctance to acknowledge guilt "was not because [church and theology] considered themselves entirely innocent but because they did not accept the collective guilt thesis and suspected that to admit to a degree of guilt would be understood by the Allies as acceptance of that thesis" (71). Yet another not insignificant concession reads: "Whether conservatives deliberately employed religious rhetoric to blur the church's failings or sincerely sought to address the frightful situation by interpreting it through the lens of the law-gospel dualism is difficult to determine" (72). "Conservative Lutherans acted as if they agreed with Voltaire's quip that 'God forgives sins because that is his business,'" but in reality there was "no unanimity among Lutherans, let alone Protestants, about the correct meaning of this doctrine [of justification by faith]" (73).

This latter acknowledgment of dispute over antinomianism is the crucial concession so far as theology is concerned: "[d]isagreement over whether confession and repentance were the precondition or the outcome of God's justification was central to the acrimonious debates about how to come to terms with the Nazi past" (74). Hence in regard to the Stuttgart Declaration of Guilt (presided over by that "increasingly conservative Lutheran," Asmussen), Hockenos concedes that "there is no doubt that the references to guilt by Allied representatives hindered attempts to convince Germans to take responsibility for the Nazi government that they brought to power" (83), especially when Allied guilt for the vindictive Versailles Treaty and its consequences in creating the conditions for the rise of Nazism had been conveniently forgotten on the side of the victors. Yet, Hockenos opines, Germans who reacted against the Stuttgart Declaration were "blinded by the idea that a confession would not lead to forgiveness but rather serve as justification for revenge" (88), as if this can be called "blindness" rather than a very precise memory of Versailles. Hockenos is correct in observing that the "feeling was ever present that since the Allies also committed war crimes, this fact should somehow lessen the gravity of the crimes perpetuated by Germany." But, recalling Arendt's precise judgment on Eichmann and the aforementioned dispute about justification, the proper distinction between the degrees of guilt in crime *coram hominibus* and the absoluteness of sin *coram Deo* is exactly what was (and still is) being disputed, as Hockenos's also vaguely concedes: "Confessions of guilt are hard even under the best of circumstances ... conditions in Germany in autumn 1945 were, for three reasons, highly unpropitious..."; namely, that 1) real Nazis were unrepentant, 2) that the extent of the atrocities was difficult to comprehend and

3) that Germans "naturally" prioritized their own sufferings (89). Acknowledging these three difficulties, Hockenos in fact acknowledges that there was a difference in criminal guilt between real Nazis and those in the church who in widely varying degrees were complicit in it; that there was actual confusion and ignorance regarding the radical extent of Nazi criminality; and that in their present sufferings Germans in the church reflected not least on divine retribution upon their own sins (though this final reflection does not occur to Hockenos).[12]

These concessions to reality by Hockenos come to a focus in his discussion of the postwar Dahlemite Darmstadt Statement, in which it was asserted that "dogmatic anticommunism and conservative Lutheranism had restricted the moral leadership of the church during the Nazi era and was jeopardizing the process of repentance, reconciliation, and reformation..." Here for the first time postwar "political Barthianism" articulated its own agenda and corresponding interpretation of the past in the ruins of the "destroyed" Prussian Union. It is to his credit that Hockenos reports how in the process of Darmstadt's formulation and reception, several members of the Council of the Brethren from the eastern zone, "having experience the brutality of Soviet troops in 1945," expressed "shock over the council's defense of facile Marxist political and economic theory... [and failure] to recognize that the Soviet secret police were as insidious a threat to Christianity as the Gestapo had been" (120, see also 130). Thus "a broad range of churchmen," including Asmussen and Künneth as well as the east German theologians, "subjected the radical statement to trenchant criticism for both political and theological reasons." So much to his credit Hockenos concedes to reality before the spin returns: "Intentionally or not, attention to the brutality of Soviet communism in the eastern territories had the effect of distracting attention away from Germany's wartime atrocities in eastern Europe," thus also from Darmstadt's ambition for a "fundamental transformation in the church's mission—from one of private piety and conservative nationalism to one of reconciliation, social concern, and critical engagement in the political sphere" (121). But such resort to spin turns what must be argued theologically into something that can be assumed as if it were historically evident, namely, that the political-Barthian framing of the issues in theological dispute is simply and obviously the case.

Yet Hockenos provides the rudiments of the theological debate that actually occurred, even as he reduces it to Lutheran-Calvinist confessional differences. "The roots of this theological discord were firmly embedded in

---

12. I find evidence for this in the records of German POWs who reflected that the Nazi crimes in Poland and the east would surely be avenged, e.g., Neitzel and Welzer, *Soldaten*, 162.

the centuries-old debates between Lutherans and Calvinists on the nature of salvation and the church's relation to the public sphere" (122). Hans Iwand, principle author of Darmstadt (who was the object of Barth's teasing when he called him a "Reformed Lutheran") expressed dismay at how his conservative Lutheran co-religionists "sided unabashedly with the 'Christian' West while demonizing the 'Bolshevik' East" (127). Darmstadt's third thesis, that "we have betrayed the Christian freedom which enables us and commands us to change the forms of life, when such a change is necessary for men to live together" (128), thus assigned "culpability to the church's decision to eschew the responsibility that comes with Christian freedom and instead to ally itself with conservative political forces . . . [I]n Germany since the Reformation, one heard virtually only the commandment: one must submit to the unjust political and social order'" (129). Not for a moment reflecting on the irony that Iwand in this way was now calling on German Christians in the east to submit to the political and social order of Stalinism, Hockenos tells us that the "reforms" proposed by Darmstadt "defined the church by its service to God and man—not by its confessions, offices, organizational structure, or alliance to the conservative state." One wonders how this counsel is at all different from Goebbels's disdain of theological hair-splitting in favor of "practical Christianity." But following an idea of Barth's, Iwand urged: "As disciples of Christ, the members of His church do not rule: they serve" (131). *Diakonia*, not creed and confession, is to be the sign of the church. In this Christian freedom the Christian can serve also in socialism—just as she had in National Socialism.

In response to Iwand's argument, Künneth and Asmussen said that it was a mistake to denounce "all national endeavors as precursors to National Socialism . . ." What was particularly offensive to them was the teleology, "Luther to Bismarck to Hitler," and therewith Darmstadt's devious "form of self-absolution," implying "that whoever did not share the brethren council's historical view of the church's sins and its newly formulated mission would not receive absolution" (132). The phenomenon now long since familiar in Protestant churches of publishing a ideological manifesto in the liturgical guise of a litany signaled to Künneth a real loss of theological existence: "We are standing before a theological derailment, which carries the characteristics of a new German Christian theology but from the opposite political direction" (133)—a veritable prophecy of the ostentatious Christian service that closed ranks with Stalinism in acts of humble service to build the Workers' Paradise of the GDR. This posture but amounted to a left-wing clone of the right-wing German Christianity under Hitler. It was but an equal and opposite reaction. The thesis lived on in the antithesis.

Contested Topics in Theology

Penetrating past these surface dynamics, we can indeed follow Hockenos in pinpointing the source of the theological confusion at the core Protestant doctrine of justification by faith alone, where on the one side faith is known by its public confession of Christ as Savior and Lord of sinful and oppressed humanity and on the other by the visible sight of Christ-like works of service, that is, by faith operative in its works—if that is indeed an adequate portrait of the Lutheran-Calvinist confessional difference. In my view, it is not. Indeed, that these should be pitted against one another is already the sign of a mortal illness in a body divided against itself. On these confessionalistic grounds, Asmussen wrote against Darmstadt in old Lutheran fashion: "One can go astray as a believer and still be blessed. One cannot, however, be blessed by doing good works without faith." The dispute about this, he continued, is thus "first and foremost a confessional—that is, denominational—dispute . . . [F]or Luther, [the emphasis] was on man's inward condition of faith; for Calvin, on outward signs of justification" so that "political actions reveal the grace of God working through man as signs of salvation" (133). Thus in the process of pinpointing the source of the confusion in divergent understandings of the doctrine of justification, Asmussen also contributed to the re-confessionalizing of the dispute that Darmstadt had initiated. This confessionalist overlay added but further acrimony that obscured his very insight into the source of the confusion.

Without endorsing the adequacy then of Asmussen's restatement of the Lutheran-Calvinist divergence, we may note that this turn in the debate is surely getting to the heart of the matter theologically, just as the interpretation of the doctrine of justification directly bears upon the problematic distinction between anti-Judaism and anti-Semitism going back all the way to Paul the Apostle's interpretation of the Christ-event and its ecclesial sense that all are one is Christ, no longer Greek or Jew, slave or free, married or single (Gal 3:26–28). For this reason, despite the irresponsible and misleading ways in which he frames his own discoveries, we can be grateful to Hockenos for his research. It serves to expose the theological quandaries at the heart of our inquiry in this book, even as our critique of the way in which he perpetuates the polemic allows us to refilter the filter by which the topics in dispute have been read. Given all the concessions to historical reality that Hockenos has been forced to make along the way, as pointed out above, we can now try to set aside the bitter polemical framework of mutual recrimination that has stained the postwar discussion of what Christian theology must learn from the rise of Nazism and replace innuendo with argumentation. In what follows I make succinct interventions on disputed topics that have arisen in the course of our study that point in the direction of theological reformulation in critical dogmatics after Christendom. These can only be suggestive since the problems involved are historically complex, as we have seen, and not amenable to sloganistic reductions posing as ready solutions. What follows amounts to initial proposals for new thinking about controverted topics in Christian theology in the light of those things that Christian theology has learned from the rise of Nazism.[13]

THE END OF CHRISTENDOM

Auschwitz has fundamentally changed the situation of Christian theology in Euro-America. The import of theology after Auschwitz is theology after Christendom. But the theological critique of Christendom has the integrity of antecedents within Christendom itself, as the discerning theologians during the rize of Nazism already realized.

In a chapter entitled, "The Myth of Poitiers," historian David Levering Lewis in his illuminating study, *God's Crucible: Islam and the Making of Europe, 570–1215*,[14] re-describes the famous battle at Tours/Poitiers in 732 in what is today modern France. Here Charles "the Hammer" Mantrel, grandfather of Charlemagne, united the Franks to defeat the Muslims spreading north from modern Spain in a battle that has been regarded as crucial to halting the spread of Islam by force. The event, Lewis argues, did not so much save Christian civilization as make "possible the invention of a Europe of Europeans." He points to Isidore Pacensis's "neologism" in calling the victors "Europenses for the first time," introducing "a holistic concept that transcended (definitionally, at least) the savage particularisms of his century, a meta-category to replace the lost, lamented civitas romanum."[15] Precisely as such, however, the defeat of the Muslims at Poitier is not an event, in Lewis's estimation, worthy of celebrating; echoing the speculations of Roy and Jean Deviosse about the benefits to civilization had the Muslims instead triumphed, Lewis writes that Charles's victory contributed greatly "to the creation of an economically retarded, balkanized, fratricidal Europe that, in defining itself in opposition to Islam, made virtues out of religious persecution, cultural particularism, and hereditary aristocracy."[16] Two generations later, when the Pope crowned grandson Charlemagne emperor of a new, that is, a "holy" Roman Empire, the birth of a civilizational ideal was complete. In imitative rivalry with Byzantium and in holy war

---

13. I hope to make good on these suggestions in my forthcoming systematic theology *Beloved Community*.

14. Lewis, *God's Crucible*, 160–83.

15. Ibid., 172.

16. Ibid., 174.

Contested Topics in Theology

against Islam, the new ideal would be *Imperium Christianum* or *Renovatio Romani Imperii*—the terms reciprocated to sketch "a social order within an empire . . . : a hierarchical religious institution obedient to a supreme pontiff dependent on and defended by the king of the Franks."[17] The ideal of course was rarely realized and in fact subsequent history saw repeated power contests between emperor and pope. To the extent that it succeeded, however, the domestic policy of the emergent Holy Roman Empire bore implications that still elicited the admiration centuries later of Adolf Hitler over table:[18] Charlemagne's policy of "scourging the Saxons in order to bring the benefits of faith and order . . . 'stands as a blueprint for the comprehensive and ruthless Christianization of a conquered society.'"[19] Hitler, it may be safely said, admired the ruthlessness, not the Christianization. Just so, Christendom as a political ideal had to institutionalize "difference" as "unassimilable 'otherness'" by the "exclusion of Jews and Muslims from the *societas fidelium*."[20] "Uniform, undeviating, militant Catholicism"[21] gave birth to European "unity" at the price of these external and internal political exclusions.

This ideal of Christendom is finished. Saying this is not to make an historical claim, though that would be arguable. Not even Lewis, who manifestly wishes it so, claims that. It is rather a theological one, a judgment of theological knowledge based on the study of the gospel's history in the world. It is the judgment that Dietrich Bonhoeffer argued in the subsection, "Inheritance and Decay," of his posthumously published *Ethics*: "The *corpus christianum* is resolved into its true constituents, the *corpus Christi*, and the world. In His Church Christ rules not by the sword but solely with His Word. Unity of faith exists only in obedience to the true word of Jesus Christ. But the sword is the property of the secular government, which in its own way, in the proper discharge of its office, also serves the same Jesus Christ."[22] In this succinct statement, Bonhoeffer at once repudiates yearning "for the lost western Empire, the *corpus christianum*, in which Emperor and Pope were together the defenders of the unity of the Christian west,"[23] and at the same lays claim to the proper interpretation of the Reformation's teaching of the Two Kingdoms. But this latter is Bonhoeffer's critical retrieval of

---

17. Ibid., 232–33.
18. Trevor-Roper, ed., *Table Talks*, 220, 287–88, 319.
19. Lewis, *God's Crucible*, 267.
20. Ibid., 379.
21. Ibid., 377.
22. Bonhoeffer, *Ethics*, 94–95.
23. Ibid.

Luther's meaning at the time in Europe when this inheritance of Christendom was in mortal decline.

Not to be one-sided, Bonhoeffer's judgment applies equally to the German Lutheranism so often under the microscope in this study. Reformation theology in the sixteenth century was an attempt to reform and renew Christendom,[24] as John Witte has so well exposed in his study of sixteenth-century jurisprudence.[25] Witte sees that the sixteenth-century version of the Two Kingdoms doctrine was intended to reform and renew both church and society, each in appropriate ways according to an appropriate, theologically normed distinction of temporal and spiritual power. Thus Christian engagement in society and politics is not and never was the problem of the Reformation version of the Two Kingdoms doctrine, which was informed and motivated by a heated polemic against monastic escape from the world for pursuit of personal sanctity. The problem in it is something quite different. This is the dark side to the Reformation's fusion of state paternalism, now expected to function in analogy with the beneficent reign of the heavenly Father, with the modern state's increasing monopoly on the means of coercion in a fusion that inevitably rationalized oppression and stifled dissent.

The ancient commonwealths were, in the view of Philip Melanchthon, Luther's partner in reformation, "incomplete. They can speak only to a 'civil goodness,' not to a 'spiritual goodness' . . . For none of these classical civilizations had the full biblical revelation of the heavenly kingdom on which the earthly kingdom must be partly modeled" (147). For Melanchthon's student, the reforming jurist "Eisermann, this meant that the law of the prince must coerce citizens to a 'civil goodness,' and also cultivate in them a 'spiritual goodness'" (151). "Eisermann went beyond Luther . . . in articulating the divinely imposed task of Christian magistrates to promulgate what he called 'rational positive laws' ('*rationes iuris positivi*') for the governance of the earthly kingdom" (129). Melanchthon had regarded the Christian magistrate as "the 'custodian' of both tables of the Decalogue, 'a voice of the Ten Commandments' within the earthly kingdom . . . [M]agistrates must pass laws against idolatry, blasphemy, and violations of the Sabbath — offenses that the First Table prohibits on its face. Magistrates are also, however, to pass laws to 'establish pure doctrine' and right liturgy, 'to prohibit all wrong doctrine,' 'to punish the obstinate,' and to root out the heathen and the heterodox" (131). Witte rightly notes that "Melanchthon's move toward

---

24. Hendrix, *Recultivating the Vineyard*, 37–68.

25. Witte, *Law and Protestantism*. All subsequent page citations given in the text by parentheses. This paragraph is drawn from the author's review of Witte's book in in *Sixteenth Century Journal*.

the establishment of religion by positive law was a marked departure from Luther's original teaching ..." (131) on the freedom of faith and conscience as implications of the gospel and its theology. The *cuius regio, eius religio* ("whoever the ruler, his religion") principle of the 1555 Peace of Augsburg and at length of "the Peace of Westphalia" (1648), rested ultimately on Melanchthon's theory that "the magistrate's positive law was to be guided by the First Table of the Decalogue to establish for the people proper Christian doctrine, liturgy, and spiritual morality" (132).

Thus, in theory, the Lutheran state "has a role to play not only in fighting wars, punishing crime, and keeping peace, but also in providing education and welfare, fostering charity and morality, facilitating worship and piety ... [L]aw has not only a basic use of coercing citizens to accept a morality of duty but also a higher use of inducing citizens to pursue a morality of aspiration" (296). Education and welfare, charity and morality, worship and piety form a seamless whole, a socially cohesive force that cannot be dissected with parts removed without killing the organism, the reformed *corpus christianum*. Just so, deviation is not tolerable. Heresy undoes cohesion. Consequently modern "Germany and other Protestant nations have been locked in a bitter legal struggle to eradicate state establishments of religion and to guarantee religious freedom for all ..." (303). Liberal individualism, tolerance, and the separation of church and state may be born on the Christian soil of Protestantism, but they signal the end of Christendom in the death throes of its own internal contradictions—ironically, the contradiction that Luther first discovered in arguing that genuine Christian faith must be free and cannot in principle be compelled. It is impossible to sustain the model of Christendom, when the state, as informed by the Decalogue and its official interpreters, the theologians, cannot actively shape the ethical aspiration of the nation, but must assume an official posture of neutrality towards the multitude of competing aspirations and visions of the good, as modern liberal democratic pluralism requires. That this liberalism brings its own set of endemic problems is true, but for the moment beside the point (see the Conclusion to this book).

Whatever else Adolf Hitler accomplished at Auschwitz, his unprecedented violence kicked the tottering model of Christendom to the ground and broke it to pieces that cannot be put back together again. (It is not so clear, however, the Hitler's violence has brought an equal recognition of the contradictions embedded in *imperium* and political sovereignty that beset triumphant secularism-cum-capitalism). Contrary to its own pretensions, on which the privileging of Christianity was based (in the teaching office, be it Catholic pope or Protestant theological faculty), Christendom was able effectively neither to recognize nor oppose Hitler's evil but was inevitably in institutional symbiosis with it, as Max Horkheimer acutely observed at the time.[26] On the contrary, in its decay this inheritance provided a habitat in which Hitler could hatch his dream of superseding Christendom just as Christianity claimed to have superseded Judaism (as Heschel so acutely observed). In the end, moreover, his Third Reich was defeated militarily by an alliance of secular powers whose only unity was the unity Hitler himself fantasized in ascribing both liberal capitalism and Bolshevism to a world-wide Jewish conspiracy. The massive crime of the Holocaust ever since forces recognition of the Achilles's heel in the Christendom model, the injurious social stigmatizing of others that is inevitable when the social cohesion necessary for political functionality is subjected to a creedal test. Theologically, Christendom was not capable of recognizing or resisting Nazism because the concept of Christendom embodies a theological category confusion. The adjective, Christian, cannot modify an ethnic group or a state apparatus or even a cultural tradition; it can only modify an assembly gathered freely around the gospel's word and sacraments in the gospel's own mission of address to the nations. Nor may this truly Christian assembly proclaim itself the fulfilled Reign of God. Rather the gospel it bears to the nations in mission is the promise of that coming of God's Reign and its reality already now only in the paradoxical forms of repentance and faith, wherever and whenever this promise take form socially as belief in God's just and loving purpose for all. What replaces Christendom socially, then,

---

26. If I may cite from Adkins and Hinlicky, *Rethinking Philosophy and Theology with Deleuze*: Horkheimer argued that "even under Fascist persecution the churches" would not "regain once again the vital reality" that once was theirs. The reason he gave for this bitter judgment is that the churches simply cannot any longer give up their parasitical relationship to the state, even at the humiliating cost of theological bankruptcy manifest when the bureaucracy of the "authoritarian state" takes over and "reorganizes the old ideological apparatus in which the church had its share." Referring to the Nazi policy of *Gleichschaltung* (the "coordination" of institutions with the Nazi worldview), Horkheimer aptly observed that even though this traitorous accommodation of the community of the gospel to the Nazis state "involves hardship[,] the church must eventually see that its own social position depends on the continued existence of the basic traits of the present system." If that system were to change, "the church would lose all and gain nothing." For the church's position entirely depended on "the belief that absolute justice is not simply a projection of men's minds but a real eternal power." Yet no one any longer holds that belief as true, even if not especially in the churches. If it were held as true in the churches, dependence on the state would be expendable as in fact was once believed in this particular church: "Take they goods, fame, fortune, child or spouse, they yet have nothing won. The kingdom ours remaineth." But the church today only pretends to hold such a belief, that is to say, holds it "as if" it were true, ideologically then, for the purpose of securing and influencing the real political power of the sovereign state. By exchanging its former belief in God's coming reign for transcendent and intangible "values," the church "survives" in its new role as an obedient chaplaincy of the sovereign state, be it fascist or liberal or communist or whatever (182–83).

is the Beloved Community, of which Martin Luther King, Jr. spoke so eloquently[27] and for which he died at a critical juncture of American history, when awareness of the contradictions between its popular Christendom assumptions and its brutal social reality could no longer be suppressed. It is in this social space, the Beloved Community, moreover, that Jews and Christians may yet meet in friendship before the same God whom differently they acknowledge. That precarious prospect is the Pauline hope against hope of Christian theology after the end of Christendom.

THE PROBLEMATIC DISTINCTION BETWEEN ANTI-JUDAISM AND ANTI-SEMITISM

The hidden assumption in this problematic distinction is that Christian theology must be against Judaism without differentiation. Antinomian interpretations of justification by faith are guilty of a categorical and unjust stigmatization of Judaism as legalism. Justification by faith can only be rightly understood when it upholds the law, entrusted to Judaism as light to the nations, albeit in a new Christological key. This Christological key, furthermore, must account for the divergence between Christianity and Judaism without stigmatizing Jewish unbelief or questioning God's irrevocable calling of his ancient people, Israel. It must rather take Jewish unbelief in Jesus as the Messiah as a principle internal to its own theology.[28]

Susannah Heschel's indictment of German Protestants after the war includes a weighty criticism of this problematic distinction. "The sharp division made by most historians, theologians, church officials and scholars of religion between Christian theological anti-Judaism and modern racial anti-semitism has fostered the postwar myth that theologians did not contribute to the Nazi murder of the Jews, and also the widespread notion, common among Jewish theologians as well, that Nazism represent an anti-Christian pagan revival movement."[29] It is certainly true that European history, where the political ideal of Christendom had to make second-class subjects out of religious others, notably Jews, and where biblical calumny against the Jews could and did foster their demonization in the popular imagination, is a necessary though not a sufficient condition of the Nazi mass murder. The Holocaust did not happen on the soil of just any culture but on one claimed as "Christianized." On the other hand, however, the Holocaust did

---

27. *Beloved Community*, 348–54.
28. Following Moltmann, *The Way of Jesus Christ*, 28–37.
29. Heschel, *Aryan Jesus*, 286.

not happen on every such "Christianized" soil, but on a specific one under specific circumstances. We have noted how some traditional Christians on this same soil, in the name of normative Christianity even with its traditional anti-Judaism nevertheless discerned theologically the evil of anti-Semitism and in varying ways resisted it. To account for this difference, and develop it properly, we need some such distinction, then, so important for any kind of immanent criticism of Christian theological failure in relation to the Jewish question.

It is also true that it is misleading to think of Nazism as essentially a pagan revival, as that is usually thought in terms of Rosenberger's and Himmler's endeavors in Wagnerian remythologizing following the lead of the Pan-Germans and the Thule Society. Hitler, as we have seen, shared the latter background but utilized a thoroughly modern version of the Two Kingdoms dualism both to suppress any kind of religious interference with the scientifically guided public policies of National Socialism and to delay further development of a Nazified public theology to his victorious postwar retirement. Yet the "pagan" connection is not so misleading from another angle. As we saw in the previous chapter, "repaganization" can represent a retrieval of ancient Greco-Roman imperialism as championed by the epigones of the European Enlightenment and modeled in Napoleon, the first of Europe's modern military dictators wanting to drive the people to happiness with an iron fist. In this respect it can be viewed as another, perhaps culminating chapter of the rivalry between pope and emperor in the context of Christendom's unstable synthesis. In this connection, moreover, we learned from Heschel's study, as she put it, that certain Christian theologians "considered racial theory a tool to grant scientific legitimation to religion."[30] It was precisely those theologians—not "ironically," as Ericksen would have it,[31] but quite fittingly and precisely just those—who embraced National Socialism as the brilliant and progressive way forward between the Scylla of savage capitalism and the Charybdis of bloody Bolshevism in building the Kingdom of God on earth—the society in which the separated existence of the church would cease, but as *Volkskirche* would be absorbed by the perfected *Volkswerdung*.

---

30. Heschel, *Aryan Jesus*, 286.

31. It was not so much the theological "conservatives" but "ironically those Protestants most attuned to the problems of the poor—and to the questions of Christian ethics—[that] proved to be among the most likely to greet Hitler and National Socialism enthusiastically." Ericksen, "Emerging," 371–72. This is only "ironic" on the false supposition that Nazis and their sympathizers did not see themselves as modern, revolutionary, progressive, and socialist.

The slippery slope argument that Heschel implies here is to be sure logically fallacious. It does not follow that a distinction like that between anti-Judaism and anti-Semitism, being employed in a certain way with nefarious results, invalidates the distinction itself. It is another argument to say that the distinction is problematic, unclear, open as such to nefarious abuses. The latter is the argument I now propose. If it were simply so, however, that the very distinction must lead to or has to contribute to Nazism, we would, contrary to hypothesis, have no way to account for Christian resistance to Nazism and defense of Jews at personal risk, precisely on traditional Christian theological grounds, such as actually occurred in "Lutheran" places like Denmark, Norway, and among Osuský's Slovaks, not to mention those genuine theological Lutherans outspoken during the rise of Nazism in Germany, such as Asmussen, Künneth, Bonhoeffer, and Sasse. It is an old, tried and true axiom: *abusus non tollit usum*. History, on the other hand, does not often abide the rules of logic and Heschel has established the historical fact that the distinction between religious anti-Judaism and allegedly scientific anti-Semitism was and is used to obfuscate Christian complicity in Nazism and thus moral responsibility for the Holocaust. Thus we have little choice but to probe further. To be sure, in probing theologically the problem of the distinction between anti-Judaism and anti-Semitism, we enter a minefield.

Hockenos's discussion provides an entree. He reliably voices a present-day "progressive" consensus: "To conceptualize Christian-Jewish relations as a 'Jewish question' or 'problem' is no longer acceptable" (135), though as we have seen in Chapter 3 the so-called "Jewish Question" is a political question that arose with emancipation and the nineteenth century's discovery of an ethnic right of self-determination. In just this fashion it was asked and answered also by Jews. Indeed, the rise of Zionism and the postwar establishment of the State of Israel are inconceivable except as a Jewish answer to the Jewish question (not least in defense against the Nazi attempt to answer it once and for all in quite a different way). More deeply, just as there is a Christian question about the place in this world of the pilgrim people gathered from the nations wherein they have no permanent dwelling, there is also and indeed in the first place theologically a Jewish question about the offspring of Abraham blessed in order to be a blessing to all the peoples.

Yet Hockenos denounces the 1948 statement of the "progressive" Dahlemite Council of Brethren "to renounce the church's antisemitism while reaffirming its traditional anti-Judaism" as contradictory and reinforcing of the myth of supersessionism (136). One wonders about the pejorative, "myth," here. If it means a falsehood that has been believed with injurious results, then on what grounds is the falsehood known as false? By what truth is this falsehood deemed false? The same question arises in the following claim. "The realization that the church's widely accepted anti-Judaic myths provided fertile ground for the growth of antisemitism in nineteenth- and twentieth-century Germany culminated in the repudiation of supersessionism by the churchmen at the EKD's Berlin-Weissensee synod in April, 1950" (137). This statement is no less tendentious than the previous.

It is one thing to demand a surrender of the Christian claim to truth on the grounds of other claims to truth that are found superior. That today is entirely legitimate and politically protected disbelief. Following Luther's disturbing for his times discovery (disturbing also for Luther!) that Christian faith must be free over against Christendom's attempt to enforce faith in legal symbiosis with the state, today theology in Luther's tradition acknowledges in principle, for example in Pannenberg, that the Christian claim can be disputed. Indeed it welcomes that disputation as its very vocation. In a context of freedom no one, least of all Christian theologians who know that faith is faith and its claim to truth disputable, could or would repudiate that possibility.[32] Indeed, politically, for the sake of the integrity of faith as faith (as also in Vatican II's *Dignitatis Humanae*), such theologians would be bound to support freedom of conscience, freedom of assembly, freedom of speech, and freedom of religious exercise in the context of civil society, including the multitude of ways in which the Christian claim to truth can be disbelieved.

It is quite another thing, however, to reject supersessionism as false teaching by the standard of the Christian claim to truth, as self-critical theology today should do and must learn to do on the basis of what it has learned from the rise of Nazism. That is a matter of theology as the ongoing and unfinished work for the truth of the gospel and its rule (Gal 6:16) in the domain of those called out and assembled by that gospel's mission to the nations. In Hockenos, as in Ericksen, it is never made clear which of these demands is being made in this connection. Indeed this clarification cannot be made when one simplistically denounces the Two Kingdoms distinction between temporal and eternal powers in itself and as such. To this degree, Green is right: one-kingdom theologies whether of the left or of the right end in theocratic politics not fit for life between the ages.

---

32. On the important idea of the disputablity of Christian truth as a principle internal to Christian theology, see Pannenberg, *Systematic Theology*, I: 8–17. I should note here for what follows that the term, "disputation," may have unsavory resonances for some Jews, recalling the Inquisition's staged "disputations with the Jews." As I am critiquing the very model of Christendom in which the Inquisition was lodged, I am simultaneously transferring the process of disputation from that staging to the open-ended processes of dialogue and debate in critical pluralism as theoretically explored by Vilhauer and others.

There are good grounds in Pauline theology for rejecting supersessionism, as Wolfhart Pannenberg had superbly argued,[33] grounds that are made compelling when reinforced by the experience of the Confessing Church. But this entails as a consequence something that Pannenberg does not, perhaps, fully grasp: the finish of Christendom as a political ideal, its theological finish as an experiment in Christianity judged by God as finally a perversion of the gospel because it forces faith, however subtly, by the power of the sword that the modern state holds by monopoly. The fleshpots of Christendom are not any longer to be hankered after theologically and Christian theology in the future needs to turn a spotlight on the ambiguities, not to say contradictions, in the secular ideals of *imperium* and political sovereignty, as these were defined for modernity by Hobbes and Spinoza.[34]

Though Hockenos is utterly innocent of such considerations, he once again slips in through the back door a series of important concessions to historical reality in this regard. Consider for example the complication that it was German missionaries to the Jews who maintained against the German Christians that "'race' was no reason to exclude [Jews] from conversion to Christianity; not to preach the gospel to Jews would be a sign of antisemitism since it suggested that Jews were undesirable in the church for racial reasons." Supersessionism, in this light, is not so simple a matter as the slippery slope imagines. In one significant iteration it can intend the unity of Jew and Gentile in Christ, as in the deutero-Pauline letters to the Colossians and the Ephesians, although in others it can reactualize the invective that occurs in Matthew 23 and or the demonization that occurs in John 8. But this for Hockenos is mere quibbling, "because [mission] is an attempt to rid the world of Jews, albeit by nonviolent means" (139). Of course, it is also an attempt to rid the world of pagans or any other pre-existing subjectivities that do not conform, as Bonhoeffer put it, to the cross and resurrection of Christ.[35] With typical self-confidence, Hockenos concludes: "Of course, the church's antipathy toward Jews was a consequence of both its anti-Judaism and its antisemitism" (169)—and with just as typical inconsequence perpetuates the very distinction that he thinks himself to have crushed with bombast.

Hockenos, for all his proper attention to theology, is demanding the global surrender of any Christian claim to truth as something manifestly

33. Pannenberg, *Systematic Theology*, III: 470–77.

34. On this claim, see Hinlicky, "The Reception of Luther in Pietism and the Enlightenment."

35. " . . . formation comes only by being drawn into the form of Jesus Christ. It comes only as formation in His likeness, as conformation with the unique form of Him who was made man, was crucified, and rose again." Bonhoeffer, *Ethics*, 80.

refuted by history (as Ericksen at times implies[36]), *though at the equal cost, too little noted in discussions of this problematic distinction, also of Judaism's claim to truth,* and hence of its honest hearing as a principle *internal to Christian theology*. In other words, the reduction of anti-Judaism to anti-Semitism reduces therewith also Judaism from the people chosen of God for blessing to all to merely a people alongside others with an equal claim to nationalistic self-determination, thus no longer the bearer of that special vocation, the yoke of the Torah with its claim to truth, in distinction from all other peoples. The cost of this homogenizing move at the hands of contemporary secularism is that Christian theology never after has to hear living Judaism's dispute with its claim to truth, the one that in truth comes on solid scriptural and messianic grounds. That disputation consists in attesting the sad fact that the world remains in sorrow and unredeemed, such that one crucified cannot be the expected Messiah, but at best just another of the world's righteous waiting in the grave for true Messiah's coming to bring his redemption along with all the righteous. The fundamental disputability of the Christian gospel is first and foremost and with continuing force attested by this original and abiding Jewish disbelief in it. Just so this disbelief is and remains essential to authentic Christian self-understanding of faith as faith. Without it the passage from faith to triumphalism is well nigh irresistible.

Thus the problem of the distinction between anti-Judaism and anti-Semitism is far more precise than progressivism either sees or allows. Heschel is closer to the truth when she notes how it was the new "scientific" racism, congenial to the modernizing project of the Protestant progressives in general, that catalyzed the fateful transition from theological dispute to final solution. If traditional Christian anti-Judaism was a necessary precondition of the Holocaust, the modernizing project in theology was its sufficient condition. Just this resistance to modernizing kept the "conservative Lutherans" from jumping on the German Christian bandwagon to complete the transition from anti-Judaism to anti-Semitism. Neither stance of course is satisfactory, but just this much must be firmly grasped before new progress on the problematic distinction is theologically possible. As just indicated, progress in theology in part consists in making the original Jewish disbelief in the gospel a principle internal to the gospel's own theology so that faith in it remains faith and does not pass into triumphalist self-confidence in place of the personally risky self-venturing after the One who came not to be served but to serve, trusting in God's ultimate vindication—the faith that is obedience, as Bonhoeffer insisted, and the obedience that is faith. But progress here will also consist in questioning an assumption embedded in the

---

36. Ericksen, "Emerging," 360.

problematic distinction, namely, that it is essentially the case that Christian theology must be and forever remain categorically anti-Judaic. The difficult and ever-recurring disputes within Christian theology about antinomianism reflect this nearly universal but very much still unclarified operating assumption about what is, and what is not, preserved in Christianity from its Jewish matrix and why. That immediately touches as well on the contending interpretations, especially within Protestant theological traditions, of the core doctrine of justification by faith alone. Seen in this perspective, there is a veritable mountain of work awaiting penetrating insight that actually moves these old disputes forward.[37]

By the same token, then, a principled theological discussion of the matter opens up the volatile question to what extent Zionism too is a form of modern völkisch thought that wanted and wants to fight fire with fire in the contest of the nations for *Lebensraum*. This is a topic painfully but unavoidably connected with the present questioning of the problematic distinction between anti-Judaism and anti-Semitism. It is the double-sided problem of Zionism and the Christian theology of Israel. I would refer the reader to the exemplary discussion of the issues here by Rikk Watts that could constitute a starting point for further work.[38] For the rest, let me make plain that I do not raise this problem for theological inquiry to question the legitimacy of the State of Israel. But rather I introduce this problem from within a political stance of solidarity with embattled Israel, there to ask in all humility as a separated brother about the true, that is, about the theological nature of Israel's Jewishness, namely, the calling in her very election to be blessing to all the nations of the earth. This is not merely an outsider's question. John the Baptist was not a Christian, but Jew among other Jews. He speaks within Israel when he says, "Do not begin to say to yourselves, 'We have Abraham as our ancestor'; for I tell you, God is able from these stones to raise up children of Abraham. But bear fruits worthy of repentance" (Luke 3:8, word order altered). Prophetic Judaism's gift to the world is this demand in God's name for self-criticism (cf. Amos 3:2). In asking this question, I would honor that gift.

I do not presume to have answers to the question that I raise. It is an honest question addressed to Jewish theologians in order better to inform the Christian theology of Israel. I would thus raise this question in dialogue

---

37. After the inconclusive debates of the past several decades about the "new perspective on Paul" (see *Beloved Community*, 221–57), I would point to Westerholm, *Perspectives Old And New on Paul* as affording a fresh start.

38. Watts, "Israel and Salvation." See also Jenson and Korn, *Covenant and Hope* and especially Gerald McDermott's contribution in it, which takes up Watt's discussion as a starting point but qualifies his understanding of supersessionism.

with theologians of living Judaism,[39] in order to reclaim the prophetic and messianic heritage of the Hebrew scriptures first of all for Christians situated today in the ruins of the profoundly flawed but now dying and dead political model going back to Charlemagne. Jews know painfully the failure of this model from the inside, so to say, and in face to face dialogue with them Christian theologians can and must still be sensitized to the historical legacy they consciously or unconsciously inherit through their own tradition. These motives have nothing to do with blindly defending the behavior or thinking of Christians under Nazism, but rather of judging their behavior precisely in order to learn from a culminating episode where in fact the gospel as normatively understood was "betrayed"—the trope employed by Ericksen and Heschel that unconsciously but with poetic justice casts these German Christians but also their conservative Lutheran fellow-travelers in the narrative role of Judas Iscariot, who betrayed his Lord with a kiss. On the basis of this kind of Christian self-critique, Jewish-Christian theological dialogue bears in the very act far reaching implications for embracing the genuine and critical pluralism of these times before the Kingdom's coming, a challenge Christians and Jews share and best face prayerfully together.

MISSION TO THE NATIONS AND THE CONSTRUCTION OF RACE

The end of Christendom in the theological recognition of the disputability of the Christian claim to truth demands reconstruction of Christianity from its present debased state as chaplaincy to political sovereignty (as Volkskirche) to its true being in the missionary act of the Son in the Spirit to the nations as sent by the Father for the world's salvation. The communion so drawn from the nations is the harbinger of the coming in fullness of the Beloved Community that is from all eternity and to all eternity the blessed life of the Holy Trinity.

So repulsive today is the notion of *Volk* as an order of creation, as that was theologically endorsed and developed especially by Paul Althaus in seeking a point of contact with rising Nazism, that a genuine and important theological issue that is embedded in this topic is hardly recognized any longer. John Flett incisively retrieves this issue in express criticism of the employment of the concept of *Volk* by German missiologists during the time of the rise of Nazism in his post-Christendom missiological treatise,

---

39. Following the initiative of theologians Novak, *Jewish-Christian Dialogue* and more recently, Ochs, *Another Reformation*.

The Witness of God.[40] His thesis is that proper contextualization of theology and also proper indigenization of the gospel freely and creatively take place by the Spirit through the Word whenever and wherever the church's being is found strictly in its participation in the mission of the Triune God to the nations. The tendency in Althaus's doctrine of the *Völker* (the peoples) moves in a quite different direction than Flett's, who is dependent on Barth's mature theology. But Althaus, as Nathan Yoder has clarified, is guilty, though not quite precisely guilty as Ericksen charged, of appropriating racial theory and Social Darwinism to an extent that gives "tacit approval of the racial discrimination policies of the Third Reich,"[41] even though, as we have seen, the Ansbach Memorandum and the Erlangen faculty opinion openly crossed this line.

The grounds for claiming this subtle clarification on behalf of Althaus by Yoder are that, despite inconsistencies and the notorious transgressions just mentioned, Althaus does not simply equate God's present and active ordering of peoples with a fixed, "natural," biological-genetic or racial status, as he shows by citing Althaus's words even from the 1933 treatise, *The German Hour of the Church*: "Race is a natural, *Volk* a natural/historical term."[42] The distinction, in the context of the time of the rise of Nazism imperceptive and overly subtle, is that God's creative orderings of peoples is "more than nature—they are historical in character and demand active human involvement" to form human community in ever new ways in the dynamism of historical processes, albeit on the assumption of abiding natural regularities.[43] The consequence is that for Althaus, taken at his best, "Race remains passive and superficial, and therefore by no means constitutes a form of community"[44] To say otherwise, according to Yoder, "is unjustly to oversimplify facts, to conflate original ideas with their subsequent distortions, to gloss over significant subtleties and embrace half-truths"—a litany of scholarly sins, as we have seen throughout this book, that attends our volatile subject on all sides.[45]

The point in this, however, is not at all to come to Althaus's personal or professional defense, but to show how superficial theologically is the indictment of the "orders of creation" doctrine and its expansion to include the

---

40. Flett, *The Witness of God*. Subsequent references are provided parenthetically within the text.

41. Yoder, "Ordnung in Gemeinschaft," 132.

42. Ibid., 134.

43. Ibid.

44. Ibid., 135.

45. Ibid.

historical dynamics of ethnicity as a culture process mediated by tradition passed on in a particular language. We have not gotten to the bottom of the problem when we condemn *Ordnungentheologie* but in the same breath demand contextualization and indigenization in mission theology, moves that presuppose the very things theologically affirmed in *Ordnungentheologie*. Gaining the latter contextualization is actually the very motive of theologically attending to the existing cultural forms in family life, economy, religion and politics by which the Creator, before ever sending his Son in the Spirit through the mission of the gospel, already is forming nations and thus preparing for them to hear the gospel. That is why in principle missiologists were so interested in *Ordnungentheologie* and its recent, creative expansion by Althaus to include the historical and dynamic category of *Volk*. Seeing the theological issue embedded here, rather than merely indulging in the conventional bromide about "cultural conservativism," is why Flett's contribution will prove to be the one that advances the argument, rather than merely repeats sterile, shallow, and inconsequent reductions on all sides.

But it helps first to call upon the work of another scholar, Colin Kidd, whose *The Forging of Races: Race and Scripture in the Protestant Atlantic World, 1600–2000* helpfully locates the modern emergence of the category of race in "the eclipse of biblical narrative" (Hans Frei). "Race," writes Kidd, "was not a central organizing concept of intellectual life or political culture during the early modern period," not at all before that, but rapidly became one in the course of the nineteenth century.[46] The relevance of this observation is that, because Israel has always existed as the physical descendants of Abraham as signaled by rite of circumcision, it has always also existed as the Jewish people, separated from other peoples by the sign of circumcision and the keeping of kosher. As such a people, Jews were always also the potential object of the range of ethnic animosities and tribal conflicts of which human history is full. All the same, however, this existence as a separated people was rarely viewed in racial terms, in that "race" as a concept awaits modern notions of genetic pools interacting by natural selection with particular environments, the Nazis' *Blut und Boden*. The term, anti-Semitism, is thus of nineteenth-century coinage, invented to transcend merely religious anti-Judaism and garden-variety ethnic rivalry and to achieve racial hostility in the framework of the war of life-forms for survival and mastery on a shrinking and stingy earth. Indeed, there is an interesting story in this connection about the very terminology of "Semite," as we shall shortly see.

---

46. Kidd, *Forging*, 54. The following paragraphs are drawn from the author's review in *Sixteenth Century Journal*.

How we get from anti-Judaism to anti-Semitism in the course of modern Western history, then, is not a simple story that runs in a straight line. Religiously, the Christian Bible—which appropriates the Hebrew scriptures as its own Old Testament, is monogenetic, not polygenetic, i.e., it traces all the families of the earth to one origin in the legendary Adam and Eve (Gen 1–3). As Paul the Apostle purportedly preaches to an assembly of Greek philosophers at the Areopagus in Athens: "The God who made the world and everything in it, he who is Lord of heaven and earth . . . gives to all mortals life and breath and all things. From one ancestor he made all nations to inhabit the whole earth, and he allotted the times of their existence and the boundaries of the places where they would live, so that they would search for God and perhaps grope for him and find him—though indeed he is not far from each one of us. For 'In him we live and move and have our being'; as even some of your own poets have said, 'For we too are his offspring'" (Acts 17:24–28). Though we should note that Apartheid theologians in South Africa[47] could grasp at the straw in this text about God establishing "the boundaries of the places where they would live," Colin Kidd has rightly hypothesized that biblical monogenism militates against any kind of serious racialism, so that it is only "with the dethronement of scripture from its dominant position in western intellectual life following the Enlightenment" that ideological space opened up "for the uninhibited articulation of racialist sentiments."[48]

Prior to the scientific victory of Darwinian biology the monogenetic biblical theology, especially of Protestantism in both Europe and America, had to teach that skin color could only be skin-deep, since all had descended from Adam, all were in bondage to his fall into sin and equally in need of the Redeemer, who in the fullness of time had assumed not white, or black, or Greek or Jewish nature, but Adam's human nature. As Kidd points out, the whole theological structure of Protestant biblical theology turned upon this unity of the human race, unity in sin and unity of redemption. Against this presumption in Protestant Biblicism, Kidd shows us in figures like Voltaire and Hume how the "Enlightenment incubated both naturalistic theories of racial degeneracy from a white norm and polygenist theories of multiple, separate origins for the races of mankind."[49] In the first case, a new interpretation of scripture came about in tandem with the Atlantic slave trade to account especially for African blackness as "degenerated from a white norm."

---

47. I am indebted to Sarah Hinlicky Wilson for this tidbit, who learned it from her South African professor at Princeton Theological Seminary, Dr. Wentzel van Huyssteen.

48. Kidd, *Forging*, 19.

49. Ibid., 82.

According to the Book of Genesis, the human race was destroyed in a universal flood, from which only Noah and his three sons, Ham, Shem, and Japeth survived to repopulate the earth. A peculiar incident occurred after they disembarked the ark. Noah makes wine and gets intoxicated. His son Ham sees his father naked and drunk and in this way shames him. The text of Genesis 9:24–27 continues: "When Noah awoke from his wine and knew what his youngest son had done to him, he said, "Cursed be Canaan; lowest of slaves shall he be to his brothers." He also said, "Blessed by the LORD my God be Shem; and let Canaan be his slave. May God make space for Japheth, and let him live in the tents of Shem; and let Canaan be his slave." Degeneracists seized upon this obscure passage to claim that Ham turned black under the curse and so was designated by God for slavery; Shem (=Semites) would go on to father the Jews, while Japeth, destined for world mastery, would be the one to preserve the original white race from Adam. As influential as this racial exegesis came to be in rationalizing the slave trade, Kidd firmly locates it in the broader historical development of one Enlightenment tendency (quoting Fredrickson): "'to achieve full potential as an ideology, racism had to be emancipated from Christian universalism.'"[50] The Ham, Shem, and Japeth theory of race diversity is a halfway step in this trajectory, as we recall how the Enlightenment was not only a critique of Christendom but also a rationale for neo-pagan imperialism in its place.

Of course, as Kidd hastens to qualify, "the Enlightenment" is not one thing. In fact, it largely took place "within churches" and at its best "aimed not so much to make the world anew [i.e., into "races"] as to effect a reconciliation between the best of the new philosophy [of nature] and the core truths of Christianity."[51] But polygenism was not so easily reconcilable. In the words of Lord Kames: "Empirical evidence drawn from geography and biology seemed to indicate that God created many pairs of the human race, differing from each other both externally and internally; that he fitted those pairs for different climates, and placed each pair in its proper climate; that the peculiarities of the original pairs were preserved entire in their descendants."[52] This foreshadows the Nazi doctrine of *Blut und Boden*. It taught, as Kame saw, "a different lesson" than the book of Genesis. Kidd is cautious in his conclusions. But to the extent that theological liberals sought to deliteralize the reading of scripture to accommodate the rising natural science by insisting that "Judaic legends are not binding on our faith," science became the constant and scripture the variable—though the protest

50. Ibid.
51. Ibid., 83.
52. Ibid., 97.

Contested Topics in Theology

against scripture's traditional canonical-doctrinal authority was packaged and sold by way of an anti-Judaic smear. In this the way was prepared by "an enlightened critique of scripture" for "the rise of modern racialist doctrine."[53]

What causes Kidd to qualify this conclusion is the vulnerability of the Bible to reappropriation, as we saw in the new interpretation made of Noah and his sons. "Racists, it seems, will reach for any tool, including the Bible, to justify racial segregation or subordination. By the same token, certain passages of the Bible have provided not only reassurance but also inspiration for racists."[54] Theologically put, Kidd's insight here is that there is never any such thing as the "Bible alone," i.e., an uninterpreted or unappropriated Bible as Protestant primitivism contends. The monogenist reading of human unity in Adam and in the New Adam, Christ, derives from the classical normative and ecclesial interpretation of the Bible, namely the theological one that beginning with the second century church father, Irenaeus, construed the combination of apostolic writings and the Hebrew scriptures together as a whole forming a single story. This canonical whole is the story, summarized in the baptismal creed, of the one God's universal purpose of salvation. Irenaeus, of course, was not simply inventing this out of thin air. He was drawing upon like themes first worked out by the Apostle Paul, for example, in the Adam-Christ typology of Romans 5.[55]

In any case, the Bible here is not the Bible alone, but the Bible read from the definite perspective of the church in mission to the nations, as its normative self-understanding is articulated in the baptismal creed by which the church is gathered from them. Apart from this kind of basic construal, on the other hand, the Bible is a very big and very incoherent book that can be made by selective proof-texting to say almost anything, not to mention provide inspiration for almost anything in accord with various religious experiences or perceived needs, such as the need of early modern Europeans to salve their Christian consciences in the new and very profitable business of conquest and slave trade.

Race, it is often averred today, is not a biological given, but a social construction of certain facets of the human race's genetic diversity; in Kidd's words, "attitudes to race are determined both by real—but inconsistent—physical features and by the symbolic universes, the culture, in which human translate the misleading facts of physical difference into racial ideologies,

---

53. Ibid., 110.
54. Ibid., 272.
55. Hinlicky, *Divine Complexity*, 137–59.

stereotypes and folklores."[56] This statement, while true, lets science or better, scientists, off the hook just a little too easily. Social constructions, after all, are not pure inventions but interpretations of appearances, buildings "constructed" of certain raw materials including in our modern culture the often sacrosanct data claimed by scientists. Consider for example the latest scientific thinking on human racial diversity:

> Races certainly vary in physical appearance. Nor are the differences just skin deep; there are also variations in susceptibility to disease and in the response to drugs. The overarching similarity of all races is just what would be expected, given that the ancestral human population existed only 50,000 years ago, and given that human nature must to a great degree have been molded before the ancestral dispersal, since all its principle features are found universally. Proof of the continuing unity of the human family is that people of different races have no difficulty in interbreeding, and that the members of any one culture can, absent discrimination, function in any other. But the existence of considerable variation between races should not be any surprise either, given that the human family has long been split into separate branches, each of which has evolved independently for up to 50,000 years or more, buffeted in different directions by the random forces of genetic drift, and the selection pressures of different climates, diseases and societies.[57]

This author is admirably sensitive to the racialist potential of the science he lays out in his book. The point here is merely to lift up the still contemporary plausibility of something like the Nazi interpretation of Wade's acknowledgement of "considerable variation between races" due to the evolutionary interface of genes and environment, *Blut und Boden*.

The antidote to this plausible appeal to science for nefarious purposes is the recognition that the discoveries of science do not speak for themselves but always require interpretation that exceeds the specific expertise of scientists per se. In genuine pluralism we all have to be philosophers in this sense, Christian theologians and scientists too. Moreover, as still providing a, if not the chief "cultural universe" of Western civilization (even if it is no longer the politically enforced mechanism of social cohesion), the Bible as understood missiologically is both a resource for the theological interpretation of the unity of humanity but also, and for the very same reason, the target of those who intend religiously-culturally to divide, whether by the selective

56. Kidd, *Forging*, 18.
57. Wade, *Before the Dawn*, 194.

Contested Topics in Theology

reading and proof-texting of fundamentalists or by the hostile assault of those who want to stifle the gospel's public claim to truth, our present-day "secularists." Abuse of the Bible comes as much from the side of its would-be zealous defenders as from its declared enemies.

These considerations lend support to the claim that Flett's work really puts the central problem of the gospel mission to the nations, as the act in which the being of the church consists, on a new basis by exposing the inadequate Trinitarianism of both defenders and opponents of mission. According to Flett, the defenders think of a God, and hence of a church, that statically has its being and thence may or may not add as something accidental to its being a work or a mission external to its self-identity. To think this way is to think then inevitably of the work or mission as an expansion or reduplication of this pre-existing identity, a self-cloning by means of others, so to say. Taking up the very same assumptions about God's static self-identity and an optional mission, opponents see in this scheme narcissism and imperialism in the arbitrary decision to expand oneself by incorporation of others as replications. The shared assumption of friend and foe of mission alike is thus inadequate Trinitarianism, as if the economic Trinity in mission were something additional, and accidental in relation to, a timeless self-identity. By contrast, following the lead of Karl Barth's retrieval of the doctrine, an adequate Trinitarianism would see that God is eternally a missionary God, i.e., the Father who sends, the Son who obediently goes, the Spirit who brings the Son's obedience home to disobedient humanity, so that united with him they return freely and joyfully to the waiting arms of the sending Father. The Triune God lives eternally and thus also temporally in these joyful exchanges. The "economic" externalization of this God in mission is not anything other than this God for God in God eternally now becoming this very God for creatures in space and time.

These rather demanding theological reflections bear immediately upon the controverted topic of the status of the nations or peoples and the nature of the gospel's mission to them. As Flett shows by a detailed analysis of the German missiologists with whom Barth debated, the effect of their inadequate Trinitarianism was to think that as God has a pre-existing, static identity to which God arbitrarily adds something external in mission, so also God's creatures, the peoples reflecting God in whose image they are made, have such a set, pre-existing völkisch identity that must first come to a civilized self-awareness as a particular *Volk* before it can likewise replicate Christendom on its own new soil in its own unique way. Flett cites as the representative of this widely shared line of thought the missiologist, Siegfried Knak, who wrote to Barth on March 22, 1931, that while God gives faith, "[o]ne must, nevertheless, ground mission in the preexisting social

173

structures because it is not possible for the gospel to be understood by 'the heathen' without the possibility of harmony between the revelation of Christ, which newly approaches him, and the revelation, which had already sought him[,]" namely, in and through the social-historical experience of being formed as a "people" (115). Thus such missionaries thought that the natives had first to be civilized, i.e., Europeanized, before they could be evangelized.

But for Barth, Flett explains, "the necessarily contextual nature of Christian faith and the need for missionary translation are not at issue" in the way that Knak thinks. Rather Barth disputes this "grounding of mission in *Volkstum*" because it "leads to the method of Christianization[,]" that is, of mission in the sense of replicating Christendom (117), transparently an act of cultural imperialism piggybacking on Western colonialism. As Flett notes, Barth's sharp critique of "totalizing logic at any point" seemed to imply to the missiologists a denial of the very possibility of mission. But Barth, as usual, is taking the critics of Christian proselytizing more seriously than they take themselves in order to make their critique fruitful for progress in Christian theology and thus of missiology informed by the imperative of the gospel, not that of the modern Western imperial project. The critics have rightly seen, though they have not recognized, the inadequate Trinitarianism implicit in mission as Christianization. The mission of the gospel to the nations undertakes something that cannot be pre-programmed according to this existing, faulty, indeed tottering model. It would take us far afield here to explore Flett's intriguing proposals for an alternative missiology in this regard, though they have everything to do with keeping the adjective, Christian, as a proper modifier of the gospel's own action in assembling a people from all nations. The missiologist's problem with how Barth's position, and Flett's development of it, has the "capacity to connect with the context" (117) is a real one, not lightly to be dismissed. But what has been certainly gained here and points the way forward is the insight that the attempt to ground mission in a pre-existing *Volkstum* cannot but make Christian mission the cart that follows the horse of colonialist nation-building—whether at home in the Germany of the 1930s where Nazi "coordination" and *Volkswerdung* were underway, or abroad. For Barth, as for Flett, the issue is not "whether the missionaries theologically should translate the gospel using the resources—including the religious [or national] sources at hand." No, Barth insists on freedom for this task. Rather, "the issue is that one translates the gospel and that one does not identify the gospel with some partial and derivative version" (112). But how is that to be known?

CHRISTOLOGY AND THE JEWISHNESS OF JESUS

The external Word of the gospel concerning Christ includes the Jewishness of the man Jesus, because the ambiguity of his appearance in history is constituted by the well-grounded scriptural refusal of living Judaism to believe him. Only in the light of this refusal can Christian faith in Jesus as the Messiah and Son of God understand itself properly as faith, not sight.

An objection may arise to the foregoing suggestion about the Barth-Flett way forward: "And just how is the gospel to be known apart from our appropriation of it, appropriation that is driven and determined by our own needs in our own context?" This objection is at the heart of the postwar divergence between Barth and Bultmann in theology. The latter correctly insisted that as historical beings we always encounter the gospel with a definite "pre-understanding" of God, world, and self and that while the gospel "corrects" this pre-understanding, the pre-understanding also corrects the gospel, i.e., requires its demythologization. Bultmann thought that Heidegger's existential analysis of human existence provided a serviceable framework for systematically translating the gospel out of the mythological language of the first century in which it was encoded to make it intelligible to contemporaries according to their modern pre-understanding. This would work because we today share with the New Testament witnesses the timeless and universal concern with one's own existence as uncovered by Heidegger's existential analysis. This analysis, moreover, has the virtue of avoiding all the dubious claims for *Volk* and worldview that theologians like Hirsch and Althaus, who shared the same theological concern for translatability or mediation, fell into. Since Bultmann's time, his claim for existential analysis has fallen on hard times, but not his basic hermeneutical model of theology as the mutually correcting synthesis of gospel and pre-understanding. The issues here are subtle.

Jack Forstman has made the best contemporary defense for Bultmann's approach in connection with the rise of Nazism. As we shall see, Bultmann makes an abiding contribution to the construction of the theological subject by his insistence on, and interpretation of, theological subjectivity on the model of Paul the Apostle. For Bultmann the theological subject is not the posture of the witness, as assumed in the theocentrism of the Dialectical Theology of the 1920s, the human crater left behind by the bombshell of revelation, as a pure pointing to the Wholly Other, the Unknown God, as occasioned by the testimony of the cross as a sign of the nothingness of all things human. Rather, the theological subject arises as the concrete conformation of the believer to Christ's death and resurrection (as above we heard Bonhoeffer describe). Bultmann found this theological subjectivity articulated in Galatians 2:19b-20. This new identity as conformation to the crucified and risen Christ is an advance over against Barth's view (which Flett more or less follows) that regards the theological subject as the subordinated, secondary human agency that exists purely in the action of imitative following after the superordinated, primary agency of God disclosed in the free event of his self-revelation. More on this will come below. For the present, however, this much of the argument about theological subjectivity indicates how the problem of Christology in general, and of the Jewishness of Jesus in particular, dogs Bultmann's alternative future for Christian theology in the light of the rise and fall of Nazism.

Thanks to Forstman there can be no doubt of Bultmann's profound and insightful theological critique of Nazism in the church. "In a direct attack on the enthusiasm" of that time, Bultmann affirmed that "In a day when the nation has again been generously recognized as an ordinance of creation, the Christian faith has to prove its critical power precisely by continuing to insist that the nation is ambiguous and that, just for the sake of obedience to the nation as an ordinance of creation, the question must be asked what is and what is not the nation's true demand" (227). The Christian's patriotism, according to Bultmann, is this critical obedience that subordinates theologically the claim of the state to God's institution. Uncritical obedience would be enthusiasm that identifies the claim of the state carte blanche with God's institution, that is, apart from its conformity, as known by God's word, with God's purposes, "a rigorous understanding of justice [as] we find in the prophets and Jesus and in love for other people" (228). Hence, "Christian faith and uncritical enthusiasm are incompatible" (228). We must, Bultmann declared in a public lecture, "scrupulously guard ourselves against falsifications of the faith by national religiosity as against falsifications of the national piety by Christian trimmings" (229).

These statements come from the time when the controversy about the introduction of the Aryan Paragraph into the church was breaking out. Bultmann authored the opinion of the Marburg Faculty about it; he forthrightly opposed the Nazi law—quite in contrast to Althaus, who drafted the statement of the Erlangen faculty surfeit with "unhistorical appeals to the New Testament and ... pathetic appeals to the requirements of the German *Volk*" in support of Jewish exclusion (230). As the controversy unfolded, a colleague of Hirsch, Georg Wobbermin at Göttingen, attacked Bultmann for trying to trump racial science with the outmoded views of the New Testament: "the present day German Jewish question was an issue of race, the New Testament is irrelevant" (231). To which Bultmann countered with all the simplicity and radicalness of the Pauline gospel that he so cherished,

"Does the proclaimer of the gospel in the church speak out of his being as a member of a *Volk* or out of the spirit of Christ?" The first is enthusiasm, because "the essential nature of the German people is not present as a clear criterion by virtue of which we may clearly judge the rightness of our action" (237). The second is the Spirit who is holy, who speaks by the Word concerning Christ the crucified—the Christ whom we cannot have without the mediation of Paul (239, this said in the context of the Grundmann school's historical reconstruction, according to which Jesus was an Aryan fighter against the Jews and Paul the "Judaizer" who turned him into an otherworldly god).

Forstman concludes his excellent study reminding of Ericksen's double crisis of modernity: "To live in this world is to live in an uncertain present" (244). But unlike Ericksen, he does not despair of theology. He confesses that "we who are concerned about Christian faith want to know more . . . [that] there are in Christian faith understandings of God, self and world that help one to recognize the demonic before it shows itself boldly and whether Christian faith helps one find courage to name it for what it is and say, 'No!'" (244). Christian theology proves itself by its critical prowess. The critical principle in theology means, as Tillich understood, the "commitment to shrink from no question and to subject everything to criticism, including the faith itself and its sources, to radical criticism" (249). The attempts in contrast to link positively political sovereignty with God's Lordship in Althaus and Gogarten by means of analogy in this light prove to be uncritical. As Barth rightly saw, the principle of radical criticism indigenous to theology in the train of the biblical prophets consists in the dogma that God is God and we are not: to "confess that God is Lord is to acknowledge that neither oneself nor anyone else is God" (254). Thus analogical attempts to link something in the world directly with its Creator are idolatrous. That insight was Barth's great passion, his mighty *Nein!* to the mediating theology and metaphor mongering of his times. As Forstman very helpfully unfolds, it was the ground for Barth's sharp break with his erstwhile comrade in dialectical theology, Gogarten.

Yet while honoring Barth's identification of the Lordship of God made known in the event of revelation as theology's critical principle (254), Forstman insightfully explicates the precise difference from Bultmann's teaching on the theological subject (as mentioned above), that "Barth could not speak about redemption as a present reality, not even with dialectical reservations as a having and not having at the same time" (255) as did Bultmann. Just here, moreover, Forstman finds in Barth at his strongest point a dangerous equivocation by which the critical principle is compromised, even potentially surrendered. This is the claim to have *witnessed* God's revelation, namely, the claim, *Deus dixit*, "God has spoken," which is also inevitably the claim of the theologian, "I have heard, understood, believed, obeyed." Witness is how Barth constructs the theological subject. Forstman comments: "The problem with this position is that from any point of view other than its own, it is arbitrary and provincial" (256). Thus Barth's theology, for all its power and its historical place of honor in potently challenging Hitlerism, in some abstract way imitates Hitler's enthusiasm and makes its own dialectical claim to religious experience. But this leads theology into a self-validating ghetto. "To make acceptance of the Bible a first act of faith is provincial" (257) and a "sacrifice of the intellect . . . not formally different from the sacrifice of the intellect theologians who supported Hitler made as they gave themselves enthusiastically to his leadership," a similarity that is "deeply troubling" (258–59). The alternative is to see with Bultmann that the material content of the Bible, the gospel, "not only makes radical criticism possible and necessary; it provides criteria for that criticism," the test of which is the theologian's integrity also in self-criticism, what Bultmann called *Sachkritik*, criticizing the Bible itself where and when it strays from the theological subjectivity given and identified with life in Christ as love of neighbor (260–61). It is by virtue of *Sachkritik* that one can, for example, criticize the invective in Matthew 23 and the demonization in John 8 as inconsistent, but affirm Romans 11, as consistent with the gospel.

With this outcome we have a very insightful and well-grounded intervention on the topic engaged in this book about what Christian theology must learn from the rise of Nazism. The problem Forstman puts his finger on in comparing the intellectual provincialism of Barth's bald claim that God has spoken in the Bible in comparison with Bultmann's material appeal to the Pauline gospel as something knowable with the help of anthropological analysis will lead us in the next section on theological existence to the mediating path between Barth and Bultmann represented by Dietrich Bonhoeffer. While Forstman acknowledges this divergence in postwar paths of theology between Bultmann and Barth, he considers it as beyond the scope of his study.

The particular concern left hanging then has two sides. On the one hand, Forstman acknowledges how Bultmann restricted his interventions to the life of the church. He accounts for this by the fact that Bultmann, unlike Tillich and Barth, remained at risk of career and even life itself in Marburg through the end of the Third Reich. While prudence under such conditions may count as an explanation of Bultmann's strictly one-kingdom interventions, it does not count in Forstman's own terms as a properly rigorous and unrestricted application of the critical principle in theology. It uncritically leaves the political kingdom to its own devices (even though

Bultmann knows better in his account of the state as an order of creation subject to its divine institution and just so the object of the church's public and prophetic interrogation). One has to wonder, then, whether an unspoken or tacit version of the (modern) Two Kingdoms doctrine is at work here that restricts the claim of God's Lordship, so essential to Barth's alternative.

On the other hand, Bultmann's response to the Aryan Jesus phenomenon does not so much consist in an affirmation of the Jewishness of Jesus as in the irrelevance of the Jesus of history for Christian faith and finally also of the Jewishness of his messianic title, the Christ of Israel. It is the Pauline kerygma, not the (for Bultmann historically dubious) gospel narrative that provides the content of Christology. Forstman helpfully adds a number of small details (240–42) that blunt some of the concerns about Bultmann's later theology along these lines, namely, that it in a neo-docetic way he denarrativizes Christology,[58] and Hellenizes soteriology, as in Bultmann's famous statement that Jesus of Nazareth is but the presupposition of proclamation, "the That," *das Dass*. Here Jesus is but a sheer and otherwise empty fact presupposed in Christ's actual coming through the contemporary kerygma. The reference to Jesus provides an earthly occasion for existential encounter with the preached claim of God demanding daring faith, now transposed and generalized into an existentialist dying to all possibilities in order to decide for one and only one way forward. Bultmann's motives in this later turn towards docetism—again, not the direct subject of Forstman's account—are several: skepticism about liberalism's attempt to ground faith in the knowledge of a reconstructed historical Jesus (including, we may note, Grundmann's bizarre but not atypical discovery of Jesus "the Galilean"); existential concern to let faith be purely faith without false reliance on historical evidence; and above all a theological passion that the newness of the Christian theological subject as freedom from the law on account of dying and rising with Christ be preserved by radicalizing of the old Lutheran teaching of justification by faith alone to now include historical skepticism within itself. Yet all of these concerns, proper in their own way, effect a de-Judaizing of Jesus that is deeply problematic.

Christology is that by which theology knows that the gospel is being translated not substituted or replaced. What Christian theology must learn from the rise of Nazism in this regard is not that the historical Jesus is utterly uncertain, or that history is irrelevant to faith, or that gospel narrative must be abandoned because in bad faith it tries to ground faith on historical evidence, but that the Jesus of history, precisely in his particular Judaism, is ambiguous in just the ways that his Jewish contemporaries found him to be.

---

58. See Hinlicky, *Divine Complexity*, 49–60.

That is to say, knowledge of Jesus as a first-century Palestinian Jew is historically certain enough that it establishes the theological ambiguity of his life and the dubitability of his claim. It is by seeing his own Jewish claim for the reign of God and yet his abandonment and betrayal and denial by his own Jewish followers, and rejection by his own Jewish authorities, and according to the memory of the Hebrew Psalm 22:1, the Cry of Derelicton, voicing his final earthly prayer to the One whom he called, Abba Father, his abandonment also by the God of Israel. This was Dietrich Bonhoeffer's insight and central Christological claim[59] amid the Christological debates between Bultmann and Barth on the one side and Hirsch and Grundmann and their German Christian allies on the other. Pursuing it allows us properly to place Jesus historically in the contest of Second Temple Jewish sectarianisms, where knowledge of what it might mean to call a man crucified, dead, and buried nevertheless the Messiah of Israel will be found—or not at all.

THEOLOGICAL EXISTENCE

The freedom of Christian theology in obedience to the external Word of the gospel opposes in the domain of the church any and all appeals to perceived needs and/or religious experiences and casts a skeptical eye upon, and critical questions to, any and all public appeals to privileged insights or special intuitions.

The alternative to "religious experience" or "enthusiasm" or "perceived needs" as a source of theological knowledge is a word that comes to us from outside ourselves telling news that otherwise we cannot have known. This report of something new is the *Verbum externum* of Reformation theology, the key principle that Sasse and Bonhoeffer lifted up against German Christianity's embrace of the Hitler who claimed to be sent by Providence to save Germany (as we saw in Chapter 4, deriving from his own "strange nocturnal experience"). In this stand against enthusiasm on the basis of the external word of the gospel, Barth, Bonhoeffer, Sasse, and Bultmann are agreed. As Forstman puts it in regard to Bultmann, "Christian faith is neither a worldview nor a form of mysticism. On the contrary . . . [it] is an event in response to the proclamation of Jesus Christ in which a person is turned outward from the self and both called and freed to live here and now on behalf of others in the consciousness of living in the presence of the God of grace and justice" (238). Thus the theological subject is just this one who is formed by, and so also recognized by, the gospel proclamation in time and space,

59. Bonhoeffer, *Christ the Center*, 37–39. See the discussion in Hinlicky, *Beloved Community*, 32–46.

the "Word of God" taken rigorously as a word external to a subject who is confronted and thus transformed in its subjectivity by it. The nuances distinguishing these theologians in this consensus on the *Verbum externum* pale in comparison to the opposition it afforded to German Christianity in its uncritical enthusiasm. Yet, these nuances do matter. In the later postwar conflict between the dogmatic way of Barth and the existentialist way of Bultmann, subtle differences on just this point of the common convergence against the German Christians came forth with a vengeance. When we explore these nuances we discover that Barth's "provincial" appeal to the *Deus dixit* is not quite as fundamentalist and uncritical as Forstman portrayed from what is in fact substantively Bultmann's perspective.

For Barth the godliness of God, our acknowledgement of God's majesty in God's free condescension, is at stake in the fact that the defenseless theologian in the world can give no account for the mercy of this free event of God's revelation that comes freely from above where and when God makes the merely human words of the Bible into the living voice of his own address in promise and demand. It is not that Barth fails to see the rational demand to justify appeal to the Bible as authoritative, as opposed to the holy Qur'an or any other putative revelation. It is rather that in a way that anticipates postmodern themes he rejects the epistemological pretense of the Cartesian-Kantian subject to know timelessly and universally the conditions of knowledge. Thus he rejects in principle any thinking as theology that would by submitting to the philosophical demand for epistemological justification in this way subject God's Word to human judgment and in this very act turn God into something that God is not, in the process turning theologians into free-thinking philosophers rather than listeners and witnesses to revelation. Only God can speak God, only God can justify God and therefore the theologian must say, quite defenselessly, nothing other than, "This claim I have heard and dare to believe and so I speak after the event as its witness. It is not for me to verify the claim."

To put the point formally, for Barth the externality of the Word of God lies in the deity of Jesus Christ. The eternal Son of God, who as true God cannot be contained or captured in any creaturely form, is the Subject who freely according to divine good pleasure assumes flesh in the man Jesus Christ and speaks here that we may know that God is God and we are not. Establishing this austere starting point of theology as knowledge of the godliness of God is the indispensable and never to be taken for granted basis for theological subjectivity. A true and free fellowship of God and creature in a communion not of being but of act can only proceed on this basis. Behind this are the old Calvinist principles, *finitum non capax infiniti* and Christologically what the old Lutheran opponents called the *extra-Calvinisticum*, that is, Calvin's denial that the deity could be contained in the incarnate humanity, his affirmation that the divine Son of God exceeds the human being Jesus Christ.

As mentioned, Bultmann agreed with Barth against the liberal quest for the historical Jesus that finding such a Jesus would give neither God nor faith nor fellowship. But his solution to the externality of God's Word was to find it in more Lutheran fashion, not in God's transcendent majesty as revealed in Christ's deity, but in God's condescending love as proclaimed here and now *pro me*. Taking this Lutheran insight into true faith as the *pro me* appropriation of the presently proclaimed promise of God's love, as occasioned by the remembrance of Jesus, Bultmann pursued a correspondingly radical reduction of Christology to the event of contemporary proclamation. Christ exists *pro me* not as an historical figure in the past but in the event of proclamation. Here and now there is no worry about captivating God in a human or creaturely form, because God is present solely in the non-objectifiable event of proclamation, where the humanity, Jesus of Nazareth, is mentioned only to launch the address and just as quickly left behind. That is why we are justified in describing Bultmann's Christology as neo-docetist. Christ only seems to be Jesus, a figure of the past and hardly knowable. But the living Christ uses the memory of Jesus as a vehicle of human communication to tell a message of divine love that is timeless and universal, even though it breaks through to us only as event in proclamation and thus as a gift of divine grace.

Dietrich Bonhoeffer's innovative way between Barth and Bultmann in Christology was motivated among other things by resistance to the de facto evacuating of Jesus's Judaism from Christological significance in both of these elder theologians. As Michael P. DeJonge has traced this out in an incisive and penetrating analysis, *Bonhoeffer's Theological Formation: Berlin, Barth, and Protestant Theology*, Bonhoeffer locates the externality of the divine Word not in the transcendent deity of the eternal Son, nor in a kerygmatic event making known the truth of timeless divine love, but in the one, undivided person of the Incarnate humanity, not a What or a How but a Who that is personally present, as promised, in his Word and sacraments. Here "person" (as opposed to Barth's more Kantian "subject," as in the divine agency that is the condition for the possibility of God's self-revelation in Christ) means the unity of act and being[60] that constitutes a narrative identity established by its course in space and time. Thus Jesus Christ unavoidably entails the history of the first century Jew who came in the name of Israel's God but ended on the cross abandoned by the same. Here Christian

---

60. DeJonge, *Bonhoeffer's Theological Formation*, 71.

theology finds the divine Son of God (cf. Mark 15:39) or not at all in that this ambiguity is not humanly resolvable but only on the third day. Thus we would hold with Paul in Romans 11 that Jewish disbelief in Jesus as the Messiah cannot be other than God's own doing, intended for good, and just the same, that Christian belief in Jesus as the Messiah cannot be other than God's own doing, also for good. What matters in either case are not our religious claims, whether Christian is right or Jew is right about Jesus, but that by this one and same Jesus about whom we achieve disagreement a theological subjectivity is granted that freely and joyfully justifies God in his judgment in defiance of the judgments of political sovereignty. Like Barth, Bonhoeffer thinks that only a work of the Spirit resolves the ambiguity into a new knowledge of God. But unlike Barth, Bonhoeffer finds this work of the Spirit, like Bultmann, in the conferring of theological subjectivity by conformation to Christ's death and resurrection where and when the contemporaneous Jesus Christ is present by Word and Sacrament in the assembly, "Christ existing as community," as he so powerfully expressed it.

While Bonhoeffer arguably points the way forward for Christian theological subjectivity after Christendom in this fashion, it remains to be said that to his eternal honor it was Karl Barth who demanded "theological existence today," meaning just that defiance by Christian faith that refused to treat Nazi claims to the revolutionary turning point in history with the ultimacy that they demanded, that rather attends to the arduous and unfinished business of theology in hearing and understanding the one Word of God that Christians are to hear, believe, and obey in life and in death, here and now, in a world where Hitlers still can and do arise, devils disguised as angels of light.

THE TWO KINGDOMS DOCTRINE AND POLITICAL SOVEREIGNTY

The proper distinction between God's institution of political sovereignty as an emergency measure for the sake of God's appeal to the peoples of the world in Christ to be reconciled with him is not between realms spatially imagined, such as places of creation and places of redemption, nor is it between a public secular space and an inward religious one. It is a distinction between two kinds of divine power, temporal, coercive, and demanding and spiritual, persuasive, and promising. These two powers appear, intersect, collide and diverge throughout both Testaments and their proper distinction and relation comes by the revelation in the gospel of the righteousness of God apart from the law, though the law and the prophets bear witness to it.

In this very distinction, however, these two powers of God are both directed against the structures of malice and injustice under which the good though fallen creation groans in eager longing for the redemption of the body.

As mentioned above, at the Synod of Barmen in 1934 unity between Reformed, United, and Lutheran delegates was achieved by the adoption of a Two Kingdoms distinction in Theses 5. It was only much later, after 1939, that Barth virtually repudiated this move and began his polemic connecting Martin Luther's failure on gospel and law, as he put it, with the Trojan Horse of natural theology by which the natural paganism of the German people could invade and repossess the churches. Dubious as is this global judgment, and unconvincing as many theologians Reformed, United, and Catholic as well as Lutheran have found Barth's categorical denial of theological significance to the human encounter with the Creator before the coming into their lives of the gospel, Barth was right to detect that something had gone terribly wrong with the so-called Two Kingdoms doctrine. The complication, however, is that what went wrong was a definite modernization of Luther's distinctions which recast them according to the characteristic dualism of Enlightenment culture, namely, the one between the extended things in space and time over which reason presided and the thinking thing itself that transcends space and time intuiting timeless and eternal verities like its own substantiality as soul, its natural immortality, and its Creator's existence as the perfect being.

This basic Cartesian dualism suffered a variety of permutations through the course of its history. Immanuel Kant's transcendental version of it has been the most influential in German Protestant theology. Here it is the transcendental Subject, a hypothetical being Kant posited to figure the timeless and universal condition for the possibility of scientific knowledge of objects of sense experience in time and space, that entails a dualism between the knowable sensible and the unknowable supersensible. Transposed to theology, we have with this a new version of the Two Kingdoms doctrine, namely, the one that excludes religious claims to truth from the political and scientific realm subject to reason and privatizes them in a region of intense but inconsequential interiority. Here, as one might still piously put it, God-given reason presides over the public realm and rules out of place impossible claims to know the supersensible there. It relegates such claims to reason's interior realm of self-reflection, where the Transcendental Subject asks, so to say, about the conditions of its own possibility in ideas about God, the soul, and immortality. But it cannot answer these questions in any kind of public truths because it can have no sensible experience of these supersensibles as is required in the synthesis of category and sense perception that is valid as knowledge in the public domain where others can look, see and verify the claim to truth. Only privately, then, can the Transcendental Subject adopt ideas of God, soul, and immortality as practical postulates with which to guide the conduct of life.

By the time these modern dualisms percolate into the habitat in which Nazism arose, there had come the second crisis of modernity by which the children of the rationalists (in sum, Marx, Nietzsche, and Freud) exposed the dubiousness of rationalism itself (as, in sum, Descartes and Kant) in constructing thinking things and Transcendental Subjects. As a result of this collapse of the modern subject into the waves and currents of chaotic becoming, enthusiasm was making a strong comeback. Occultism was rampant and, as we have seen, such theosophical speculation was the matrix in which Nazism was born. It would also have been the matrix in which Nazism died a premature death of its own speculative absurdities, as we have also seen, had not Hitler rescued the movement from dissipation by means of this modern iteration of the Two Kingdoms doctrine. To the extent that objectively confused but subjectively strident Lutherans claimed this modern version of the Two Kingdoms as Luther's great contribution to civilization, Karl Barth was not amiss to attribute blindness to the danger of Nazism and incapacity for resistance against it to the great mistake of Martin Luther on gospel and law. But if we step back from this later cycle of polemic, as argued in the first part of this chapter, and reach back behind it, for example, to the Appeal of the Second Confessing Synod of the Evangelical Church of the Old Prussian Union that took place in Berlin-Dahlem on March 4–5, 1935, we find a rather different interpretation of the problem of the Two Kingdoms.

In its first part grounding its claims in a Christian interpretation of the First Commandment in opposition to the "new religion" sweeping Germany, II.1 of its statement reads: "The state receives its sovereignty and power by the command of God, as part of his gracious order. It is this alone which creates and limits human authority. He who would let blood, race, and nationality take the place of God as the creator and master of political authority, undermines the state." And in III.1 we read that the church therefore "must not allow itself to be pushed from the public market-place into some quiet corner of private piety, where, self-satisfied it would betray its mission."[61] The logic is as sound theologically as the argument is simple. There is one God before whom we are to have no others. This one God graciously institutes political sovereignty to limit human sin because in fact we do hold sinfully to other gods before him with disastrous consequences

---

61. Remak, *The Nazi Years*, 100–101.

for world, others and self. This gracious order limiting human sin, however, depends epistemically on the public witness of the church, which knows God's will for justice in the law because it knows God gift of justice apart from the law, be it in the preface to the Decalogue regarding the God of the Exodus or now in Christ reconciling the world to himself.

That this latter is in sum and substance the actual teaching of the historical Martin Luther on the so-called Two Kingdoms can hardly be denied today. What is equally clear from the statement of the Confessing Church in Prussia in 1935 is that it is not Luther's teaching but the modern version of the Two Kingdoms doctrine that is in its cross hairs.

Political sovereignty was not one of the original Lutheran orders of *creation*, for its institution arises *after the fall* of the first couple.[62] It exists temporarily, then, as a *Notordnung*, an "emergency order." That is because the state is, as Romans 13 explains, a monopoly on the means of coercion, God's sinful antidote for the time being to sinful violence. The state's violent suppression of violence is a kind of surd, a salvation history paradox, a perpetual state of emergency, an ongoing exception to the rule of law by which the rule of law is decided and applied.[63] Because of this endemic paradox of violence at the very heart of political sovereignty, it cannot inherit the kingdom of God. Marx was not wrong to say that with the coming of the Beloved Community, the state will wither away. In the interim, however, the state in all its lethal ambiguity must not be abandoned to the violence in which it is ensconced. Theological subjects work within it to turn this frequent servant of the devil against the devil, into service of the one God. This too happens as an event, when political ambition for gain and glory is subordinated ever again to God's purposes of grace and justice for all as known in the gospel. Christian people therefore can fulfill their baptismal calling to self-giving love of neighbor also in the governing and policing offices of the state. Just as in their personal existence they will risk their own peace to reconcile with enemies, so also in governing and police work they will risk themselves bodily in the same love for neighbors, to prevent evils by good government

---

62. Bayer, *Luther's Theology*, 147–52. Acknowledging that Luther's view is that the state is a post-lapsarian order of preservation, Bayer regards it as deficient for today because it does not sufficiently distinguish domination from dominion, mere coercion and just coercion. In this, Bayer continues in Althaus's line of interpretation, a trajectory that still assumes, in my judgment, the positive possibilities of Christendom.

63. It is intriguing to note here how Neitzel and Welzer conclude their alternative account of Hitler's willing executioners in challenging our complacent liberalism: "If we cease to define violence as an aberration, we learn more about our society and how it functions than if we persist in comfortable illusions about our own basically nonviolent nature ... Modernity's faith in its own distance from violence is illusionary." *Soldaten*, 343.

and to thwart evils breaking out in harm on others, especially the weak and the innocent. To succeed in this complex and morally ambiguous work of love by re-tooling the state's monopoly on violence, Christian people need to hear anew and anew the story of Christ who was crucified for love of neighbor, but vindicated in the Spirit as the beloved Son of the God and Father of us, all in this same morally ambiguous self-giving.

This more than anything is the critical point about the Two Kingdoms doctrine for theology in the tradition of Luther. Christian faith really is not a philosophy, a worldview or a mysticism, and when considered under these terms its claims cannot even be heard today, let alone considered in its particular claim to truth. But the claim to truth is heard when we hear Jesus Christ say, "I am yours and you are mine." This claim to truth is believed when auditors obediently surrender their own burden of guilt and sorrow to Christ and receives in their place his justice and joy and the easy yoke of following him in the power of the Spirit into the mission of God as ones beloved and just so gifted. When this is not happening, on the other hand, when just this event in the power of the Spirit is not transpiring in the communities that still out of habit call themselves "Christian," then the event of God's merciful reign is not breaking into this demonized world nor reordering the powers to serve as his instruments on the way to the best of all possible worlds. If Christian theology has learned anything from the rise of Nazism, surely today under the hegemony of the victorious and insatiable market, where even political sovereignty—that ought by God's institution to put the market in its place and keep it there—is rather bought and sold, then Christian theology must learn again by the Spirit in the gospel to create communities of faithful resistance in its midst, in just this way poking a stick into the spokes of the wheel.

Conclusion

Inheritance, Decay and, Renewal

"To the Christian doctrine of the infinite significance of the individual human soul . . .," we have heard the theologian Hitler opine, "I oppose with icy clarity the saving doctrine of the nothingness and insignificance of the individual human being, and of his continued existence in the visible immortality of the nation."[1] The source of liberalism's exalted individual is widely forgotten today with deleterious consequences. Hitler, avowed enemy, knew that it came from Christianity, and that Christianity got it from Judaism. In neither biblical tradition is the individual exalted apart from the community; rather true community, not the collective, but the Beloved Community of the covenants, is the free sharing of selves made strong in love and justice. This vocation to the Beloved Community comes from the lofty calling of the human couple (Gen 1:26–28) in the creative action of God, and it is ever restored when forfeited in sin by the seeking and finding of every single lost person (Luke 15) in the redemptive action of God, so that already now in meaningful struggles of history the people of God live politically by anticipation of the fulfillment and vindication of each with all in the messianic promise of the coming in fullness and power of that Beloved Community. When this theological grounding of liberalism's exalted individual is forgotten,[2] however, liberalism comes apart into the sibling rivals of liberal liberalism, conservative liberalism, and radical liberalism.

---

1. Cited in Burleigh, *Third Reich*, 256.

2. It is not forgotten in John Locke, *Second Treatise of Government*, the second chapter of which on the "state of nature" rather invokes the opening chapters of the book of Genesis in manifest polemic against Hobbes.

Conclusion

In all three versions of our decadent liberalism, the individual exalted by the calling, the love and the promise of God morphs into the sovereign self of Cartesian-Kantian modernity.[3] Here the individual does not stand in nature with others in covenantal history with God, but over nature, others included, in place of God. As a result of our forgetfulness, the prophetic resources for renewal in the North American tradition—I think especially of Lincoln in the Second Inaugural Address and of Martin Luther King, Jr.'s great orations—that could at least stiffen resistance to the market-machine are rather overwhelmed by it.

I want to qualify the conclusions I am about to draw by recalling two items from the preceding study. The first concerns what Peter L. Berger[4] once described as the "heretical imperative" of modern life and comes from Ericksen's note on Hirsch's Kierkegaardian observation that modern "reason and freedom lead ultimately to 'the all-encompassing debate about everything.'"[5] This pluralism of contemporary life in the age of the Internet and other communication technologies is de facto, if not everywhere de jure, our situation for the foreseeable future, especially in Euro-America. The political price we pay for it here is endemic dysfunction—the "chaos of parliamentarianism" that Hitler hated. The spiritual price we ought to pay for it is patiency, that heavenly virtue of longsuffering love for foolish opponents and even malicious enemies, who remain human sisters and brothers with us in the covenant of creation, prospective children of the same heavenly Father. But genuine love hates what is evil (Rom 12:9) and theology today must labor publicly for a critical pluralism.

The second concerns the true freedom of theological subjectivity and comes from the ironic warning that Künneth had to issue to the postwar political Barthians about a "theological derailment" insofar as the German Christian thesis lived on in the Christians in Socialism antithesis. I say "ironic," because no theologian of the twentieth century contended more than Barth for the freedom of theology grounded in the freedom of God, whose coming by the Word and the Spirit is always a free act of grace that only free theologians can freely and joyfully follow. These two notes qualify the claims that follow: 1) that theology cannot intervene in today's pluralism with the purpose of ending discussion but only in the hope—the hope of the gospel—of reframing it, and that 2) in such interventions, theology follows, and does not lead, but follows the God who comes by Word and

---

3. Elshtain, *Sovereignty: God, State, and Self*. See also Oehlschlaeger, *Procreative Ethics* and the analysis of the "sovereign self" in this author's review essay in the online *Journal of Lutheran Ethics*.

4. Berger, *The Heretical Imperative*.

5. Ericksen, *Theologians under Hitler*, 151.

Spirit. That means that the particular interpretation of mangled Christian theology during the rise of Nazism on the preceding pages cannot be meant as conversation stopper, but only, so far as it has succeeded, as reframing a debate about Nazism that must continue indefinitely. It also means that no one, friend or foe, should regard that particular interpretation as any simple equivalent to the Word and Spirit that in fact inform and inspire it. Interpretations are not matters of faith, even when they are borne of faith and concern faith. Interpretations are matters of reason, subject to philosophical criticism.

The perceptive reader will by now have long since realized that this book is not only about the rise of Nazism but about us and how we today take the rise of Nazism. This "we" is the "we" of Euro-America, after 1989 triumphant not only over Nazism but also over Stalinism, yet a "we" that has not yet grasped the genuinely tragic truth embedded in Francis Fukuyama's proclamation thereupon of the "end of history."[6] Instead, our liberal liberals in their denunciation of it for supposed neo-conservative cheerleading of the triumph of capitalism have misunderstood his diagnosis, just as they perpetually misunderstand their own deep dependence on triumphant capitalism, that is, of an impending state of biopolitical stasis that must homogenize coercively in order to manage its endemic crises. It is deeply anti-Messianic to think of the end of history and the triumph of political sovereignty as one and the same thing. But this antiChrist is nothing new. It is a thinking that is deeply engrained in the Western tradition going back to Greco-Roman imperialism.

Picking up on Emmanuel Levinas's 1934 dissent from a "dangerous" element in Heidegger's thought along these lines, Giorgio Agamben approved the radical insight embedded in Levinas's diagnosis with the acute observation that "if Nazism was able to coincide—at least at its point of departure—with the great philosophy of the twentieth century, it would be foolish to believe it is possible to extricate oneself from this uneasy proximity by condemning one philosopher and absolving another."[7] Foolish, indeed, because this individualistic and ideological blame-game perpetuates our three liberalisms in their intramural quarrels and hinders deeper understanding, while as a juggernaut the omnivorous and insatiable market silently and relentlessly works the commoditization of all things according to an increasingly open and articulate biopolitical calculus. On the one hand, if the crises become unmanageable because the model is unsustainable, the recurring temptations to fascism, indeed to some new Nazism, as

---

6. Fukuyama, *The End of History and the Last Man*.
7. de la Durantaye, *Giorgio Agamben*, 308–9.

well as communism arise. If the crises are managed, however, the captivity before us is final. It *is* the tragic end of history.

Can a renewed and purified Christian theology arise under these circumstances? It certainly cannot by way of nostalgia for the medieval synthesis. Christendom is finished. But something from Christendom can be retrieved and projected forward. That is to venture anew into metaphysics philosophically and messianism theologically, as this author and colleague Brent Adkins have proposed in our *Rethinking Philosophy and Theology with Deleuze*. Metaphysical naturalism and theological messianism are alike as dangerous as fascinating.[8] Naturalism is the "dehumanizing" truth of the biology that increasingly determines politics. Messianism is the underground hope of a "vindication of the meaningfulness of history" (Niebuhr) despite all sound and fury signifying nothing. It is the hope that drove in perverted form the secularized political religions of fascism and communism, just as it had been the force driving Pope Urban II's equally perverse call to holy war against Islam in response to Islam's holy war against Byzantium and the ruins of the Roman Empire in the West and elsewhere. It is the driving force also in modern Zionism as also in today's iterations of Islamic fanaticism. Messianism is the hope that Nietzsche satirized when he said that man is such a being that he would rather have nothingness for a meaning than no meaning at all. Disgust with messianism is not least of the attractions that seduce us, as Nolte saw, to biopolitical homogenization and the stasis of political sovereignty.

Reinhold Niebuhr captured this messianic hope for a meaningful vindication of humanity in the struggles of covenantal history to and for the Beloved Community in his powerful analysis on the cusp of World War II, "Where a Christ is Expected."[9] And he pointed Christian theology in the right direction there when he wrote that "[t]he fact that there can be no Christ without an expectation of Christ relates Christianity as founded in a unique revelation to the whole history of culture; the fact that the true Christ cannot be the Messiah who is expected separates Christianity from the history of culture." By this dialectic, Niebuhr sought to express the Pauline metaphor, "Christ crucified," meaning that Christian theology cannot even ask its own questions, let alone demonstrate its critical power in the world, except in dialogue with living Judaism, not only the bearer of Torah values to the world, but the suffering servant of them. Christ crucified may be a "stumbling block to Jews," as Niebuhr explained, "but he is not

---

8. Lilla, *The Stillborn God*.
9. Niebuhr, *The Nature and Destiny of Man*, II:15–34.

'foolishness'" to Jews, as he is to the Greeks.[10] He is, perhaps, as Maurice Samuel intimated, all too familar.

Hope arises from creation's groaning (Rom 8:19), its grief and sighing for the revelation of the glorious liberty of the children of God (Rom 8:21), the redemption of the body (Rom 8:23). We Euro-Americans are situated today in an unfolding biopolitical captivity, on the horns of the dilemma just described. Within this captivity, here hoping against hope, and thus not by some flight in imagination to another world or any theoretical transcendence, but from within this captivity we theologians must discover again the One, who if he is to plunder the strong man's house must first break in and bind him up (Mark 3:27). That, or rather this One, is what Christian theology must learn anew after the rise of Nazism.

---

10. Ibid., 16.

Appendix

The Philosophy of Bolshevism, Fascism, and Hitlerism

A Lecture presented at the Academic Conference of the Ministerium of the Liptovsky, Oravsky, Turiec and Zvolen Districts of the Evangelical Lutheran Church of the Augsburg Confession[1] on November 22, 1937 in Ružomberok, Czechoslovakia, by Bishop Professor Dr. Samuel Štefan Osuský

[Translator's note: This translation first appeared in a two part series in *Lutheran Forum* (Winter, 2009) 50–58 and (Spring, 2010) 50–58 and is reprinted here with permission. A few notes on translation. Always problematic is the rendering of *evanjelický* (= German, *evangelisch*) into English: translating that word as "evangelical" brings incorrect associations in English, but "Protestant" likewise is incorrect, since the reference is to the historic confessions of the Reformation period. The official name of Osuský's church is "*Evanjelická* Church of the Augsburg Confession in Slovakia"; hence *evanjelická* stands as an abbreviation for this church-confessional identity. I have thus taken the liberty of translating "evangelical" as "Lutheran," to conform to American usage. I have left Osuský's inconsistent manner of citation as it is found. Anyone interested in pursuing his sources would have to be fluent in Czech or Slovak, and as such can consult the original text for such few clues as are provided. I have disregarded Osuský's irregular paragraphing and removed some obscure allusions to footnotes to make for a smoother read. I have also taken the liberty of modernizing somewhat the rather archaic (even in Slovak) expressions into contemporary idiomatic English, e.g., the biblical "Behold!," which Osuský uses ironically, I usually render as "Look!" I would like to thank my Slovak friend and theological

---

1. Subsequently published in *Styri Prednasky* [Four Lectures] (Mikulas: Tranoscius, 1940).

Appendix

colleague, Dean Lubomir Batka, for his counsel on matters of this translation and the librarian at the "Lutheran" Theological Faculty of Comenius University in Bratislava, Jan Badura, for his assistence. —PRH]

I HAVE RUMINATED FOR A long time about what to lecture on at this academic meeting of pastors. Three circumstances made my choice easy and decided for me. Since this is an academic meeting for pastors, the first of these is that I should accordingly lecture from a discipline which is assigned to me at the Czechoslovak State Evangelical Theological Faculty in Bratislava, namely, from philosophy, psychology or sociology. I cannot then lecture on more narrowly theological problems, about which the other brothers from the Faculty will lecture for you, but I must keep to my own area. Again considering what field of study I should choose from those just mentioned, a second circumstance came to my aid, namely that at the first such academic conference for pastors in 1926 I lectured on the development of socialism from the side of social theory.[2] This lecture then will be a continuation of that one. Which side of this complex of thought to continue today is decided by a third circumstance, namely, a very interesting book, which I have read and commend to the attention of all participants: Konrad Heiden, *Europe as It Is*.

Under the influence of this book and of experience, I have come to the conviction that Bolshevism, fascism and Hitlerism belong among the most potent currents of our century. We feel their activity, dynamism, and power on every side; hence I regard it necessary that we become familiar with their ideologies or worldviews in their basic thoughts. Originally they were only political parties, yet from political parties they have developed great political movements in such order as I have named them, i.e., the first of these entered on the stage of history in Russia in the second decade (1917), the second in the third decade (1922) in Italy and the third in the fourth decade (1933) in Germany. Their literature is by now well distributed, so it does no harm to occupy ourselves with the philosophy of Bolshevism (as I call in brief Russian Communism), fascism (as I call the philosophy of Mussolini), and Hitlerism (as I call German National Socialism).

THE PHILOSOPHY OF BOLSHEVISM

The philosophy of contemporary Russian Communism, abbreviated Bolshevism, can be expressed by two words: *dialectical materialism*.

---

2. *Cirkevny Listy*, 1926, 173–75, 199–201, 224–26, 265–67.

The *philosophy of materialism* forms the foundation of Bolshevism. The history of this idea is well known, beginning from Democritus through the Epicurean materialists, the Renaissance Epicureans of the fifteenth and sixteenth centuries, the followers of Gassendi in the seventeeth century of the French Enlightenment: Diderot, Holbach, Lamettry in the eighteenth up to the materialists of the nineteeth: Vogt, Buechner, Moleschott, Colby. These form one source of the philosophy of Bolshevism, except that there is a certain difference. We ordinarily call these metaphysical, mechanical, or vulgar materialists, whereas we name the philosophers of Bolshevism dialectical materialists. Vulgar materialists acknowledged only matter, and they explained all phenomena, all change—also in psychic and spiritual life—as the motion of matter, as a change of place in space. Thus they reduced everything to quantitative magnitudes. Such materialism partly theoretically, but even more practically, developed also in the first phase of Bolshevism and even maintains itself up till now; it is in opposition to dialectical "official" materialism.[3]

Contemporary "official" materialism is *dialectical*. It originates from the dialectical philosophy of Heraclitus, Neo-Platonism, Hegel, Feuerbach up to Karl Marx and Friedrich Engel. Already in Heraclitus's philosophy, life is understood as like the flow of water between the banks of a river; among the Neo-Platonists as the development of thesis and antithesis; with Hegel as the battle with the thesis through the antithesis to the synthesis. Etymologically, "dialectic," coming from the Greek word, *dialogo*, means taking things apart by analysis. Hegel, as is well known, explained the development of things as the posit of the absolute spirit as thesis in the first place, and then, nature/matter as the antithesis, and then out of these two the dialectic continued further to their synthesis. So also Bolshevism. But where Hegel posited absolute spirit in the first place as the thesis, Bolshevism posits matter. Therefore Lenin called Hegelianism inverted materialism. Fr. Bicek in his essay, "On Dialectical Materialism,"[4] rightly lifts this up: just as there was no dialectic among the pre-Hegelian vulgar materialists, so also there was no materialism in the Hegelian dialectic.[5] So we see that already in its foundations two contradictory sources flow together in the philosophy of Bolshevism: the source of materialism and the source of dialectical idealism.

This conflict in the very foundations becomes a danger for dialectical materialism. The question is how would it be possible to attain to a

---

3. Osuský notes. "Such are Boricevskians, Timirjazevians, Sarabjanovians, Stephanists, Alexrodians, etc."

4. Fr. Bicek, "On Dialectical Materialism,"*Ceska Mysl.* 1931 Annual, 385–408.

5. Ibid., 423.

Appendix

combination of these two contradictory tendencies, i.e., to the transformation of mechanistic materialism into dialectical materialism. Mechanistic materialists understand life and man as a machine. In so far as this worldview is not undermined, mechanistic materialism can remain. When, however, after the progression of physics and mechanics, chemistry and biology also develop, and these show the unsustainability of the mechanical view with regard to organism, mechanistic materialism must also proceed and change into dialectical materialism. Dialectical materialism retained to be sure the basic idea of mechanistic materialism, that the fundamental element of existence is matter, although mental life, thought, knowledge could not be understood as the mere movement of matter. According to dialectical materialism, mental life and everything connected with it is a special property of matter. In Spinoza's language: matter does not have only the property of special extension, but also of thinking; it does not have only the property of movement, but also something more, thinking. Thinking, as a property of matter, is not something incidental or accidental, but a property which develops at a definite stage of development as an effect of matter. Between matter and mind there is a relation of thesis and antithesis. Namely matter is the first reality, out of which develops a second reality: mind. Between them is a relation as between cause and effect. Dialectical materialism in this way receives the idea of evolution or development out of the philosophy of evolutionism and expresses it precisely by dialectic. That is why it is called *dialectical* materialism.

Dialectical materialism understands all of existence thus—natural and mental life, also history—as the constant metamorphosis with the movement from thesis to the antithesis. According to it, everything is in a constant process—metamorphosis, one form of being dialectically passing into a second form. All things are composed from antithesis and in knowledge the antitheses have to be transcended. Bicek characterizes it this way: "Dialectical materialism looks on the universe as an infinite universal process, in which one thing inevitably passes into a second thing, everything is in activity, everything in formation."[6] Everything real is in change and everything which is in change is real. Where there is no change there is no life. Hence dialectical materialism repudiates the thought of an absolute and immutable being. Deveopment or change, as I said, take place dialectically, namely, with a thesis to an antithesis and thus to a synthesis, to new, mutual influencing union of antitheses. The most general form of disintegration is the antithesis of being and nonbeing. Existing things are the union of being and nonbeing. What exists forms the new which is not yet. A boy is

---

6. Ibid., 394.

already not a child but not yet a man. Process, metamorphosis lies in the unity between being and nonbeing, that is, between what was and what will be, what becomes and between that which is. There is no present, only the passage from the past to the future. Antar in his book *ABCs of Dialectical Materialism*[7] considers as the chief antitheses the following: matter-mind; quantity-quality; cause-effect; part-whole; male-female; individual-collective; theory-praxis, etc.

Dialectic, that is dialectic of development, does not relate only to being in the kingdom of space, in nature, but also to being in the kingdom of mind and to history in the kingdom of time. The dialectic of dialectical materialism is occupied with problems in the kingdom of mental life. Dialectic namely does not mean only a method or means of development, but also means a doctrine about acquiring knowledge, thus a theory of knowledge. In this sense we already meet with dialectic in Plato. With Plato dialectic meant reflecting through conversation in order to come to common concepts, to ideas. Dialectic is also found in Hegel, as the logic in the development of a concept. Dialectic as a theory of knowledge in dialectical materialism is distinguished from these two. In fundaments it is materialistic, sensualistic, but also in metaphysics, thus also in noetics, it overcomes mere sensualism. From the principles introduced above it follows that dialectical materialism in its theory of knowledge derives things from being and not the opposite, being from thinking, as do various shades of Idealism, for example, Plato and Hegel, as mentioned. Idealists, when starting from mind, must start from thinking, because mind thinks. Over against that, materialists when they start out from matter, must start out from being, from matter and to the same degree to that they attribute to matter the causality of thought.

But I said that they are not mere sensualists like the mechanistic materialists. They set out from material reality, but they also overcome it. They analyze being and thought and in the synthesis they remove their opposition to each other. Bicek expresses it this way: "Man himself is a part of being and therefore the forms determined for being are also determined for thought."[8] Reality works on our minds, calls forth in us impressions, representations, even though the process of thinking is still not finished by this. Thought rationally works over these impressions and perceptions. By this rational processing mechanistic sensualism is overcome. It is then empiricism, passing into the antithesis of rationalism, and being overcome in the synthesis of rational empiricism. Our thinking according to this is determined by being, impressions from the real world, not only however the world of nature, but

7. Antar, *ABCs of Dialectical Materialism* (Praha: Jaroslav Holshek, 1931), 40.
8. Bicek, "On Dialectical Materialism," 394.

Appendix

also the historical world and by our reactions to it. We react in thinking to that which happens outside of us, but according to our own selves, our own subjecthood. This "according to us" is determined by natural and historical impressions and by our subjective elements.

Bolshevism wants to create its own *psychology* suitable to this line of thought. This is the so-called "reaction psychology," started but mechanized by the psychologist K. Kornilov. As in metaphysics it stands under the influence of materialism and evolutionism, so also in psychology it stands under the influence of American behaviorism. This tendency understands mental life and its activity as the reaction of an organism to external impressions. That is why this psychology gets the name reaction psychology.[9] It criticizes the Western direction of psychology, because it does not sufficiently understand the development of psychological phenomena on the basis of the activity of labor, but operates with an abstract, not concrete human being. For example, an intelligent being reacts in a totally different way than a robot to the same thing. But the same psychology of Kornilov also reduces the entire mental life to mechanical reactions, and thus psychology to physics, and as a result further psychologists of dialectical materialism have moved beyond that, because according to them psychology also must be dialectically materialist. Kornilov does not accept phenomena on the basis of feelings and perceptions but only on the basis of reactions. But in the reactions we do not have reflections of things as if in a mirror, because they are subjectively alive also in them, which depend on the perceptive apparatus. At this point already Lenin's psychology encountered empircal criticism. These subjective elements of reactions must be investigated not only according to nature, but also according to the history of labor, according to the social environment and process,[10] Bolshevik psychology must take account of these moments, so that like other sciences, it also might help "in the realization of the practical goals of social construction."[11] Psychology perceived in this way shows that just like in metaphysics Bolshevism deviates from vulgar materialism by its dialectic, thus also in psychology as in all the sciences.

Every science, according to Bolshevism, must start out from reality, but reality must logically, systematically be worked out in knowledge, and, like American pragmatism, test this knowledge, whether it is true in the sense that one can use it to the benefit of the proletariat. According to them, every science, as also occupation, must be productive. A nonproductive science is not necessary. There is no absolute truth, truth is what development

---

9. F. Bicek, "On the Soviet Reaction Psychology," *Ceska Mysl.* 1931, 527–38.
10. Ibid., 529.
11. Ibid., 527.

demands and proves itself in the praxis of the proletariat. Anyone proficient in the history of philosophy clearly sees that we have here to do with American pragmatism.

We said above that dialectical materialism relates itself not only to the kingdom of nature and to the kingdom of thinking, but also to the kingdom of time, namely, to history. Accordingly Bolshevism creates a philosophy of history. In brief we can name this philosophy of history historical materialism. As in metaphysics materialism combined with idealistic dialectic asserting itself as a philosophy of evolution, as likewise in epistemology American behaviorism and pragmatism assert themselves, so in the philosophy of history beginning with Karl Marx and Engel the idea of historical materialism asserts itself. As in metaphysics matter is the first element, so in history the basic, motor force of history is matter, i.e. economic interest. The human being is the product of economic relations. The idea does not form relations, but relations form the idea. Everything ideological—politics, laws, morality, philosophy, religion—everything is only a reflection, reflex, superstructure of the economic. History is the contest of economic classes, which develop in time. First there was the period of primitive communism, i.e., the thesis. Then classes were created under the influence of production —as antithesis. These classes developed this way: in the ancient world there was master and slave, in the medieval world lord and serf, in the modern age bourgeois and proletariat. The proletarian was first in a relation of service to the lord and then in the relation of a worker to an employer. The problem of consumption comes to the foreground in the modern age as the synthesis. Mercantilism gave birth to the Physiocrats who gave birth to liberalism with capitalism, and then capitalism gave birth to socialism. The goal is the destruction of classes, a classless society by means of the dictatorship of the proletariat. The individual is only an atom of the total-collective proletariat. A theory of collectivism is evident, of communization; this is what statism means in Bolshevism, the nationalization of everything.

But here too we see the overcoming of mere mechanistic collectivism. At the beginning, private property was not at all allowed, but now after the breakdown of economic policy known by the name of the Soviet New Economic Policy (Lenin, 1921), Bolsheviks make a distinction between private property and capital. The question of pay, the reward for work, led them to this. Work was not any long rewarded by need but by achievement[12] and so from wages it is possible to create private property. But private property here does not mean capital in the Communist sense, namely, involuntarily creating surplus value in private property by exploiting alienated labor, but

---

12. Osuský notes: "see Stachanovshtina."

rather that one can use one's pay for non-necessities. This is a deviation from pure communism, as we know, just as on the other side, it is a deviation from the communization of the family. Elo Sandor in his book, *Bratislava –Moscow*,[13] asserts that while there are in Russia various social levels and also luxury goods, there is only one working class, because everyone is an employee of the state and of oneself, not of another.

According to this theoretical and political philosophy, a practical philosophy of Bolshevism is also formed, as it appears to us in their ethics and in their philosophy of religion. Morality is what serves the proletariat. Good is what is profitable to the proletariat. Evil is what is not profitable to the proletariat. It is the antithesis to the previous thesis. Before Bolshevism, namely, good was whatever served the employer class. Behold the dialectic! There are no absolute moral names, as there is no absolute truth. Christian ethics are also, according to Bolshevism, only relative and not absolute, but only the consequence of the proletariat movements of those times. Already Nietzsche called Christian ethics the morality of the slave class. Lunacharsky, longtime Commissar of culture, similarly explained the origin of Christian morality. It was and is the morality of the miserable proletariat in the period of the origin of Christianity. The proletariat then did not know otherwise how to change their miserable fate: they did not have the power, they were not organized, and hence they awaited the intervention of supernatural powers, which would bring the kingdom of the hungry, i.e., the impoverished proletarians. According to Lunacharsky, this is the original sense of the kingdom of God. When in the third and fourth centuries the higher classes joined Christianity, they changed the concept of the kingdom of God into a spiritual-idealistic one. Bolshevism returns the original Christian conception of the kingdom, but with this difference, that today Communism with the organization of the proletariat actualizes the kingdom of the proletarians and of equality. Everything and anything that serves this goal is good and permitted. Look! The end sanctifies the means! It is not possible to come to this understanding of the kingdom of God by means of contemporary Christian morality, which is the morality of the bourgeoisie; on the contrary, so far as Christianity nowadays is against the morality of the proletariat, it is the opium of the people and it is necessary systematically to battle against it.

It is not necessary perhaps for me to remark more broadly on their point of view regarding religion, such are things well enough known. I mention only the 124th article of the Stalin Constitution. This says literally: "To secure the freedom of conscience to the entire citizenship the church

---

13. Bicek, "On the Soviet Reaction Psychology," 20.

in the USSR is separated from the state and the school from the church. The freedom to practice religious cults just as the freedom of antireligious propaganda is acknowledged to all citizens." It is worth noting that only the practice of the cult is secured for the religions while the right to propaganda is secured for godlessness. This is a big difference. But also note that freedom here is not freedom in our sense of the word. According to their understanding freedom does not lead to the above mentioned good, but obedience to the collective. Therefore Andrej Gide could write in his book, *Return from the Soviet Union,* that in Russia conformism reigns.[14]

Further development shows us we can see already budding, that also here the dialectic breaks down the rigor of the collective, which swallows up the individual. The individual must serve the whole and the whole must serve the individual, just as determinism must be broken by indeterminism. That already shows that Bolshevism deviates from mechanistic determinism and comes to the conviction that neither determinism nor indeterminism is valid, but only the one with the other. As Antar writes, to know the necessary is needful, so that we know what is possible and to act necessarily according to the knowledge of what is possible. Therefore the philosophy of Bolshevism can be called also the philosophy of the will, voluntarism, action, activity.

Dialectic materialism regards itself as the highest synthesis of all the streams of philosophy. It fights vigorously against tendencies which deny the justification of whatever philosophy. One of them wants to replace philosophy with natural science (Minin), another wants still to suffer with philosophy in the present, but asserts that in the future philosophy will disappear into science (Vasiljev), a third accepts dialectic as a philosophical method, but not as an epistemology (the Mechanists) and they defend vigorously their perspective of dialectical materialism against all others. This work in Russia, as Bicek informs us,[15] is large and organized in Marxist-Leninist institutions, especially in the Marx-Engel Institute, concentrated in the Philosophical Institute, affiliated with the Communist Academy in Moscow. This institute for the study of philosophy has as its main sections: Dialectical Materialism, Historical Materialism, the History of Philosophy, and Contemporary Philosophy.

We will not overcome Communism by boasting of our own superiority. It is necessary to deal with it seriously and thus to overcome it philosophically. As it overcomes the oppositional streams in Russian, so I judge,

---

14. Bicek, "On the Soviet Reaction Psychology," 26–35.

15. Bicek, 'The Organization of Philosophical Work in Soviet Russia,' *Ceska Mysl.*, 1931, 330–32.

that it also overcomes itself. I point to a contradiction already in its foundations. It denies the absolute, the eternal, and yet begins with matter as its own absolute and eternal. This is the most basic contradiction. No dialectic overcomes this. Also in the very title there is a contradiction: either dialectic or materialism, not both. If dialectic is valid, why begin precisely with matter? Just so I am justified in beginning with mind. Why begin under the influence of economic relations and not with mind, i.e., the ideational side of life? The very reality of their ideology in advance of the realization of their own ideal proves best the error of their perspective. Why begin with work and not with theory like they do? Why with the whole and not the individual? Why with necessity and not freedom? Why with the inconstant rather than the constant? Why with the temporal and not the eternal? Why with the relative and not the absolute? Why with the less and not with the greater? And so on. Dialectical materialism has to fall to pieces on these contradictions. Either the dialectic or the materialism has to fall out. Thus I see that the development continues to the end. In dialectical materialism antitheses are connected, out of which it is impossible to form a unity. As dialectical materialism abandoned mechanism, so also dialectic, if it wants to be consequent, must abandon materialism, and only remain as dialecticism, relativism, and as such be satisfied only with time. If religion is an opiate, the counter question is whether Bolshevism itself is not without religious elements. Already Feuerbach, the patriarch of Bolshevism, put the human being in the place of God. Communism, as the descendent of Feuerbach, has done nothing else but collectivize this human being, divinize it or its special class and bow to it as to God. In the place of Jesus and the apostles it has Marx, Engels, Lenin, Stalin, in which they believe. The proletarian believes in paradise, in the dictatorship of the proletariat. This faith gives him power, even fanaticism, but what will it mean when here also it proves to be the case that this religion too is an opiate?

THE PHILOSOPHY OF FASCISM

Some say that the fascism of Mussolini in Italy does not have its own philosophy. Fascists would say in reply that they are proud of that because their philosophy is not in speculations but in action. So Herbert Schneider, professor at Columbia University, characterizes it in his voluminous and objective book, *Fascism: Its Theory and Praxis in Italy*.[16] A certain fascist Pellizi writes: "The thought of Fascism is Mussolini, because he thought up

16. Herbert Schneider, *Fascism: Its Theory and Praxis in Italy*, trans. Cr. V. Cizek (Prague: Orbis 1931), 368.

Fascism when he created it."[17] We might add: when he created it by deeds and speeches, less by writings. But Pellizi does not have the complete truth. Fascism neither fell from heaven, nor did Mussolini just think it up, but Mussolini also had his predecessors-teachers, from whom he learned. Schneider says in the foreword to his book that fascist theory developed out of various ideologies, under the influence of circumstances and matured chiefly from three philosophical sources in the past: from the philosophy of Machiavelli, from the philosophy of northern nationalism, and from southern, Hegelian, idealistic philosophy. Let us take a closer look at these philosophies and see with whom Mussolini went to school.

Michael Macchiavelli (1469–1527), the great Renaissance political philosopher by virtue of his book, *The Prince*, is the first teacher of Mussolini and his fascism. It is only necessary to insert the word "Duce" in place of the word "prince" to see this. The ideal of a great, united, powerful Italy stood before Macchiavelli. Powerful lords or princes would achieve this, who united divided governments and made order. His ways and means were justified by the result: a powerful Italy. After Macchiavelli, the second teacher of fascism is the first modern Italian philosopher of history, Giovanni Battista Vico (1668–1744). In his philosophy Vico took a position against the rationalistic French Enlightenment in defense of Catholic tradition. In his chief writing, *On New Science* (1725), he sought to found a new science on the creative activity of mind or spirit. We shall see later where and how the thought of the creative activity of mind or spirit was validated. Another philosophical school is the Italian nationalist philosophy, which grew out of the classical French philosophers J. De Maistra (1753–1821) and L. De Bonalda (1754–1840). These traditionalists under the Bourbons, terrified by the terrors of the French revolution, proclaimed a return to Catholic ontology, to Catholic tradition, to absolutism, to the feudal-estate arrangement, to the ideal of the theocratic state and authority, and set up obedience as the chief pillar of order. We know that they are the conceptual founders of Catholic modernism. Anton Rosmini (1797–1855) took over the opinions of these men in his own eclecticism. After the model of the French eclecticism of Cousin and in the spirit of the eternal Catholic philosophy of Thomas Aquinas, he took a stance against the critical philosophy of the Protestant philosopher, Immanuel Kant.

These ideas echoed even more distinctly in the philosophy of Vincent Gioberti (1801–1852), who connected the French ontologism already mentioned with Hegel's idealistic philosophy, introduced to Italy by Frantisek De Sanctis, and thus cleared the way for statist-nationalist Catholic philosophy

17. Ibid., 330.

Appendix

in Italy. That happened chiefly in his book, *On the Moral and Culture Primacy of the Italians*, in the year 1857. This writing contains Catholic idealism; it proclaims that Catholic religion creates morality and morality creates erudition. The European nations originated from Christianity and by this means from Italy; Italy is the firstborn, in her Christianity erected its throne, in her it obtained the height and the glory. Italy is a priestly nation, head of Christianity, the other nations have to be her hands, Europe has to return to Catholic origins, the heterodox have to be destroyed, and so forth.[18] Silvio Spaventa (1817–1882) continued in the philosophy of Gioberti. He connected the previous thoughts with the thoughts of Macchiavelli, laid down the idea of the power state, and so put in motion the divinization of the state. Thus the Catholic thought and nationalist thought combined in their philosophies. Among the older thinkers, the nation was subordinate to religion; among the recent thinkers, the relation has reversed, the nation with the state has been divinized. Don Sturzo, the Catholic populist Italian member of Parliament named this the pantheistic divinization of the nation and state.

Thus we have come to the official philosopher of fascism, Giovani Gentile (1875-).[19] Gentile, as J. Popelova has written,[20] was first a middle school teacher, and from 1903 a university professor. With his philosophy, which was contained in the writings, "Reform of the Hegelian Dialectic," (1913), "Theory of Mind" (1916), "System of Logic," (1917) and so forth, he overshadowed another great Italian philosopher, Benedetto Croce. Strangely like Communism, this Italian fascism in the philosophy of Gentile also starts out from Hegel's philosophy. Just like the philosophy of Gentile is idealistic, but over against the speculative and intellectual characteristics of Hegel, it is also voluntaristic and actualistic, so also is the philosophy of Bolshevism. The foundation of Gentile's metaphysics is the act of knowing in the sense of action and this, furthermore, in the sense of a creative action of the mind. Look! We see here an echo of Vico's philosophy. Only this is what is alive to Gentile, what exists as the ego in its act of consciousness. Reality is only thinkable to the extent that it is really thought. Thinking does not comprehend reality, as it is, but creates reality. Philosophy then is and ought to be a creator of reality. For example: music lives only when someone plays and listens. According to this concrete logic, it is not the logic of an object which is known but the logic of a knowing subject. The concrete logic of

---

18. Ibid., 29.
19. Gentile, who ghostwrote for Mussolini *The Philosophy of Fascism*, died in 1944.
20. Popelova, "Gentile, Philosopher of Italian Fascism," *Ceska Mysl.* 1934, 10–20.

Gentile is not what it is to Masaryk,[21] but a science about thinking thought. Philosophy is not the knowledge of the object known, but the knowledge of the knowing subject in its activity of knowing. Philosophy is not the understanding of what is real in reality, but of the self ("Autoconscienza"). Truth is not the identity of things and reason, nor the identity of sensations and reason, but the identity of reason and will. To know means to think and to desire and that means to act. The one and only truth is the one that I create. Truth is not that which authority, science or the church preaches, but is the act of our being. Truth does not exist always ready and available, but we each have and indeed must have our own truth.

It is evident that this philosophy agrees with the Communist doctrine about the relativity of truth and also with the famous Jesuit doctrine. As it is against absolute truth, so it is also against history in the sense that history is the sum of things which have been done (res *gestae*). History is not that which has been done, but that which lives in us from them. Between historical persons and us there must be a constant relation and only then do these historical persons become historical. History is not in the archives but in us. History then is historiography and these "writings" [the -graphy in histori*ography*] must be written by deeds. As we see, the kernel of this philosophy is not the contemplation the world, but the creation of a world, of life and that by every individual in the united whole, the nation. Moral is whatever one does in the union of the nation. The chief virtue is manliness, heroism. By this philosophy and ethic, he reforms then not only politics, but also the training of the young and the incorporation of them into Mussolini's fascism. In this way, the idealistic German philosophy of Hegel—actually more that of Fichte—reshaped itself in Italy in a particular philosophy of Catholic activism. Schneider characterizes it this way: "God, the immanent mind, has moved itself from Germany and reveals itself now in Italy, in its own new dwelling, in the creative process of history." [22] With its relativism and activism this philosophy has points of contact with American pragmatism. This is verified by the pragmatist Giovanni Papini (1881–), who converted from atheism to affiliate with the aforementioned Catholic modernism, and also Giusippe Prezzolini (1882–), by his writings on Italian culture and about the life of Macchiavelli and in addition to this again the influence of the idea of the German Nietzsche about the *Ubermensch*.

So we now come to the special representative of fascism, Benito Mussolini. We know originally he was a socialist, a revolutionary, and admirer

---

21. Tomaš Garrigue Masaryk (1850–1937), the President of the First Czechoslovak Republic, was a rationalist and humanist.

22. Popelova, "Gentile, Philosopher of Italian Fascism," 33.

Appendix

of his forerunners Marx and Blanque. He was a revolutionary socialist until 1914, when he was expelled from the socialist party, even though they say he himself did not cease to be a socialist and revolutionary. By his activity, circles were founded in 1915, "Fasci d' azione rivoluzioari." From these "fasci"—or, unions (originally in ancient Rome that meant the *lictor fasces*, the bundles of the lictors)—came the name fascism, which got its entire momentum from the union of such fascist revolutionaries. We mention from his writings, *The Doctrine of Fascism* (1932), and significantly his political speeches and appearances, because, as we said, he creates more by his speeches than by his writings. He is of the conviction that living speech is able possibly to attain more than written words. In this perspective he resembles Hitler. We do not yet have in Slovak literature a work on Mussolini's fascism, unless we want to consider the work of Karl Murgas, *The New Italy* as such.[23] But this is really a journalistic travelogue, which promises to be objective, but is far from [non-]prejudicial. He does not see any failures or inadequacies. The author praises to heaven everything he has seen in Italy, and it causes him joy when alongside his praise of the foreign land, he can "take a swing" by sarcasm or mockery at Czechoslovakia. I am curious what the divinized Mussolini would say to an author, to an Italian journalist, if he wrote this way about Italy, as this author writes about ours. From such writing we do not at all become any wiser. Fortunately, even if we do not have our own Slovak writings on Mussolini, other sources will serve us.

Mussolini in his philosophy marches in the tracks of the philosophers mentioned above, and besides these he was also influenced by the so-called poets of revolution, futurists, the post-war social relations in Italy, socialist dissatisfaction, risks, the danger of a split from Communism. In general it is necessary to understand his Fascism as a reaction to Communist action. Even though he was a socialist, and in his worldview there remain certain elements of socialism, he is nonetheless consciously antidemocratic, antirationalist, antipositivist, because according to him these tendencies are the foundation of democracy, and he is an enemy of democracy. Zdenek Smetacek calls his tendency collective spiritualism.[24] The world does not exist, it must be created by the human mind, will. Already according to this, you can see the tracks of Gentile. Chiefly these are the products of the mind of the nation: science, art, religion, culture. By this we are overcoming nature. Culture appears in the whole history of the nation, which is a revelation of the general mind. From the mind of the nation the individual comes forth and to it he must once against be subordinated. All institutions are products

---

23. Karl Murgas, *The New Italy* (Bratislava: Library of the Slovak, 1937).

24. Zdenek Smetacek, "Ideology of Italian Fascism," *Ceska Mysl.*, 1933, 208–215.

of this collective mentality and have to serve it. But the nation does not exist by itself alone; it needs the state in order to unfold its mind. The state is the incarnation of the mind. It is the greatest, holiest magnitude. This Mussolini, who on April 6, 1920 in an anarchistic spirit could still write in the magazine, *Popolo d' Italia*: "Away with the state in all its forms, with the state of yesterday, today and tomorrow, with the bourgeoisie state and the socialist state. For us last surviving individualists, there is only one religion, absurd in this age today, but ever consoling: the religion of anarchy"—this Mussolini, I say, turned 360 degrees and took a stance for the highest idol, the state. His statism, his divinization of the state, devours everything like Molloch. His ideal is, like Macchiavelli, *Stato forte*—the powerful state. The power of the state is not measured only by physical strength, but by the ability to know how to arrange, lead, and create order and so values. The state to him is the organism, which must have the central governance, and this reigns over the individual members. Chief is the head of the government and this is he—the Duce. The single limit of the government is its power. In the leader the nation comes to self-awareness, from which then it passes to the consciousness of the whole and mainly into the will of individuals. Mussolini is this leader. Smetacek rightly notes that if we would inquire why precisely Mussolini is the One, we would wait in vain for an answer.

In such a conception, democracy does not have a place nor does the philosophy of democracy, liberalism. According to him, liberalism was justified only as a rejection of Enlightenment absolutism. He certainly speaks about freedom, but he does not understand this as a right, but as a duty that the state determines according to conditions. In democracy we see the government of the majority and equality. He denies that the majority ought to reign and says that equality is unthinkable. There is natural inequality and it is impossible to equalize this. What democracy holds, that the state must build upon the sum of individuals and on the will of the majority, is an error. The representatives as they are called in the democracies of the people are in fact representatives of factions. In democracy the government of the people is in fact a conflict between political factions and not government. But government must be based on the whole, on the nation, as upon a living, ideal unit. The expression of this unit is the elite of the nation, namely, the spiritual leaders of the nation and chiefly the One, the Duce. The individual must submit to the whole—again a common point with Communism. In Communism she submits to the class, here to the nation. His motto is: Nothing for the individual, everything for Italy. Only the state has rights, the individual only duties.[25] Already according to Gentile, now

---

25. Schneider, *Fascism*, 140–42.

Appendix

also according to Mussolini, the nation does not need freedom but work and bread. According to Mussolini, freedom is only a distant goal, which the state cultivates, but there are no natural rights.[26] This is the echo of Hegel's philosophy of the Prussian state.

As he is against democracy and liberalism, so also he is against capitalism and socialism. We have an expression of this in his statist syndicalist-federative system, or as it is commonly called his corporative system, to the extent that it builds on the social *corpus*, that is, on social estates. *Corpus* is a society of producers, where there are both employers and employees, but where there are no classes. In the *corpus*, the employer and the employee are unified; they are collaborators in the framework and in the interest of the state. The Marxist doctrine about classes increased the gulf between employer and employee and Mussolini wants to remove this gulf in that he fights for a classless society—but that, I say, is utopia. The thought of a corporative system is not new—the medieval estates and guilds are revived by this idea and according to the Catholic hierarchical system it makes out of these a hierarchical organization. Mussolini removes the battle between the classes, but in place of it he introduces war between the nations. The socialist motto "International solidarity and class warfare" in Mussolini changes into the slogan, "Interclass solidarity and national warfare."[27] We see from this also that he is against the idea of internationalism. Just as he is alienated from the Socialist International, he is also alienated from the international work of the League of Nations. According to Schneider, both the Presbyterian Wilson's Christian internationalism and the Jewish International of the Bolsheviks are to him ideological nonsense.[28] We will see below how he judges papal internationalism. Thus we understand why Mussolini with his fascist state left the League of Nations and fights against its ideas.

He has in fact further reasons. According to the view of fascism, life is motion, conflict, war. Death awaits whoever does not fight. War is inevitable because in life there are antitheses—again a point of contact with Communism. Equilibrium, like equality, will never exist, neither then peace, only that, while Communists bring a Darwinist war between classes, Mussolini brings one between nations. He is an open imperialist, because, he says, imperialism is eternal and laws do not change life. Whatever is living must expand. He wants to achieve this with his nation. He wants to resurrect the old Roman Empire, the glory of the age of the Renaissance. According to his philosophy, glorious Italy did not become extinct, but only declined and

26. Ibid., 146–52.
27. Ibid., 209.
28. Ibid., 40.

now fascism will raise it to new life, because Italy has the natural right to it. From the beginning, according to Schneider, he proclaims that in doing this he will not use barbarian means like the Germans, but that they will also not be idealists, but rather will be among those nations who have a favorable situation and do not suffer from other nations. There are plutocratic and proletarian nations. The Italian nation is proletarian, injured in the world war. "We want our place in the world, because we have a right to it."[29] To speak about peace, about work in service of peace, about disarmament, is hypocrisy. I said above that his ideal is a divinized, mighty Italy. Already this becomes clear from the previously introduced information. From this perspective he looks back upon all of history and so builds his philosophy of history. In the tracks of the aforementioned predecessor philosophers, he proclaims that Italy to be the center point of all history and indeed the world. The Greeks, the Phoenicians and the northern barbarians all desired Italy. Italy led Europe in the fight for education; it first civilized and Christianized the barbarians, then stood at the head of medieval mercantilism, then came the naval conquests and discovery. Italy gave the world the Renaissance, modern astronomy, physics, and now leads the world to a new level of social and political organization.[30] A certain fascist named Volt looks on history this way: "The Cycle of a great heresy, beginning with Luther and ending with Lenin, is finished. Future society will not be built upon *The Declaration of the Rights of Man*, but on the [papal] *Syllabus [of Errors]*."[31]

We have already seen what kinds of means Mussolini uses in internal and foreign policy, how they change according to circumstances, how he has gotten rid and gets rid of his opponents. We read enough about that. What ethical principles he has besides great industriousness, efficiency, courage, fearlessness and daring, he answers himself the best: "We do not have unchanging principles, because we are not a church but a movement. Fascism has two pillars: flexibility, changing according to the times and needs—that is pragmatism (Jesuitism, according to us), and second: consciousness of the glorious past of Italy."[32] A true pupil of Macchiavelli. Alongside this Macchiavellian nature, Schneider finds also a streak of Nietzscheanism. According to him Mussolini holds to the motto: Live by taking risks. That means to be fearlessness and defiantly to reject all rest and motionlessness. Gentile gave philosophical foundation to this by asserting that life is not a game, fun, but a hard and merciless struggle. It demands work, sacrifice, heroism,

---

29. Ibid., 39.
30. Ibid., 313.
31. Ibid., 328.
32. *Popolo d' Italia*, October 17, 1920.

Appendix

physical and mental youthfulness. Their hymn, originally a student song, corresponds to this as also their greeting, "Eia-eia a la-la." Strength, energy, self-confidence, self-awareness, firm will, faith, and optimism about life—all these characterize fascism, again in resemblance to Communism. In fascism some kind of aristocracy is born, which regards itself as the creator of history. The fascist Evola writes: "The light of a sublime myth shines in us aristocrats, in beings whose visage is frightful, who breathe freely in a world freed from Providence, teachers and reasons for things, but now looking into the shadows where there is no God and where they themselves are his creators."[33] This is a definite piece of gigantism, of modern titanism.

How is it possible to square their perspective on Christianity with such principles? We said that fascism divinizes the state and in it sees the incarnation of the mind of the nation. From all that has been said we see that the gigantist mentality of the nation takes the place of God for fascism and that politics is religion for it. In what relation can the Christian-Catholic papal religion stand to such a political religion? What religious philosophy can it be and what is theirs? So far as the Catholic Church puts up with the fascist mentality, it lives in peace with it. That is rationalized by the fact that the Catholic Church is also a manifestation of this historical Italian mind. If the church took a stance against the ideas of fascism and vindicated sovereign rights for itself, that would be the end of the peace. Just so, as a papal monarchy, to the extent that the Church helps fascism it suffers from fascism. And vice versa. Murgas also in the abovementioned writing about the new Italy says: "The dictatorship of Mussolini lives by a respectful, correct relation with the Church."[34] In so far as the Catholic Church is not superior to the state, he can cooperate with her. The past testifies that if suddenly she took a stand against fascism at all (certainly not necessarily in all the Christian principles), fascism would turn against her. Actually fascism was originally against the Church. In 1919, according to Murgas, Mussolini still proclaimed that their "movement is not and would not be anti-Catholic,"[35] but already in 1921 he spoke this way: "Tell the priests, who however amount to nothing more than whimpering old celibate virgins: away with those church buildings, destined for demolition, because our victorious heresy is determined to enlighten the brains and hearts of all."[36] It is true that later he changed his view and proclaimed a synthesis of the spiritual and secular Romes. On February 11, 1929 he came to an agreement with the Vatican. After this

33. Schneider, *Fascism*, 346.
34. Murgas, *The New Italy*, 41.
35. Ibid.
36. Schneider, *Fascism*, 298.

agreement, the Pope published an encyclical, in which he carefully but very characteristically says: "Although the church does not condemn democratic governments, it is evident that in its governmental system there is favorable soil for partisan elbowing."[37] It is interesting that in democratic states, the Pope praises democracy.

After this agreement fascism did not take a stance against the Church, but fascist-ized the Church, so that it regards fascism as Catholic: "Whatever is national must also be fascist. If anyone objects that the Catholic Church is international, I reply that it is actually Roman, that is, imperialistic... The spread of the Roman church is a phase of Italian cultural imperialism, by acknowledging the moral primacy of Italy among the nations. The church is only the organized form of Italian religion... The state is spiritualized, the church nationalized."[38] Look! we saw above that Mussolini rejects Jewish international socialism, the international League of Nations and with that the Presbyterian Wilson, however, the international papacy he not only receives, but also rationalizes and politicizes. The former are nonsense, but the latter is genuinely sensible! Like the Catholic Church, fascism also rejects the idealistic philosophy of the Lutheran Hegel and gives the state as a dowry the philosophy of Thomas Aquinas. On the basis of such a combination of the spiritual and the secular, naturally, attacks against the pope and the Catholic Church are forbidden, indeed punishable just as if attacks against the king. Catholicism is the state religion and other cults are allowed, if they do not oppose laws and good morals. What that in fact means, however, according to the whole philosophy of fascism we can just imagine. The day of the Concordat with the Vatican, February 11, is not only a Church, but also a state holiday.

The development of the divinization of fascism does not cease, but continues today. In the schools, the state teaches religion with its own teachers, even though the Church authorizes the textbooks; in the classrooms next to the picture of the king is a cross, but Schneider correctly says: "This cross more and more is swallowed up and Fascism becomes religion." It is mystical, fanatical and cultivates the monastic ideal of self-sacrifice for the divnization of Italy, with Italy for the Vatican. Thus we do not wonder at what Murgas writes: "In fascist Italy the principle is valid: that a good patriot can only be a good Catholic."[39] Does anyone turn that around and say: to be a good Catholic means to be a fascist? Murgas to be sure says that a Slovak cannot be a fascist, actually, more precisely said, he says that a Slovak cannot

---

37. Ibid., 299.
38. Ibid., 301.
39. Murgas, *The New Italy*, 141.

Appendix

be for fascism among us.[40] Why? Because Czechoslovakia is not like Italy. Italy, he says, is more than 99 percent Catholic and almost 94 percent Italian. "Such a nation can be bound together 'to the fasces'— bundled together as one and the same idea and able thus to be organized into one order on the way to one goal."[41] But in Czechoslovakia, where there are more nationalities, that is impossible. But if conditions were otherwise, also this author of *The New Italy* would be a fascist, an adherent of this fascism which you see engraved upon the battle flag: "We go with Andrej Hlinka, the dictator of our hearts, souls, desires and hope."[42]

When I gather all these ideas together and reflect on this whole philosophy, I do not wonder that it is received by the Catholic brothers, even though objections would be possible from the standpoint of the doctrine of Christ, but I do wonder and I cannot understand how some Lutherans can nod Yes to fascism. Certainly they do that either of out ignorance about the essence of fascism or because the feeling of Lutheranism in them has completely perished.

THE PHILOSOPHY OF HITLERISM

The most recent of the three philosophical streams and thus one not yet sufficiently studied, with less literature as a result, is Hitlerism. As Bolshevism is typically Russian, though in origin German, as fascism is typically Italian, so Hitlerism is typically German. Hitlerism also can only be well understood in historical perspective. Originally it was the National-Socialist Worker's Party, which was formed in 1920 in Munich under the leadership of Hitler, but gradually grew, up to the revolution of January 30, 1933 when it became the pan-national German movement. J. L. Fisher in an essay about Hitlerism in his book, *The Third Reich*,[43] correctly treats and characterizes Hitlerism in stating that racial nationalism creates its conceptual foundation over against the internationalism of social democracy. In order to understand this, it is inescapably necessary to study antecedent theoretical works of such nationalism.

The roots of racism extend to the Frenchmen Joseph Gabineau (1816–1882) and his work, *Essay on the Inequality of Human Races*, which in four

---

40. Ibid., 82.

41. Ibid., 81.

42. Ibid., 171. Hlinka (1864–1938), a Catholic Priest, and head of the Slovak People's Party, advocated for Slovak Autonomy in the first Czechoslovak Republic and resisted the liberal, secular, and rationalistic tendencies of Masaryk.

43. J. L. Fisher, *The Third Reich* (Brno, Soc. Revue, 1932), 117.

The Philosophy of Bolshevism, Fascism, and Hitlerism

volumes was published in the years 1853–1855. We can probably summarize his opinion this way, that as individual races are physically different so also are they mentally different, that the mixing of more precious races with less valuable ones effects a decline of the former and finally, that the Aryan races have effected the progress in culture. After Gabineau it is necessary to mention H. S. Chamberlain (1885–1927) by origin an Englishman, but working as a German philosopher, who in his work, *Foundations of the 19th Century*, published in 1899, proclaimed the superior rule of the German race, especially the maritime Vikings. I am grateful to our late brother Jan Hrobon for pointing me to this peculiar work thirty years ago, which I read already then with peculiar interest. The Frenchman La Pouge, the German Woltmann, and Gumplowitz, who called all of history the labor of the races, continued developing these racist views. Besides these I cannot fail to mention that some theories in biology also helped these racist theories. Thus August Weismann posited the hypothesis about the inheritance of human properties. After him the Augustinian monk from Brno, the well-known Rehor Mendel (1822–1884) taught that inherited human properties cannot be changed by internal means. This in particular supported the opinion that was everywhere being introduced that there are gifted and less gifted races. From these anthropologists and biologists Hitler's National Socialism learned about the first, basic agent in the Hitlerite worldview, which we signify by the world, *Blut*, and thence on up to a mystical cult of race and blood.

A second source, as of fascism and Communism, so also of Hilterism's worldview, is the famous theory of evolution according to Charles Darwin from the middle of the nineteenth century. We know that according to this life is struggle. If it is struggle, if in the struggle of natural selection the stronger triumph and if the Germans are the higher race, so the race must go to war with the less valuable races and triumph. Look! We already have the path sketched out before us by which Hitlerism makes its way. We add to this another philosophical source. It is the well-known worldview springing up from the philosophy of Fichte, of Friedrich Nietzsche (1844–1900) who in his book, *Thus Spake Zarathustra*, published in 1883–1885, erected as the new ideal of the individual and of the nation the *Ubermensch* with his lordly morality and the Will to Power as his chief feature over against the slavish Christian morality. Alongside Nietzsche, I mention also the Vienna Professor Otmar Spann (1878–) with his National Socialist sociology, corporative system, philosophy of war and of Germanhood. It is also impossible not to mention the pessimistic philosophy of history of Oswald Spengler (1880–1936) with his writing, *The Decline of the West*, published in two volumes 1918–1922. In this work he prophesies the extinction of the West. In order

Appendix

to avoid this sad prediction, in order for the German nation to avoid it, it is necessary to protect it by purity of race and acquisition of sufficient soil. By this he gave expression to Prussian autocracy according to which the whole is sovereign and the individual has only to obey. Finally I mention Gustav Feder, an engineer who also had influence on the worldview of Hitler. According to *Mein Kampf*, Feder is actually the initiator of the economic and social program of the National Socialist party with the theory in which he distinguishes between capital arising from labor and speculative, bourgeois capital. The former supports, the latter destroys, because capital must serve the state and not rule over it.[44]

So we come to the creator of Hitlerism, to Adolf Hitler (1889–), with his book *Mein Kampf*, from 1924. Bauer says that it is the "Bible of National Socialism, published again and again, introduced into the schools, they give it as a wedding gift, etc."[45] Besides this book, the chief sources for knowledge of the worldview of Hitlerism are Hitler's speeches and deeds. According to these sources we could reconstruct his worldview in its chief thoughts as follows: Hitler even before the 1933 takeover was an enemy of democracy and parliamentarianism, because according to him in this form of government personal responsibility disappears. His perspective is aristocratic. To be sure he speaks of a true "German democracy," over against the Western democracies, but this German democracy consists in the nation which as a whole freely chooses its Leader, who resolves to take on himself all responsibility for everything that happens. In this democracy the majority does not vote, yet the individual decides.[46] He hardened himself to such views after hard tests before the war and after the war, especially after the defeat of Germany in the war. He set himself on the rebirth of the nation, the return to self-awareness of the nation, strength, unity, in order to undo the defeat. He gave himself again to the way of victory and what was it that stood in his way? Jewish Marxism, internationalism, the society of nations, France, the Slavic nations, etc., and all this has to be overcome and removed.

He builds the Third Reich on these ideas. But the state is not the goal of human life, rather the survival of the nation, of the race, is the goal. The state is the vessel, the content is the nation, race.[47] Human rights are according to him state rights. "The world is not for cowardly nations."[48] As there is war in nature, so also in life; there is struggle in history, in which the stronger

44. Adolf Hitler, *Mein Kampf*, trans. Dr. Frantisek Bauer (Prague: Orbis, 1936), 73
45. Ibid., 13.
46. Ibid., 39.
47. Ibid., 124.
48. Ibid., 41

triumphs. "The strong drive away the weak, because the life instinct always crushes the ridiculous bonds of the so-called humanity of individuals and in its place introduces the humanity of nature, which destroys and devours weakness, in order to grant a free field of play to actual strength."[49] Humanity really ought to look forward to this struggle, because it becomes great in this eternal struggle—in eternal peace humanity would sink away.[50] This law of nature justifies the policy of conquest. As nature has laws, so also does the nation. The life of nations works by the law of race. "The stronger must reign and must not mix with the weak and thus sacrifice their greatness."[51] Race creates everything on the earth: culture, technology, science. There is no equality of races. There are races which create culture, which appropriate culture, and which destroy culture.

Among the destroyers of culture belong in the first place the Jews. Hitler regards it as a great deception when Judaism is taken as a religion. To the Jew religion is nothing else than a system of teaching about how to maintain the Jewish race and its material benefits.[52] Jews are egoists, parasites on human society. The have never created anything in the two highest arts, music and architecture,[53] only in theater, yes, because there it is only a matter of imitation. Nor have they created in economics, because they only do business, bargain, and speculate. To be sure they preach freedom, but only in order to use it for their own benefit. They founded the Free Masons and socialism in order to dominate the whole world. The Jew himself protects his own race. A Jewess will marry an influential Christian out of calculation, but a Jew rarely marries a Christian girl.[54] Their final goal is the dictatorship of the proletariat, that means to rule over the entire world. Zionism is naiveté.

In order for the German nation to triumph in the struggle, it is necessary for it to preserve it purity. The nation fell physically because it is necessary to use the means which will make it youthful again (sterilization, prohibition of incest, the Aryan paragraph, assistance for population increase, etc.). Since strength comes in nature and in history, so also it is necessary to cultivate the youth in physical vigor, and with that also reticence, obedience, and self-sacrifice for the nation. Hitler is aware of the fact that the German nation is a mixed race of Nordic, Baltic lowland, Baltic

---

49. Ibid., 49.
50. Ibid., 50.
51. Ibid., 95.
52. Ibid., 58, 100.
53. Ibid., 97–99.
54. Ibid., 102.

Appendix

highland, and other races.[55] As may be seen his concept of nation is purely biological. According to him, the nation is a blood organism, the individual is only an organ of the whole without rights, but only with duties. The whole has rights, of which the Führer is the symbol with his autocracy and totalitarianism. From these principles his foreign policy also flows. *Mein Kampf* says: "It is necessary that we adopt with icy cold realism the perspective that it is not the intention of heaven that any nation on this earth have fifty times more soil than another. It is self-evident that in such a case the political border must not turn up back from the borders of eternal rights. If there is on this earth enough space for the life of all, then we must get so much soil as we need for life."[56] Probably he means Russia. He clearly expresses that this way. "If we want to acquire soil in Europe, there is nothing else to do than to conquer it at the expense of Russia."[57] "The German Reich, as a state, has to take in all Germans," to subjugate other nations, "not to Germanize the people but to Germanize the soil."[58] So we come to the second pillar of their political philosophy, to the soil, *Boden*. Fisher says that if pre-war Germany meant industrial imperialism and the social democracy connected with that, so Hilter's Germany means agrarian imperialism. Hitler wants the nation to return to the soil at home, but he also wants for it to conquer and settle new soil, because it is needed. *Mein Kampf* wants to achieve this with the help of England and Italy, reckoning with the chief enemy, France, and by annexing the soil of Slavic nations. "Human beings create the borders of states, and they can also change them." If it some nation succeeds in extending its borders, "this testifies to the strength of the conquerors and the weakness of the defeated. Rights are grounded only in such power." Look! Here we see Stirner's slogan: the right of the fist.[59] According to Hitler's views, Russia is weak and stands on the edge of destruction and therefore he turns his gaze on Russia.

If anyone would pose the question, what is the economic program of Hitler's National Socialism, since it is socialism, in brief I would answer as follows. According to Feder, in his economic philosophy he leaves private property alone on account of initiative and creativity, but he puts it in service of the nation. He want capital to be creative and not plunder (*Schaffendes nicht raffendes Kapital*). In this way the class war of social democracy would be resolved. Hitlerism also, like fascism, builds on the conditions in which

---

55. Ibid., 125.
56. Ibid., 51.
57. Ibid., 52.
58. Ibid., 126.
59. Ibid., 196.

both entrepreneur and worker have the identical social function: they serve the needs of the whole and do not exist in the service of the profit of the individual. Soil constitutes the most precious capital, which ideally belongs to the nation. The individual, or even societies, possess soil only by renting it. Any other economic programs are not yet worked out. They change according to conditions and circumstances.

Olden, Hitler's biographer, characterizes the central figure of Hitlerism, namely Adoph Hitler, with his principles in short this way. According to Hitler the masses wish for the victory of the strong and the annihilation of the weak, and to him only one law is valid and that is the law of power. He has the will for this, like Nietzsche's *Ubermensch*, the resolve and determination. He believes in terror, and chiefly he believes in himself as Führer. He is a good orator; he does more with words than with letters. Behind him as the Führer comes the entire hierarchy of underlings gradually down to the lowest local organizations. These form the elite of the nation, as also with Mussolini. National selection also dominates in the nation itself.[60] The Führer commands down to the underlings, the underlings obey and respond back up. The program of the party is inerrant dogma, in which, in the model of Catholic ideology, it is necessary to believe. The Führer is inerrant, his Rome or Mecca is Munich. Bauer says that the fanaticism of faith in the Führer and in the correctness of his principles, in the victory of German national matters fulfills their great fantasy of hatred towards others. When we analyze these ideas and their present realization in Hitlerism, and seek in the past for their model we come to what the great Hitlerite Rosenberg came to: He called the revolution of National Socialism the "conservative revolution." He was right in this sense, that they returned to the old Prussian ideas. Many German ideas may be thus characterized, that they represent the actual Prussianization of Germany.[61] The expression of the entire movement and a good symbol of it is battle flag of Hitlerism: the red background with a white circle in the middle, and the black swastika in it. It is the symbol of the old imperial colors: black, white, and red. Red symbolizes the social program, white the national, and the black swastika indicates that German-Aryan Man fights against the Jew.[62]

To this sketch of the picture it is still necessary for us to mention two significant race theorists of Hitlerism: K. Gunther and Alfred Rosenberg. K. Gunther, professor and a chief propagator of racism, wrote the book, *Race Doctrine of the German Nation*, in which the concept of race exchanges

60. Ibid., 144.
61. Ibid., 147.
62. Ibid., 159.

Appendix

back and for with the concept of nation. As a professor, he classifies and evaluates individual races. Bearing in mind that modern anthropology after Linnaeus and Blumenbach discerns three chief races, the European (white), the Negroid (black), and the Mongoloid (yellow) and more sub-races, Gunther then acknowledges the mixing of races. By race in distinction from nation we understand a group of people, who have commonly inherited bodily indicators. In nation the bond is more mental, linguistic and cultural. Gunther, in the first, that is European, white race discerns these sub-races: the Nordic, the Alpine, the Baltic highland and Baltic lowland. According to him the Germans are 50 percent Nordic, 20 percent Alpine, 15 percent Baltic mountain [*dinarsky*], and 15 percent Baltic lowland [*osticky*] and other races. As a result of the fact that it has mostly Nordic blood, it excels among all the others. Gunther's German race is characterized by lean form, long skulls, blond hair, and blue eyes. It is the most excellent, most noble, most creative—the master race. The other races are less valuable. Among these belong the French nation which is bastard and degenerate, the Czechoslovak race, the Polish, etc. Least valuable especially is the Jewish race.

True, the research of other anthropologists comes to other results. Thus according to our anthropologist, Matiejka, the percentage of races in our nation is 4.5 percent Nordic, 15 percent alpine, 35 percent Baltic flatland, and 20 percent Baltic Mountain. The volume put together by Dr. Weignerom, *The Equal Value of the European Races*, proves that there are no privileges among the Europeans. It is worth noting, that also the former Leipzig professor H. Schneider, in his 1923 book *The History of Philosophy*, proved on the basis of natural science that precisely the mixing of the races created mechanisms fitting for cultivating higher culture. Against the boasting about the inner properties of the German race, Dr. Hugo Iltis in his book, *Race in Science and Politics*, points out that physical properties are not connected with mental properties. He writes satirically: "Black skin is not connected with a black soul." There are no longer today any pure races. The closer we come to the primitive tribes, the purer the race is; the closer and higher we come to today, the more the races are mixed. The Jews also are a well mixed race. If the German racists are right that the mixing of the races works evil and the decline of nations, that it is necessary to purify the races, then how will we explain the phenomenon that culture has advanced just there where and how the races step by step have mixed together? Europe itself, North America, and even Germany itself are sufficient proof of that. Why, we saw above that they acknowledge the mixing of races also in Germany, and so is their culture thereby lower? Neither science nor statistics prove that the Nordic race would be the most valuable. It is impossible to prove that because neither history nor culture attests to it.

In order to support the theory of racism, attempts to analyze races according to blood also occur. This is what the theory of Alfred Rosenberg demands in his book *The Myth of Blood of the 20th Century*. According to this theory, the mixing of blood is a crime, incest. Iltis correctly comments on this that blood more connects us than divides us, as proved by the fact of blood transfusions. The blood types, A, B, AB and O are well known and these exist among all the races. But Rosenberg continues politically with the conclusions of Gunther. In the years of writing *Mein Kampf* Hitler treated the advocates of the old German myths ironically.[63] But that did not deceive Rosenberg from continuing in his fantasies. According to his myth of blood, we Czechoslovaks are uncultured, valueless, half-savage, with no right to exist on European soil. For example, he writes about the Hussite movement: "Here the Alpine-Baltic Mountain essence shows itself, which manifested itself in savageness, combined with a terrible superstition. From this time on, this nation remained uncreative, and it has to thank the creative German powers repeatedly flowing into it for its later cultural recovery . . . To acknowledge freedom today for Czechs and Poles means to be wed to racial chaos."[64] If he writes that way about us, we can imagine what he writes, for example, about the Jews. I cite his words: "The Jews have poisoned the world, they are the originators of Christianity as of Free Masonry, Capitalism as also of Marxism—they must be destroyed."[65] Those are the words that sound like the news reports today about the concentration camps not only of Jews, but also of Christians. We understand why we are less valuable: they need our soil.

How far they will proceed in this malice aforethought towards others and towards themselves, the following testimony serves to make clear: "The Viking appears in a singular beauty in history, since compared to him the aesthetically perfect Greek is the unfinished barbarian."[66] Look and see where Hitlerism is going! The maritime Viking pirates are victorious over the classical Greeks! And if we would go further in history, so we would finish up the sketch of them this way: the continuation of the Vikings were the German knights, who expelled the Baltic Slavs, after them came Prussian militarism which introduced a world war, and in the end come the Hitlerites, who can only introduce a world catastrophe!

---

63. Ibid., Bauer, 116.
64. *Mythos*, 23–126.
65. Iltis, *Race*, 92.
66. *Mythos*, 167.

Appendix

CONCLUSION

What can I say not only about Hitlerism but about the philosophy of all three of these tendencies? Democracy is on the defensive. These tendencies, according to their essence, are on the offensive. Our situation is not easy, but in short we must assert: in so far as Bolshevism is atheistic and materialistic, we cannot accept it from a religious standpoint; so far as Hitlerism is naturalistic, we cannot accept it from a Christian standpoint; so far as fascism is Catholic, we cannot accept it from a Lutheran standpoint. I will not analyze the matter in greater detail. But I will point further to this: the method, terror, the denial of individual freedom, we cannot accept neither as Christians nor as Lutherans, and Hitlerism we cannot accept either as Slavs. I have expressed my astonishment at how anyone from the ranks of the Lutherans could agree with fascism, and no less astonishment do I express how anyone from the Slovak Lutherans could sympathize, preach, and write sympathetically about the philosophy of Hitlerism.

Bibliography

Adkins, Brent and Paul R. Hinlicky. *Rethinking Philosophy and Theology with Deleuze: A New Cartography*. London: Bloomsbury Academic, 2013.

Adorno, Theodor W. and Max Horkheimer. *Dialectic of Enlightenment*. Translated by J. Cumming. London: Verso, 1997.

Althaus, Paul. *The Ethics of Martin Luther*. Philadelphia: Fortress, 1972.

Arendt, Hannah. *Eichmann in Jerusalem: A Report on the Banality of Evil,* revised and enlarged edition. New York: Penguin, 1994.

Aschheim, Steven E. *The Nietzsche Legacy in Germany 1890–1990*. Berkeley: University of California Press, 1994.

Barth, Karl. "Introduction" in Ludwig Feuerbach, *The Essence of Christianity*. Translated by G. Eliot. New York: Harper Torchbooks, 1957.

———. *Theological Existence To-day: A Plea for Theological Freedom*. Translated by R. B. Hoyle. London: Hodder and Stoughton, 1933.

Bayer, Oswald. *Martin Luther's Theology: A Contemporary Interpretation*. Translated by Thomas H. Trapp. Grand Rapids: Eerdmans, 2007.

Becker, Matthew. "Werner Elert in Retrospect." *Lutheran Quarterly* 20/1 (2006) 249–302.

Bell, Daniel M. Jr. *Liberation Theology after the End of History: The Refusal to Cease Suffering*. London: Routledge, 2001.

Benne, Robert. *The Paradoxical Vision: A Public Theology for the Twenty-first Century*. Minneapolis: Fortress, 1995.

Bergen, Doris L. *The Holocaust: A Concise History*. Plymouth, UK: Rowman and Littlefield, 2009.

———. *Twisted Cross: The German Christian Movement in the Third Reich*. Chapel Hill: The University of North Carolina Press, 1996.

Berger, Peter L. *The Heretical Imperative: Contemporary Possibilities of Religious Affirmation*. New York: Anchor, 1979.

Bertram, Robert W. *A Time for Confessing*. Edited by Michael Hoy. Lutheran Quarterly Books. Grand Rapids: Eerdmans, 2008.

Bielfeldt, Dennis, Mickey Mattox, and Paul R. Hinlicky. *The Substance of Faith: Luther on Doctrinal Theology*. Minneapolis: Fortress, 2008.

Bonhoeffer, Dietrich. *Christ the Center: A New Translation*. Translated by E. H. Robertson. New York: Harper & Row, 1978.

———. *Ethics*. Translated by N. H. Smith. New York: MacMillan, 1978.

Browning, Christopher R. *Ordinary Men: Reserve Police Battalion 101 and the Final Solution in Poland*. New York: Harper, 1998.

Bullock, Alan. *Hitler and Stalin: Parallel Lives*. London: Fontana, 1993.

Bultmann Rudolf & Five Critics. *Kerygma and Myth*. Edited by H. W. Bartsch. New York: Harper & Row, 1961.

Burleigh, Michael. *Earthly Powers: The Clash of Religion and Politics from the French Revolution to the Great War*. New York: HarperCollins, 2005.

———. *The Third Reich: A New History*. New York: Hill and Wang, 2000.

Busch, Eberhard. *Karl Barth: His Life from Letters and Autobiographical Texts*. Translated by J. Bowden. Philadelphia: Fortress, 1976.

Carrier, Richard C. "Hitler's Table Talk: Troubling Finds." *German Studies Review* 26/3 (2003) 561–76.

Carter, Guy C. "Martin Luther in the Third Reich: Recent Research on Luther as Iconic Force in Hitler's Germany." *Seminary Ridge Review* 12/1 (2009) 42–62.

Cornwell, John. *Hitler's Pope: The Secret History of Pius XII*. New York: Penguin, 2000.

———. *Hitler's Scientists: Science, War and the Devil's Pact*. New York: Viking, 2003.

Crowe, David M. *The Holocaust: Roots, History, and Aftermath*. Boulder, CO: Westview, 2008.

Dawidowicz, Lucy S. *The War against the Jews: 1933–45*, tenth anniversary ed. London: Penguin, 1987.

DeJonge, Michael P. *Bonhoeffer's Theological Formation: Berlin, Barth, and Protestant Theology*. Oxford: Oxford University Press, 2012.

de la Durantaye, Leland. *Giorgio Agamben: A Critical Introduction*. Stanford: Stanford University Press, 2009.

Dennett, Daniel C. *Darwin's Dangerous Idea: Evolution and the Meanings of Life*. Simon & Schuster, 1995.

Dietrich, Otto. *The Hitler I Knew: Memoirs of the Third Reich's Press Chief*. New York: Skyhorse, 2010.

Duchrow, Ulrich. *Christenheit und Weltverantwortung: Traditionsgeschichte und systematische Struktur der Zweireichelehre*, 2nd ed. Stuttgart: Klett-Cotta, 1983.

Dwork, Deborah and Robert Jan van Pelt. *The Holocaust: A History*. London: Norton, 2002.

Ellis, Joseph J. *American Sphinx: The Character of Thomas Jefferson*. New York: Vintage, 1998.

Elshtain, Jean Bethke. *Sovereignty: God, State, and Self*. The Gifford Lectures. (New York: Basic, 2008).

Ericksen, Robert P. "Christians in the Nazi Era: A Problematic Story." *Kirchliche Zeitgeschichte* 17/2 Sonderheft (2004) 352–58.

———. "Emerging from the Legacy? Protestant Churches and the Shoah." *Kirchliche Zeitgeschichte* 17/2 Sonderheft (2004) 359–82.

———. "Hiding the Nazi Past." In *A Lutheran Vocation: Philip A. Nordquist and the Study of History at Pacific Lutheran University*, edited by R. P. Ericksen and M. J. Halvorson, 137–56. Tacoma, WA: Pacific Lutheran University Press, 2005.

———. *Theologians under Hitler: Gerhard Kittel, Paul Althaus and Emanuel Hirsch*. New Haven: Yale University Press, 1985.

Ericksen, Robert P. and Susannah Heschel, eds. *Betrayal: German Churches and the Holocaust*. Minneapolis: Fortress, 1999.

Flett, John G. *The Witness of God: The Trinity, Missio Dei, Karl Barth, and the Nature of Christian Community*. Grand Rapids: Eerdmans, 2010.

Forstman, Jack. *Christian Faith in Dark Times: Theological Conflicts in the Shadow of Hitler.* Louisville: Westminster John Knox, 1992.
Frank, Thomas. *What's the Matter with Kansas? How Conservatives Won the Heart of America.* New York: Henry Holt, 2004.
Friedlander, Henry. *The Origins of the Nazi Genocide: From Euthanasia to the Final Solution.* Chapel Hill: University of North Carolina Press, 1995.
Fritz, Stephen G. *Ostkrieg: Hitler's War of Extermination.* Lexington: The University of Kentucky Press, 2011.
Fukuyama, Francis. *The End of History and the Last Man.* New York: Free, 1992.
Furet, François. *The Passing of an Illusion: The Idea of Communism in the Twentieth Century.* Translated by D. Furet. Chicago: University of Chicago Press, 1999.
Furet, François and Ernst Nolte. *Fascism and Communism.* Translated by K. Golson. Lincoln: University of Nebraska Press, 2001.
Garcia, Alberto L. and Susan K. Wood, editors. *Critical Issues in Ecclesiology: Essays in Honor of Carl E. Braaten.* Grand Rapids: Eerdmans, 2011.
Gellately, Robert. *Lenin, Stalin, and Hitler: The Age of Social Catastrophe.* New York: Knopf, 2007.
Gentile, Emilio. "Fascism as Political Religion." *Journal of Contemporary History* 25/2–3 (1990) 229–51.
———. "New Idols: Catholicism in the face of Fascist Totalitarianism." *Journal of Modern Italian Studies* 11/ 2 (2006) 143–70.
Gluchmann, Vasil. *Slovak Lutheran Social Ethics.* Studies in Religion and Society, Vol. 37. Lewiston, NY: Edwin Mellen, 1997.
Goldhagen, Daniel. *Hitler's Willing Executioners: Ordinary Germans and the Holocaust.* New York: Knopf, 1996.
Goodrick-Clarke, Nicholas. *The Occult Roots of Nazism: Secret Aryan Cults and Their Influence on Nazi Ideology.* New York: New York University Press, 1985.
Green, Lowell C. *Lutherans against Hitler: The Untold Story.* St. Louis: Concordia, 2007.
Greene, John C. *The Death of Adam: Evolution and its Impact on Western Thought.* Ames: Iowa State University Press, 1996.
Hamerow, Theodore S. *Why We Watched: Europe, America and the Holocaust.* New York: Norton, 2008.
Hanfstaengel, Ernst. *Hitler: The Memoir of a Nazi Insider Who Turned Against the Führer.* Translated by J. W. Toland. New York: Arcade, 2011.
Heckel, Johannes. *Lex Charitatis: A Juristic Disquisition on Law in the Theology of Martin Luther.* Translated by Gottfired G. Krodel. Grand Rapids: Eerdmans, 2010.
Hendrix, Scott H. *Recultivating the Vineyard: The Reformation Agendas of Christianization.* Louisville: Westminster John Knox, 2004.
Heschel, Susannah. *The Aryan Jesus: Christian Theologians and the Bible in Nazi Germany.* Princeton, NJ: Princeton University Press, 2008.
Hinlicky, Paul R. "A Lutheran Contribution to the Theology of Judaism." *Journal of Ecumenical Studies* 31/1–2 (1994) 123–52.
———. *Beloved Community: Critical Dogmatics after Christendom.* Grand Rapids: Eerdmans, forthcoming in 2014.
———. *Divine Complexity: The Rise of Creedal Christianity.* Minneapolis: Fortress, 2010.

---. "Luther and Liberalism." In *A Report from the Front Lines: Conversations on Public Theology. A Festschrift in Honor of Robert Benne*, edited by Michael Shahan, 89–104. Grand Rapids: Eerdmans, 2009.

---. *Luther and the Beloved Community: A Path for Christian Theology after Christendom*. Grand Rapids: Eerdmans, 2010.

---. "Luther's Atheism." In *The Devil's Whore: Reason and Philosophy in the Lutheran Tradition*, edited by J. Hockenberry Drageseth, 53–60. Minneapolis: Fortress, 2011.

---. *Paths Not Taken: Fates of Theology from Luther through Leibniz*. Grand Rapids: Eerdmans, 2009.

---. "Process, Convergence, Declaration: Reflections on Doctrinal Dialogue." *The Cresset* 64/6 (2001) 13–18.

---. "The Reception of Luther in Pietism and the Enlightenment," *Oxford Handbook to Martin Luther*, edited by R. Kolb, I. Dingel, and L. Batka. Oxford: Oxford University Press, forthcoming in 2013.

---. Review of *The Forging of Races*, by Colin Kidd. *Sixteenth Century Journal* 39/2 (2008) 513–14.

---. Review of *Jonas Propheta*, by Johann Anselm Steiger. *Lutheran Quarterly* 26/4 (2012) 453–55.

---. Review of *Law and Protestantism*, by John Witte. *Sixteenth Century Journal* 35/2 (2004) 534–36.

---. Review of *Procreative Ethics*, by Fritz Oehlschlaeger. *Journal of Lutheran Ethics* Online: http://www.elca.org/What-We-Believe/Social-Issues/Journal-of-Lutheran-Ethics/Issues/November-2012/Hinlicky-Review-of-A-Discussion-of—Procreative-Ethics.aspx.

---. "Staying Lutheran in the Changing Church(es)," afterword in Mickey L. Mattox and Gregg Roeber, eds., *Changing Churches*. Grand Rapids: Eerdmans, 2011.

---. "Verbum Externum: Dietrich Bonhoeffer's Bethel Confession." *God Speaks to Us*, International Bonhoeffer Interpretations, 5. Edited by R. Wüstenberg and J. Zimmermann. Frankfurt: Peter Lang, forthcoming 2013.

---. "What Hope after Holocaust?" *Pro Ecclesia* 8/1 (1999) 12–22.

Hitler, Adolf. *Mein Kampf*. Translated by R. Manheim. Boston: Houghton Mifflin, 1971.

Hitler's Second Book: The Unpublished Sequel to Mein Kampf. Translated by K. Smith. New York: Enigma, 2003.

Hockenos, Matthew D. *A Church Divided: German Protestants Confront the Nazi Past*. Bloomington: Indiana University Press, 2004.

James, William. *The Varieties of Religious Experience*. New York: Dover, 2002.

Jenson, Robert and Eugene Korn, eds. *Covenant and Hope*. Grand Rapids: Eerdmans, 2012.

Katz, Eric, ed. *Death by Design: Science, Technology, and Engineering in Nazi Germany*. New York: Pearson/Longman, 2006.

Kidd, Colin. *The Forging of Races: Race and Scripture in the Protestant Atlantic World, 1600–2000*. Cambridge: Cambridge University Press, 2006.

Klossowski, Pierre. *Nietzsche and the Vicious Circle*. Translated by D. W. Smith. Chicago: University of Chicago Press, 1997.

Knowlton, J. and T. Cates, editors and translators. *Forever in the Shadow of Hitler? Original Documents of the Historikerstreit, the Controversy concerning the Singularity of the Holocaust*. Amherst, NY: Humanities, 1994.

Kolb, Robert and Timothy J. Wengert, eds. *The Book of Concord: The Confessions of the Evangelical Lutheran Church*. Minneapolis: Fortress, 2000.

Kubizek, August. *The Young Hitler I Knew*. Translated by G. Brooks. London: Greenhill, 2006.

Kuklick, Bruce. *A History of Philosophy in America, 1720-2000*. Oxford: Clarendon, 2001.

Lazareth, William H. *Christians in Society: Luther, the Bible and Social Ethics*. Minneapolis: Fortress, 2001.

———. *Luther on the Christian Home*. Philadelphia: Muhlenberg, 1960.

Lewis, David Levering. *God's Crucible: Islam and the Making of Europe, 570-1215*. New York: Norton, 2008.

Lilla, Mark. *The Stillborn God: Religion, Politics and the Modern West*. New York: Vintage, 2007.

Lindbeck, George A. *The Nature of Doctrine: Religion and Theology in a PostLiberal Age*. Philadelphia: Westminster, 1984.

Locke, John, *Second Treatise of Government*. Edited by C. B. Macpherson. Indianapolis: Hackett, 1980.

Löwith, Karl. *Martin Heidegger and European Nihilism*. Edited by Richard Wolin and translated by G. Steiner. New York: Columbia University Press, 1995.

Luhrssen, David. *Hammer of the Gods: The Thule Society and the Birth of Nazism*. Washington, DC: Potomac, 2012.

MacIntyre, Alasdair. *After Virtue: A Study in Moral Theory*, 2nd ed. Notre Dame, IN: University of Notre Dame Press, 1984.

———. *Three Rival Versions of Moral Enquiry: Encyclopaedia, Genealogy and Tradition*. Notre Dame, IN: University of Notre Dame Press, 1990.

———. *Whose Justice? Which Rationality?* Notre Dame, IN: University of Notre Dame Press, 1988.

Marrus, Michael R. *The Holocaust in History*. New York: Meridan/Penguin, 1987.

Mauer, Wilhelm. *Historical Commentary on the Augsburg Confession*. Translated by H. George Anderson. Philadelphia: Fortress, 1986.

Mazower, Mark. *Dark Continent: Europe's Twentieth Century*. New York: Knopf, 1999.

McCumber, John. *Time in the Ditch: American Philosophy and the McCarthy Eras*. Evanston, IL: Northwestern University Press, 2001.

Menand, Louis. *The Metaphysical Club: A Story of Ideas in America*. New York: Farrar, Straus & Giroux, 2001.

Moltmann, Jürgen. *The Way of Jesus Christ: Christology in Messianic Dimension*. Translated by M. Kohl. New York: Harper Collins, 1990.

Morgan, Michael L., ed. *A Holocaust Reader: Responses to the Nazi Extermination*. New York: Oxford University Press, 2001.

Morse, Christopher. *Not Every Spirit: A Dogmatics of Christian Disbelief*. Harrisburg, PA: Trinity International, 1994.

Nagorski, Andrew. *Hitlerland: American Eyewitnesses to the Nazi Rise to Power*. New York: Simon & Schuster, 2012.

Neitzel, Sönke and Harald Welzer. *Soldaten: On Fighting, Killing, and Dying. The Secret World War II Transcripts of German POWs*. Translated by J. Chase. New York: Knopf, 2012.

Niebuhr, Reinhold. *The Irony of American History*. New York: Scribners, 1952.

Bibliography

———. *The Nature and Destiny of Man: A Christian Interpretation*. 2 vols. New York: Scribner's, 1943.

Niewyk, Donald L., ed. *The Holocaust: Problems and Perspectives of Interpretation*, 3rd ed. New York: Houghton Mifflin, 2003.

Nirenberg, David. *Anti-Judaism: The Western Tradition*. New York: Norton, 2013.

Nolte, Ernst. *Three Faces of Fascism: Action Francaise—Italian Fascism—National Socialism*. Translated by Leila Vennewitz. New York: Holt, Reinhart and Winston, 1966.

Novak, David. *Jewish-Christian Dialogue: A Jewish Justification*. New York: Oxford University Press, 1989.

Oberman, Heiko. *The Roots of Antisemitism in the Age of Renaissance and Reformation*. Translated by J. I. Porter. Philadelphia: Fortress, 1984.

Ochs, Peter. *Another Reformation: Postliberal Christianity and the Jews*. Grand Rapids: Baker Academic, 2011.

Oehlschlaeger, Fritz. *Procreative Ethics: Philosophical and Christian Approaches to Questions at the Beginning of Life*. Eugene, OR: Cascade, 2011.

Osuský, Samuel Štefan. "The Philosophy of Boshevism, Fascism and Hitlerism," translated by Paul R. Hinlicky and previously published in Two Parts, *Lutheran Forum* (Winter, 2009) 50–58 and (Spring, 2010) 50–58. Translated from *Štyri prednášky*. Liptovsky Sväty Mikuláš: Tranocius, 1940.

———. *Pastoral Letter on the Jewish Question* (1942) with Bishop Pavel Čobrda. Translated by Paul R. Hinlicky. *Lutheran Quarterly* XXIII/3 (2009) 332–42, from *Sluzba Narodu* II, edited by Dr. Samuel Štefan Osuský. Svaty Mikulaš: Tranoscius, 1947.

Pannenberg, Wolfhart. *Systematic Theology*, 3 vol. Translated by G. W. Bromiley. Grand Rapids: Eerdmans, 1991.

Peirce, Charles Sanders. *Philosophical Writings of Peirce*. Edited by J. Buchler. New York: Dover, 1955.

"The Persecution of the Christian Churches." *Rutgers Journal of Law and Religion*. Online: www.camlaw.rutgers.edu/publications/law-religion.

Pringle, Heather. *The Master Plan: Himmler's Scholars and the Holocaust*. New York: Hyperion, 2006.

Remak, Joachim, ed. *The Nazi Years: A Documentary History*. Long Grove, IL: Waveland, 1990.

Report on "The Persecution of the Christian Churches," *New York Times*. Online: http://www.NewYorktimes.com/2002/01/13/weekinreview/word-for-word-case-against-nazis-hitler-s-forces-planned-destroy-german.html?pagewanted=all&src=pm.

Rhodes, Richard. *Masters of Death: The SS Einsatzgruppen and the Invention of the Holocaust*. New York: Knopf, 2002.

Rice, Daniel F. *Reinhold Niebuhr and John Dewey: An American Odyssey*. Albany: State University of New York Press, 1993.

Rosenbaum, Alan S., ed. *Is the Holocaust Unique? Perspectives on Comparative Genocide*, 3rd ed. Philadelphia: Westview, 2009.

Royce, Josiah. *The Problem of Christianity*. Washington, DC: The Catholic University of America Press, 2001.

Rubenfeld, Sheldon, ed. *Medicine after the Holocaust: From the Master Race to the Human Genome and Beyond*. New York: Palgrave Macmillan, 2010.

Rubenstein, Richard L. *After Auschwitz: Radical Theology and Contemporary Judaism.* Indianapolis: Bobbs-Merrill, 1966.

Ruether, Rosemary. *Faith and Fratricide: The Theological Roots of Anti-Semitism.* New York: Seabury, 1979.

Ryback, Timothy W. "Hitler's Forgotten Library: The Man, His Books, and His Search for God." *The Atlantic Monthly* (May 2003) 76–90.

———. *Hitler's Private Library: The Books That Shaped His Life.* New York: Knopf, 2008.

Safranski, Rüdiger. *Nietzsche: A Philosophical Biography.* Translated by S. Frisch. New York: Norton, 2002.

Samuel, Maurice. *The Great Hatred.* Lanham MD: University Press of America, 1988; first published October 1940.

Schmid, Heinrich. *The Doctrinal Theology of the Evangelical Lutheran Church*, 3rd edition. Philadelphia: Lutheran Publication Society, 1899.

Schmitt, Carl. *Political Theology: Four Chapters on the Concept of Sovereignty.* Translated by G. Schwab. Chicago: University of Chicago Press, 2005.

Scholder, Klaus. *The Churches and the Third Reich, Vol. One: 1918–1934.* Translated by J. Bowden. Minneapolis: Fortress, 1988.

Schwarz, Hans. "Paul Althaus (1888–1966)." *Lutheran Quarterly* 25/1 (2011) 28–51.

Shirer, William L. *The Rise and Fall of the Third Reich.* New York: Simon and Schuster, 1960.

Siemon-Netto, Uwe. *The Fabricated Luther: Refuting Nazi Connections and Other Modern Myths,* 2nd ed. St. Louis: Concordia, 2007.

Snyder, Timothy. *Bloodlands: Europe between Hitler and Stalin.* New York: Basic, 2010.

Spicer, Kevin P. *Hitler's Priests: Catholic Clergy and National Socialism.* DeKalb: Northern Illinois University Press, 2008.

Stayer, James M. *Martin Luther: German Saviour. German Evangelical Theological Factions and the Interpretation of Luther, 1917–1933.* Montreal: McGill-Queens University Press, 2000.

Steiger, Johann Anselm. *Jonas Propheta: Zur Auslegungs- und Mediengeschichte des Buches Jona bein Martin Luther und im Luthertum der Barockzeit,* mit einer Edition von Johann Matthäus Meyfarts "Tuba Poenitentiae Prophetica" 1625. Stuttgart-Bad Cannstatt: frommann-holzboog Verlag, 2011.

Steigmann-Gall, Richard. *The Holy Reich: Nazi Conceptions of Christianity, 1919–1945.* Cambridge: Cambridge University Press, 2003.

Sternhell, Zeev. *Neither Right nor Left: Fascist Ideology in France.* Translated by David Maisel. Berkeley: University of California Press, 1986.

Taylor, Kressman. *Day of No Return* (org. *Until That Day*) No place provided: Taylor-Wright, 2003, org. 1942.

Telushkin, Jospeh. *Jewish Literacy.* New York: Morrow, 2001.

Tillich, Paul. *The Socialist Decision.* Translated by Franklin Sherman. New York: Harper and Row, 1977.

Tóth, Dezider, ed. *The Tragedy of the Slovak Jews.* Proceedings of the International Symposium, Banská Bystrica, March 25–27, 1992. Banská Bystrica: Datei, 1992.

Trevor-Roper, H. R., ed. *Hitler's Table Talk 1941–1944: His Private Conversations,* new updated version. Translated by N. Cameron and R.H. Stevens. New York: Enigma, 2008.

Bibliography

Ušiak, Ján. "Evanjelická Cirkev a Slovenský Štát." In *Kapitoly z Odboja na Slovensku*, edited by Jaroslav Šolc, 5–53. Bratislava: Ustav Dejín Kommunistickey Strany Slovenska, 1967.

Vilhauer, Monica. *Gadamer's Ethics of Play: Hermeneutics and the Other.* Lanham, MD: Rowman and Littlefield, 2010.

Wade, Nicolas. *Before the Dawn: Recovering the Lost History of Our Ancestors.* New York, Penguin: 2006.

Wallman, Johannes. "The Reception of Luther's Writings on the Jews from the Reformation to the End of the 19th Century." *Lutheran Quarterly* 1/1 new series (1987) 71–97.

Walmer, George J. "Hitler and the German Church." *North American Review* 237/2 (February 1934) 133–41.

Watts, Rikk. "Israel and Salvation." In *The Oxford Handbook of Evangelical Theology*, edited by G. McDermott, 177–94. New York: Oxford University Press, 2010.

Weikart, Richard. *From Darwin to Hitler: Evolutionary Ethics, Eugenics, and Racism in Germany.* New York: Palgrave MacMillan, 2004.

Wendebourg, Dorothea. "Jews Commemorating Luther in the Nineteenth Century." *Lutheran Quarterly* 26/3 (2012) 249–70.

Westerholm, Stephen. *Perspectives Old And New on Paul: The "Lutheran" Paul and His Critics.* Grand Rapids: Eerdmans, 2004.

Witte, John Jr. *Law and Protestantism: The Legal Teachings of the Lutheran Reformation.* Cambridge, UK: Cambridge University Press, 2002.

Wright, William J. *Martin Luther's Understanding of God's Two Kingdoms: A Response to the Challenge of Skepticism.* Grand Rapids: Baker Academic, 2010.

Yoder, Nathan Howard. "Ordnung in Gemeinschaft: A Critical Appraisal of the Erlangen Contribution to the Orders of Creation." PhD diss., Regensburg, 2011.

Zimmermann, Jens. *Recovering Theological Hermeneutics: An Incarnational-Trinitarian Theory of Interpretation.* Grand Rapids: Baker Academic, 2004.

Žitňan, Andrej. "Evanjelická Cirkev Augsburgského Vyznania na Slovensku v rockoch 1938–1945." PhD diss., Bratislava: Univerzita Komenského, 2008.

Index of Names and Subjects

Ad hoc apologetics, 48–50
Adkins, Brent, xi, 6, 124, 158, 191, 221
Adorno, Theodor W., 6, 21, 221
Agamben, Giorgio, 6–7, 115, 122, 190, 222
Allen, Maj, Gen, Henry T., 78
Althaus, Paul, 15, 17–18, 21–27, 33–34, 37, 45–48, 50, 53, 146, 148—9, 166–68, 175–77, 186, 221–22, 227
Ansbach Memorandum, 21, 23, 52, 57–58, 149, 167
Antinomianism, 56, 93, 150, 165
Arendt, Hannah, 3, 39, 109–17, 150, 221
Aschheim, Steven E., xi, 61, 117–18, 221
Asmussen, Hans, 52, 57, 62, 148–53, 161

Baeumler, Alfred, 121
Barmen Declaration/Synod, 21–23, 46, 51–53, 56–58, 142, 148–49, 184
Barth, Karl, 9–10, 21, 23–24, 27, 30, 33–35, 39, 45–46, 48, 51–53, 55–63, 69–71, 86, 97, 144–45, 148–49, 151–52, 167, 173–75, 177–85, 189, 221–22, See Political Barthianism
Bayer, Oswald, 46, 186, 221
Beblavý, Ján, 97
Becker, Matthew, 50, 221
Bell, Daniel M. Jr., 6, 221
Beloved Community, 134, 159, 166, 186, 188, 191

Benne, Robert, xi, 47, 221, 224
Bergen, Doris L., 7, 15, 28–35, 37, 48, 142, 144–47, 221
Berger, Peter L., 189, 221
Bernhard, Leopold W., 71, 86–87, 93
Bertram, Robert W., 22, 50–52, 67, 221
Bielfeldt, Dennis, 16, 221
Bolshevism, 8–9, 17–18, 21, 24, 67, 72, 78–81, 94, 133–34, 158, 160
Bonhoeffer, Dietrich, xii, 9, 25, 35, 49–52, 56–57, 60, 63, 66, 71, 148, 155–56, 161, 163–64, 175, 178, 180, 182–83, 221–22, 224
Bormann, Martin, 32, 39, 135
Browning, Christopher R., 55, 76, 221
Bullock, Alan, 100, 106, 117, 222
Bultmann, Rudolf, 9, 32, 34–35, 58, 63, 71, 123, 132, 145, 149, 175–83, 222
Burleigh, Michael, 2, 89, 102–3, 109–12, 115–16, 121, 129, 188, 222
Busch, Eberhard, 59, 222

Carrier, Richard C., 135, 222
Cartesian (-Kantian) dualism, 46, 60, 106, 181, 184, 189
Christendom, 11–12, 46, 66–67, 84, 153–63, 166, 170, 173–74, 183, 186, 191, 223–24
Christian Platonism, 110–11, 119, 123
Christology, 10, 12, 23, 31, 60, 63, 146, 159, 175–82, 225
Cliché-thinking, 20, 53, 65–67, 77, 110, 140
Cornwell, John, 9, 76, 222

229

Index of Names and Subjects

Critical dogmatics, 11, 16, 48–49, 67, 95, 100, 107, 153, 223
Crowe, David M., 7, 222

Dahlemite Front/Dahlemites, 51, 56, 142, 144, 151, 161
Darwin, Charles, 1, 22, 107–20, 123–24, 213, 222, 228
Darwinism, 22, 61, 108, 123, 167
Dawidowicz, Lucy S., 7, 9, 96, 100, 125–28, 130, 222
de la Durantaye, Leland, 190, 222
DeJonge, Michael P., xi, 5, 45, 63, 182, 222
Dennett, Daniel C., 108–11, 222
Dietrich, Otto, 138, 222
Donovan, Gen, William J., 14, 16, 35–36, 141
Duchrow, Ulrich, 47, 222
Dwork, Deborah, 7, 222

Eckhart, Dietrich, 139–40
Eichmann, Adolf, ix, 3, 39, 112–14, 116, 150, 221
Elert, Werner, 21–23, 33–34, 37, 45, 50, 52–53, 57–59, 62, 148–49, 221
Ericksen, Robert P., 11, 15–28, 30–31, 35, 41, 48, 71, 83, 85, 97, 102, 109, 128, 142, 145–47, 160, 162–63, 166–67, 177, 189, 222, See Left-Right Binary
External Word (*Verbum externum*), 40, 48, 63, 175, 180

Flett, John G., 166–68, 113–15, 222
(das) *Volk* (*völkisch*, *Völker*, *Volkskirche*, *Volkstum*, *Volkswerdung*), 19, 22–26, 29–32, 37–38, 40, 51–52, 58–61, 64, 66, 103, 109, 116–17, 119, 139–40, 145, 149, 160, 165–67, 173–77
Forstman, Jack, 16, 20, 34, 45, 71, 175–81, 223
Friedlander, Henry, 6, 223
Fritz, Stephen G., 7, 223
Fukuyama, Francis, 190, 223
Furet, François, 20, 223

Garcia, Alberto L., 10, 223
Gellately, Robert, 17, 223
Gentile, Emilio, 89, 223
German Christianity, 6, 10, 15–16, 22–25, 28–33, 35–41, 45–46, 48, 51, 57, 61–64, 71–75, 88, 97, 109, 142–49, 152, 163–64, 166, 180–81, 189, 221
Gluchmann, Vasil, 97, 223
Gogarten, Friedrich, 26, 34, 45, 58, 71, 148, 177
Goldhagen, Daniel, 55, 101, 223
Goodrick-Clarke, Nicholas, 139, 223
Green, Lowell C., 49, 52–64, 67, 122–23, 143, 162, 223
Greene, John C., 122–23, 223
Grundmann, Walter, 25, 32, 39–40, 177, 179–80

Hamerow, Theodore S., 67, 72, 77, 80–86, 91, 93, 223
Hanfstaengel, Ernst, 99, 223
Heckel, Johannes, 47, 223
Heidegger, Martin, 26, 175, 190, 225
Heschel, Susannah, 16, 25, 31–32, 39–43, 76, 109, 142, 145–47, 158–61, 164, 166, 222–23
Himmler, Heinrich, 32, 114–16, 139, 160, 226
Hinlicky, Paul R., x, 4, 6, 10, 16, 25, 33, 45–46, 49, 69, 71, 124, 158, 163, 169, 179–80, 221, 223–24, 226
Hirsch, Emmanuel, 15, 17–18, 25–28, 34, 71, 146, 148, 175–76, 180, 189, 222
History of Religions school, 39–40
Hitler, Adolf, 1–2, 4, 7–12, 14–15, 17–18, 20–22, 25–28, 32, 36, 39, 43, 45–47, 49, 51–61, 63–67, 72–76, 78–85, 87, 89–92, 94, 96–98, 99–140, 144–45, 148–49, 152, 155, 157–58, 160, 178, 180, 183, 185–86, 188–89, 206, 212–20, 228–28
Hlinka, Andrej, 98, 212
Hockenos, Matthew D., 51, 142, 144, 147–53, 161–63, 224

Index of Names and Subjects

Horkheimer, Max, 6, 21, 157–58, 221

Intentionalism, 7, 8, 36, 45, 96, 124–31
Iwand, Hans, 152

James, William, 101, 108, 224
Jamnický, Ján, 97
Jefferson, Thomas, 5–6, 68, 77, 110–11
Jenson, Robert, 165, 224
Jewish question, xii, 7, 18–21, 83–85, 94, 160–61, 176, 226

Kant, Immanuel, 105–6, 109–10, 113–16, 122, 126, 136, 184–85, 203
Katz, Eric, 76, 224
Kidd, Colin, xii, 22, 168–71, 224
King, Jr., Martin Luther, 6, 158, 189
Kittel, Gerhard, 15, 17–21, 25–27, 108, 145–46, 222
Klossowski, Pierre, 120, 224
Knickerbocker, Hubert Renfro, 80–81
Kolb, Robert, 49, 224–25
Korn, Eugene, 165, 224
Kubizek, August, 101–2, 116–17, 125, 131, 225
Kuklick, Bruce, 124, 225
Künneth, Walter, 45, 49, 54, 60–61, 71, 151–52, 161, 189

Lazareth, William H., 46, 225
Left-Right binary, 11, 20–26, 35, 67, 110, 143, See Ericksen, Robert P
Levinas, Emmanuel, 190
Lewis, David Levering, 154–55, 223, 225
Liberalism, 5–6, 8–9, 15, 17, 27, 53, 65–74, 76–86, 91–92, 95, 97, 99, 102–3, 110–111, 116, 124, 131, 133, 143, 157–58, 186, 189–90
Liberal Protestantism/Theology, 16, 21, 23, 25–26, 30, 33–34, 36–39, 41, 45, 48, 56, 64, 88, 93, 97–98, 144–45, 148–49, 170, 179, 182
Lilla, Mark, 191, 225
Lincoln, Abraham, 6, 189
Lindbeck, George A., 48, 50, 225
Lindberg, Anne, 80

Locke, John, 5–6, 68, 77, 110, 157, 188, 225
Löwith, Karl, 26, 225
Ludendorff, Erich, 79–80
Luhrssen, David, 139, 225
Luther, Martin, ix, 1, 15, 21, 24–25, 33–35, 37, 40, 65–67, 69, 73, 76, 97–98, 148, 152–53, 156–57, 161–63, 184–87
Lutheranism/Lutheran theology, ix, xii, 21–26, 29, 31, 37–38, 44–64, 66–67, 71, 86, 88, 94–98, 142–45, 147–53, 156–57, 164, 166, 179, 181–82, 184–86

MacIntyre, Alisdair, 68–69, 102, 106, 127, 225
Marrus, Michael R., 125, 225
Mattox, Mickey, 16, 221
Mauer, Wilhelm, 47, 225
Mazower, Mark, 17, 225
Melanchthon, Phillip, 48–50, 156–57
Menand, Louis, 124, 225
Moltmann, Jürgen, 159, 225
Morgan, Michael L., 13, 131, 225
Morse, Christopher, 71, 225
Mowrer, Edgar, 81
Mussolini, Benito, 78, 98, 106, 117, 194, 202–12, 217

Nagorski, Andrew, 8, 72, 77–78, 80–81, 86, 225
Napoleon, 110, 134–38, 140, 160
Neitzel, Sönke, 55, 70, 113, 151, 186, 225
Niebuhr, Reinhold, 69, 124, 191, 225–26
Niemöller, Martin, 10, 51, 71, 88, 142, 149
Niewyk, Donald L.
Nirenberg, David, 18, 226
Nolte, Ernst, xi, 17, 20, 107, 119, 131–34, 191, 223, 226
Novak, David, 165, 226

Oberman, Heiko, 90, 226
Ochs, Peter, 165, 226
Oehlschlaeger, Fritz, v, vi

231

Index of Names and Subjects

Oehlschlaeger, Fritz, xi, 224, 226
Orders of creation, 22, 25, 148, 166, 179
Osuský, Samuel, x, xii, 8, 12, 72, 85, 94–98, 100, 161, 193, 221

Pannenberg, Wolfhart, 162–63, 226
Plato, 119, 122, 197
Political Bartianism, 62, 144, 151, 189, See Barth, Karl
Pringle, Heather, 76, 226

Race, 8, 12, 22–23, 30, 40, 55, 58, 60–61, 78, 84, 90, 98, 107, 118, 121, 129, 134, 139–40, 163, 166–74, 176, 185, See Racism, Scientific racism
Racism, 32, 41, 58, 64, 98, 102, 149, 170, See Race, Scientific racism
Remak, Joachim, 76, 226
Retrospective fallacy, 2–5, 11, 16, 44–45, 52–53, 55, 65, 70, 77, 145
Rhodes, Richard, 7, 116, 129, 226
Rosenberg, Alfred, 29, 109, 139, 160, 217, 219
Royce, Josiah, 11, 226
Rubenfeld, Sheldon, 76, 226
Rubenstein, Richard L., 10, 12–13, 67, 128, 227
Ruether, Rosemary, 8, 10, 227
Ryback, Timothy W., 105, 108, 135, 227

Safranski, Rüdiger, xi, 119, 121, 227
Samuel, Maurice, 18, 71, 85, 91–93, 192, 227
Sasse, Hermann, 25, 30, 56–58, 60–61, 71, 148, 161, 180
Schaeffle, Albert E. F., 106–7
Schmid, Heinrich, 46, 227
Schmitt, Carl, 26, 227
Scholder, Klaus, 29–30, 32, 35, 62, 76, 139–40, 227
Schopenhauer, Arthur, 61, 105–6, 117
Schwarz, Hans, 58, 227
Scientific racism, 22, 41, 164
Shirer, William L., 1, 65, 77, 81, 227

Siemon-Netto, Uwe, 20, 25, 49, 52, 64–67, 77, 87, 227
Snyder, Timothy, 17, 227
Spicer, Kevin P., 8, 227
Stalin, Joseph, 17, 25, 55, 81, 83, 100, 102, 124, 200, 202, 222–23, 227
Stayer, James M., 15, 33–35, 37, 44–46, 50, 65, 227
Steiger, Johann Anselm, 110, 224, 227
Steigmann-Gall, Richard, 15, 28, 31, 35–41, 64, 67, 92, 134–35, 140, 142, 146, 227
Structuralism, 45, 124–28

Taylor, Kressman, 71, 85–91, 227
Telushkin, Joseph, 131, 227
Theological existence, 10, 12, 24, 33, 50, 60, 62, 69, 95, 152, 178, 180–83, 221
Tillich, Paul, 22, 25, 27, 70–71, 97, 115–16, 148, 177–78, 227
Tiso, Jozef, 96, 98
Tóth, Dezider, 95, 227
Trevor-Roper, H. R., 32, 99, 106, 134, 136, 227
Two Kingdoms doctrine, 12, 23, 32, 37, 46–47, 51–52, 56, 60, 62–63, 66–67, 75–76, 87, 140, 143, 148, 155–56, 160, 162, 179, 183–87, 228

Ušiak, Ján, 95, 228

van Pelt, Robert Jan, 7, 222
Vilhauer, Monica, 5, 49, 162, 228

Wade, Nicolas, 172, 228
Wallman, Johannes, 65, 228
Walmer, George J., 72–77, 228
Watts, Rikk, 165, 228
Wedemeyer, Albert C., 79
Weikart, Richard, 1, 22, 106–7, 123, 228
Welzer, Harald, 55, 70, 113, 151, 186, 225
Wendebourg, Dorothea, 65, 228
Westerholm, Stephen, 165, 228
Wiegland, Karl Henry von, 78–79

Index of Names and Subjects

Wilson, Hugh, 80
Wilson, Sarah Hinlicky, xii, 169
Wilson, Woodrow, 208, 211
Witte, John Jr, 156, 224
Wood, Susan K., 10, 223
Wright, William J., 46, 228

Yoder, Nathan Howard, 58, 61, 167, 228

Zimmermann, Jens, 5, 224, 228
Zionism, 19, 60, 64, 84–85, 161, 165, 191
Žitňan, Andrej, 95–96, 228